Education for the
Intercultural Experience

Education for the Intercultural Experience

Edited by
R. MICHAEL PAIGE

INTERCULTURAL PRESS, INC.

For information, contact:
Intercultural Press, Inc.
P.O. Box 700
Yarmouth, Maine 04096 USA

© 1993 by R. Michael Paige

Book design by Patty J. Topel
Cover design by Ralph Copeland

Printed in the United States of America.

98 97 96 95 94   1 2 3 4 5

Library of Congress Cataloging-in-Publication Data

Education for the intercultural experience / edited by R. Michael Paige.
   p.   cm.
   Includes bibliographical references and index.
   ISBN 1-877864-26-9
   1. Multicultural education. 2. Cross-cultural orientation. 3. Ethnopsychology. I. Paige, R. Michael, 1943—

LC1099.E347   1993
370.19'6—dc00   93-31313
                        CIP

Table of Contents

Preface

This volume, *Education for the Intercultural Experience*, is based on two fundamental premises: first, intercultural experiences are emotionally intense and profoundly challenging for the participants and second, education for intercultural experiences requires content and pedagogy radically different from traditional instructional practices. The purpose of this book is to explore these premises in depth. The contributing authors examine (1) the nature of intercultural adjustment, culture learning, and the stages of personal development associated with movement toward intercultural sensitivity, (2) the domestic and international contexts within which intercultural relations occur, (3) the pedagogy of intercultural education, training, and orientation, (4) the cultural immersion and reentry phenomena, and (5) the experience of being culturally marginal.

This book is a compilation of writings which originally appeared in the University Press of America volume entitled *Cross-Cultural Orientation: New Conceptualizations and Applications* (R. Michael Paige Ed., 1986) and in the special issue of the *International Journal of Intercultural Relations* (IJIR) devoted to cross-cultural orientation (Judith Martin, guest editor, Vol. 10, no. 2 1986).

Cross-Cultural Orientation was well received, but by 1989 it had gone out of print. The IJIR issue was distributed for some time by the Intercultural Press, but it too is out of general circulation. It was my feeling as the editor of Cross-Cultural Orientation that these writings deserved wider distribution. David Hoopes and Margaret Pusch of the Intercultural Press shared this view and expressed keen interest in a new volume. Thereupon, selected authors from the two collections were asked to revise their original articles to bring them up to date with respect to the literature, research findings, refinements in their own thinking, or more recent practical applications. That was done, a new introductory chapter was prepared, and a new chapter on cultural marginality by Janet Bennett was added.

This book is the result of the authors' labors, and it brings together in one volume some of the most insightful writing on intercultural training and education available. I am pleased to have been associated with this project and wish to thank all of the authors for their contributions.

R. Michael Paige
Minneapolis, Minnesota

1

On the Nature of Intercultural Experiences and Intercultural Education

R. Michael Paige

INTRODUCTION

Intercultural education is a highly specialized form of instruction designed to prepare persons to live and work effectively in cultures other than their own. Its curricular content and instructional methodologies have developed over the years in response to the needs of learners and the demands intercultural experiences place upon them. Professional intercultural educators know that communicating and interacting with culturally different others is psychologically intense. The process of adapting to a new culture requires learners to be emotionally resilient in responding to the challenges and frustrations of cultural immersion. It also requires sojourners to be capable of utilizing their own culture-learning skills to master appropriate target-culture behaviors and acquire the insider's knowledge of the culture. Intercultural education, if it is to be effective, must help learners develop these culture-learning skills and enable them to manage their emotional responses. It must therefore incorporate cognitive, behavioral, and affective forms of learning into its structure.

1

The purpose of this chapter is to explore in greater detail these ideas regarding intercultural experiences and intercultural education. The chapter includes an examination of situational variables and personal attributes, referred to as *intensity factors*, which influence the psychological intensity of the intercultural experience. Attention is then focused upon intercultural education with a discussion of *risk factors*, i.e., the ways in which intercultural learning activities challenge and confront learners. The position this author takes is that intercultural education must be inherently provocative, by necessity and design, if it is to be an appropriate preparation for the intercultural experience. This chapter presents a rationale and an explanation for that proposition.

Intercultural Experiences

Intensity of emotions is considered to be one of the three main factors that comprise the intercultural experience (Brislin et al. 1986). (The other two are (1) knowledge areas that incorporate many cross-cultural differences that sojourners find hard to understand, and (2) some bases of cultural differences, especially concerning how people think about and evaluate information.) Culture shock, defined as emotional reactions to the disorientation that occurs when one is immersed in an unfamiliar culture and is deprived of familiar cues, has been an organizing psychological concept in intercultural relations since the term was originally coined by Cora DuBois in 1951 and popularized after Kal Oberg's 1953 speech in Brazil appeared in *Practical Anthropology* in 1960. But culture shock is not a singular event. It occurs as part of a broader culture-learning process. This process, this progression through the different stages of personal development, challenges one's sense of self, cultural identity, and worldview. Consequently, sojourners can experience intense psychological stress. Similar stress arises as individuals reenter their home cultures and seek to comprehend what has happened to them, integrate what they have learned into their lives, and readapt to their home cultures. The realization that one has become marginal in one's own culture adds a new and challenging dimension to the reimmersion experience. Having been marginal to the host culture, the expectation is that one will be able to be in the center at home.

Individuals who have undergone long-term cultural immersion understand how emotionally powerful intercultural experiences can be. They know there are significant risks involved when confronting a new culture as they move outside the comfort zone of their own cultural milieu. During the past several decades, the people who have had these kinds of experiences have been articulating them and examining their implications for intercultural education programs. In many instances, they have become intercultural educators and trainers themselves and have helped the intercultural education profession to refine its program design, curricular content, and instructional methods.

Intercultural Education

Intercultural education is intense for a number of reasons. Its content can be difficult to grasp, its process demanding. First, it requires learners to reflect upon matters with which they have had little firsthand experience. Second, unlike more conventional approaches to education, which tend to emphasize depersonalized forms of cognitive learning and knowledge acquisition, it includes highly personalized behavioral and affective learning, self-reflection, and direct experience with cultural difference. Third, "learning-how-to-learn," a process-oriented pedagogy (Hughes-Weiner 1986), replaces learning facts, a product-oriented pedagogy, as a major goal. Fourth, intercultural education involves epistemological explorations regarding alternative ways of knowing and validating what we know, i.e., the meaning of truth and reality. In the intercultural framework, human reality is viewed as socially constructed (Berger and Luckmann 1967), a function of perception and of culture-group membership (Singer 1987), and something which varies considerably across human communities. In this vein, learners study the impact that culture, race, ethnicity, gender, politics, economics, and other factors have on the perceptions of the world which individuals and groups come to hold. Finally, these inquiries lead logically to the idea that cultures are social inventions which address, in vastly different ways, how basic human needs are met and how meaning in life is derived. Cultures possess their own internal logic and coherence for their members and, hence, their own validity. Making judgments about them is hazardous when the criteria for evaluation come solely from another culture.

Inevitably, learners struggle with these ideas. The ambiguities surrounding truth, knowledge, and perception are disturbing to them. The searching self-appraisals are painful and difficult. Moral certainty about rightness and wrongness becomes less absolute; indeed, it is a common phenomenon for learners to find themselves becoming temporarily immobilized in a state of extreme cultural relativism, hesitant or unable to make judgments. Put simply, intercultural education, as a function of its content and pedagogy, is psychologically challenging.

INTENSITY FACTORS AND THEIR IMPLICATIONS FOR INTERCULTURAL EDUCATION

Attention will now be turned to those factors which heighten the psychological intensity of intercultural experiences. The purpose in delineating these is to provide intercultural educators with conceptual tools for

- predicting the level of psychological intensity that will be present in a particular cultural immersion and taking this into account for program-design purposes;
- conducting research designed to test hypotheses regarding intercultural learning;
- "inoculating" learners, i.e., setting the stage for the learning that will occur in order to minimize counterproductive responses to the host culture.

Figure 1 presents a set of factors which can raise the level of psychological intensity for sojourners. These are derived from the intercultural literature, this author's personal intercultural experiences, and the experiences of colleagues. Some are situational, i.e., engendered by the setting. Others are personal qualities or traits possessed by the sojourner. As the following discussion suggests, situational and personal variables interact to contribute to the overall intensity of the experience. In this section, the intensity factors are identified, relevant hypotheses are stated, and their implications for intercultural education are discussed.

Experts are generally agreed that sojourners experience unusually strong emotional highs and lows. The factors I am most concerned with here are the predictably *most* challenging, difficult, and stressful.

Figure 1:   Intensity Factors

Cultural differences	Prior intercultural experience
Ethnocentrism	Expectations
Language	Visibility and invisibility
Cultural immersion	Status
Cultural isolation	Power and control

Cultural Differences

Hypothesis 1: The greater the degree of cultural difference between the sojourner's own and the target culture, the greater the degree of psychological intensity.

This is the major hypothesis appearing in the intercultural literature. As M. Bennett (this volume) observes, it is not cultural similarities which challenge us, but cultural differences. And the greater those differences in value orientations, beliefs, attitudes, behaviors, patterns of thinking, and communication styles, the more challenging and stressful the intercultural immersion will be.

Every effort should be made to assess accurately the target culture and prepare sojourners for the specific differences they will encounter. It is equally important for learners to understand the nature of culture and its influence in their own lives and to be aware of the characteristics of their own culture they value most and the strength of their personal attachment to them. These are essential program content items because they enable learners more accurately to assess the areas of greatest difference and similarity between their own and their host cultures.

Hypothesis 2: The more negatively the sojourner evaluates the cultural differences, the more psychologically intense the experience will be.

Cultural differences can be the source of extreme psychological dissonance when learners find them objectionable for moral, religious, or philosophical reasons. However much they accept the principles of cross-cultural adaptation, their inability to suspend judgment and their negative responses to certain cultural differences will make the intercultural experience more intense.

It is very important for intercultural educators to familiarize learners with specific aspects of the target-culture value orientations, for instance, which can reasonably be expected to stand in sharp contrast to those of the learners and to provoke a negative response. Intercultural educators should identify those cultural elements which will be the most difficult to accept, help learners explore their responses to them, and aid learners in devising strategies for dealing with them.

Ethnocentrism

Hypothesis 3: The more ethnocentric the sojourner, the more psychologically intense the experience will be.

Milton Bennett's discussion of ethnocentrism (this volume) is particularly instructive on this point. Sojourners in the ethnocentric states of denial, defense, and minimization can be expected to have a difficult time adjusting to new cultures. They are not yet at the point of even accepting, much less adapting to, cultural difference and are most likely to view their host cultures as inferior and their own as superior. If they are in the minimization stage, they may simply deny the existence of any significant differences and behave just as they would at home. These attitudes are likely to produce a negative response on the part of their hosts, and the stage will have been set for difficult intercultural encounters.

Intercultural programs generally provide numerous opportunities for learners to assess their own biases, likes and dislikes, and overall level of ethnocentrism or ethnorelativism. For example, the study of cultural differences provides an opportunity for learners to evaluate their own and the target culture's value orientations. As a follow-up, instructors can ask them to examine how they responded to these value differences, how negatively or positively they viewed certain aspects of the target culture, how attached they found themselves to certain value orientations in their own culture, and so forth. It is important for intercultural educators to encourage such honest self-reflection and to provide a conceptual framework for doing so, such as M. Bennett's (this volume) intercultural sensitivity model.

Hypothesis 4: The more ethnocentric behavior the host culture exhibits, the more psychologically intense the experience will be.

All cultures are ethnocentric, but some demonstrate greater resistance to outside influence and greater reluctance to accept strangers. Extreme nationalism, suspicion of outsiders, and defense against difference are among the more visible manifestations and are demonstrably more prominent in certain cultures. In these cultures, sojourners will have a harder time being accepted no matter how hard they try. If they are not accepted, they will feel isolated.

This is a particularly delicate issue for intercultural educators to address because any portrayal of a given culture's ethnocentrism could be offensive to representatives of that culture and to the learners as well. In addition, such portrayals may create operative stereotypes that are not only negative, but fail to account for the diversity and the significant individual differences that exist within cultures. However, to ignore the fact that certain cultures are likely to demonstrate more ethnocentric behavior than others could lead prospective sojourners to underestimate the difficulties they will have adjusting to those cultures.

Hypothesis 5: The more racist, sexist, and in other ways prejudiced the host culture, the more psychologically intense the experience will be.

All cultures have their particular "isms," but in some these run deeper, are expressed more openly, and are institutionalized to a greater degree. Exposure to outright prejudice and bigotry can have a debilitating effect on sojourners, particularly when they are trying to overcome their own biases by involving themselves with other cultures. If they have unrealistic expectations about this aspect of the new culture, they can become very disillusioned when they encounter the prejudices held by people in the culture. In some cases, sojourners who share characteristics of the disenfranchised group may experience prejudice directly. Others, especially if they resemble the dominant group, may be assumed to share its prejudices, a situation which can also be very offensive. Interestingly, sojourners who are sensitive to prejudice and bigotry in their own societies tend to think that other cultures will be less so. It comes as a shock to discover that prejudice exists elsewhere and is not unique to their own country.

Intercultural educators should present concepts that permit learners to see how, in what ways, and toward which groups prejudices are manifested in different societies. Almost every society has its disenfranchised groups who are discriminated against culturally, socially, politically, and economically. While those groups will vary from society to society, the fact of their existence is nearly universal. These phenomena should be explored with respect to the specific target culture.

Language

Hypothesis 6: The less language ability the sojourner possesses, the greater will be the psychological intensity of the experience.

The ability to speak the target language is not always absolutely essential, nor does it assure wholly effective intercultural communication or cross-cultural adjustment, but lack of language skills can lead to social isolation and frustration. Language is the major mechanism by which culture-group members communicate and share meaning. For the sojourner, language is a means of entry into the culture and as sojourners gain enhanced language skills, they will have greater access to it. Language learning is also a major source of personal satisfaction.

If possible, language-learning opportunities should be integrated into program design. Where time does not permit extended language study prior to immersion in the culture, in-service language training should be provided.

Hypothesis 7: The more essential language ability is to functioning in the target culture, the greater will be the psychological intensity of the experience.

Some intercultural situations definitely require sojourners to speak the target language. Initially, using a language other than one's own day in and day out can be quite fatiguing, particularly when the sojourner is not yet proficient in it. But not knowing and not using the target language in such situations is to risk severely limiting one's ability to function effectively.

It is important for program planners to assess the language requirements of the intercultural assignment. If the situation clearly requires language proficiency, participants should be selected who already have it, or they should be offered the opportunity to acquire it through intensive language study prior to departure.

Cultural Immersion

Hypothesis 8: The more the sojourner is immersed in the target culture, the higher the degree of psychological intensity.

Full immersion in a new culture, i.e., extensive interaction with host-culture members, is psychologically stressful. As Grove and Torbiörn (this volume) point out, cultural differences constantly challenge the appropriateness of the sojourner's behavior, the sense of clarity the sojourner has regarding the host culture, and the expectations the sojourner has of being able to function effectively. It takes some time for sojourners to learn the appropriate behaviors, to develop the insider's knowledge of how the culture functions, and to revise their expectations about how quickly they will be able to be successful. The more immersed they are, the more imposing are these alternative cultural characteristics and realizations. Most research indicates that greater immersion in the culture, while more stressful, leads to a greater amount of learning in the long term.

One objective of intercultural education programs should be to give learners the opportunity to develop and practice skills which will be useful when they are immersed in another culture. Experience-based learning activities such as role plays, cultural excursions, and simulations are effective ways to accomplish this objective. Program content should also include a discussion of strategies for actively participating in the target culture and of coping mechanisms, such as periodic retreats back into their own culture, which are important for dealing with the stress of intercultural encounters.

Cultural Isolation

Hypothesis 9: The less access sojourners have to their own culture group, the greater will be the psychological intensity of the experience.

Sojourners who are isolated from their own culture-group members are more likely to experience stress, homesickness, and loneliness than those who are not. One reason for this is that they do not have the opportunity to reconfirm their cultural identity. Another is that they are deprived of a chance to relax, regain a sense of cultural equilibrium, and experience the ease of communicating they are used to in their own culture. Culture fatigue, language fatigue, and adaptation fatigue are very real phenomena for intercultural sojourners. The fewer the opportunities to connect with their own culture group, especially in the initial stages of the sojourn, the more psychologically stressful the intercultural experience will be.

While it is difficult to replicate the experience of cultural isolation and fatigue, intercultural educators should at least introduce these issues as discussion items in their programs. It is very important to conceptualize the impact of cultural isolation and explore alternative ways to cope with the stress it causes. Prospective sojourners can thus begin to anticipate how they will react to these circumstances and can start inventing ways to respond to cultural isolation and fatigue.

Prior Intercultural Experience

Hypothesis 10: The less the amount of prior, in-depth intercultural experience, the greater will be the psychological intensity of the experience.

Sojourners with a great deal of previous intercultural experience will, in general, experience less stress in the new culture. They will already have developed coping strategies, will be familiar with the cross-cultural-adjustment process, will have set realistic expectations of themselves and the culture, and will have intercultural communication skills to help them in the initial stages.

It is impossible in intercultural education and training programs to compensate for a lack of prior intercultural experience, but it is essential to take into account the amount of such experience the learners have when designing the program. Milton Bennett (1986) is particularly instructive on the sequencing and inclusion of specific learning activities for learners at different stages of intercultural development.

Expectations

Hypothesis 11: The more unrealistic the sojourner's expectations of the host culture, the greater will be the psychological intensity of the experience.

Brislin et al. (1986), Grove and Torbiörn (this volume), and Martin (this volume) address the importance of realistic expectations about what will be encountered in the host culture, the nature of the upcoming intercultural experience, and the sojourner's own ability to function effectively in the new setting. Sojourners who have positive but unrealistic expectations will experience what Brislin and his coauthors refer to as "disconfirmed expectancies" and a psychological letdown. They will likely be disappointed with the culture, the experiences they are having, and their own performance.

Intercultural education programs should require learners to reflect carefully upon their expectations. What do they expect to gain from the experience? What do they think the host culture will be like? How personally satisfying do they think the host culture will be for them? What do they expect of themselves in the intercultural situation—for example, how culturally sensitive or adaptable do they think they will be? Do they think they will experience culture shock? When discussing these questions, intercultural educators must help sojourners maintain their enthusiasm while at the same time thinking realistically about the upcoming experience.

Visibility and Invisibility

Hypothesis 12: Being physically different from members of the host culture and feeling highly visible to them can increase the psychological intensity of the experience.

One of the more interesting intercultural phenomena is the sense sojourners in a foreign land sometimes have of "living in a fishbowl" because they are physically different from members of the host culture and are objects of curiosity. Many sojourners report feeling quite awkward in such circumstances because they are physically different from members of the host culture. In some cultures children may follow the sojourners around and adults watch them or comment on their behavior, making them feel they are constantly being observed.

It is difficult to prepare someone for this experience who isn't already familiar with it. One technique used in intercultural programs is to send learners into a local community or neighborhood where they are distinctly different from the residents and then discuss in depth what they felt.

Hypothesis 13: Feeling invisible to members of the host culture because they do not know or cannot accept important aspects of the sojourner's identity can increase the psychological intensity of the experience.

This problem occurs when an important aspect of the sojourner's identity (for instance, being gay or lesbian) is concealed or, if known by members of the host culture, is not accepted. Concealing something about oneself for fear that it could harm one's standing or reduce one's effectiveness can cause considerable psychological stress. Moreover, host counterparts may ignore a belief or principle important to the sojourner (e.g., Western feminism) because it conflicts with their culture; they know the sojourner possesses those views, but they expect the sojourner to sublimate them. In each of these experiences, whether self-imposed or otherwise, a central element of the sojourner's identity is devalued.

It is important to discuss these issues in training programs. Virtually all sojourners have to make decisions about what they will and will not reveal about themselves, to whom they will disclose certain things, and under what circumstances. They need to have enough culture-specific knowledge to be able to weigh the consequences of their choices. They also need to understand which personal revelations are most likely to cause discomfort among their specific hosts.

Status

Hypothesis 14: Sojourners who do not feel they are getting the respect they deserve or, conversely, who feel they are receiving undeserved recognition will find the experience more psychologically intense.

A person's status in the community is, to a certain degree, a function of what the host culture values and defines as important. Age, ethnicity, religion, nationality, gender, family background, occupation, and race are just some of the personal characteristics which confer status on the individual. Unlike personal accomplishments or hard work, many of these are inherited qualities which cannot be controlled. Qualities that are valued in the home culture may not be important in the new one; the result can be a loss of status. Alternatively, the sojourner may be granted standing on the basis of inherited characteristics, not personal achievement, and feel the conferred status is undeserved. In either case, serious psychological discomfort can result.

Intercultural programs can prepare sojourners for these status-related phenomena by discussing the status indicators that are important in the target society and by having the learners reflect on the status position they expect to occupy there. Interviews with returnees and host-country nationals can help clarify matters and bring expectations in line with reality.

Power and Control

Hypothesis 15: The less power and control one possesses in the intercultural situation, the greater the psychological intensity of the experience.

One of the most consistent research findings regarding intercultural immersion is that sojourners feel they lack control. As Grove and Torbiörn (this volume) point out, people do not initially understand the cultural dynamics of the host society. Behaviors which worked in their own culture do not now produce the expected results, and their sense of personal efficacy is diminished. The power they had to influence events and other people in their own environment is reduced. These things are very disconcerting, especially for individuals who need to be and are used to being in control. The more power and influence one is used to exercising, the more disturbing is the loss of power.

It is very difficult to adequately prepare sojourners for this experience. At a minimum, loss of power and control should be discussed as a general phenomenon. Beyond that, role plays and simulations can be valuable in providing some exposure to unfamiliar circumstances.

As we have seen, intercultural experiences provide many challenges for the learners. The overall level of psychological intensity and the sojourner's feelings of psychological stress will, at times, be considerable. The more of these intensity factors the intercultural experience possesses, the more challenging it will be for the sojourner.

The sojourner's attitude toward the intercultural experience can be a powerful mediating influence. If intercultural adjustment, as stressful as it might be, is viewed as a valuable learning opportunity, the sojourner will be better equipped to handle its psychological intensity.

Intercultural educators have many roles to play in assisting sojourners before, during, and after intense intercultural experiences. First, they can help the learners maintain a high level of motivation for the experience; this may be one of the most important sources of support educators can provide. Second, they should accurately represent the psychological dynamics of the intercultural experience; sojourners need to know about the challenges they will be facing. Third, they can help sojourners determine how much stress or intensity they are ready to handle by weighing the intensity factors against the sojourner's personal qualities and background. There may be an intensity threshold beyond which a given learner cannot reasonably be expected to proceed because a sufficient foundation of prior experience is lacking. Fourth, having identified the amount of challenge the sojourner is able to bear, they can provide advice on the specific intercultural learning experiences which will best fit his or her needs, interests, and background. Fifth, they can design appropriate intercultural education programs which prepare participants for the intercultural experience and which enable them to continue their learning after their return. Sixth, Janet Bennett (this volume) suggests that intercultural educators can validate those who live intercultural lives daily and who do not have a choice in the matter, such as minorities and refugees.

RISK FACTORS IN INTERCULTURAL EDUCATION AND THEIR IMPLICATIONS FOR EDUCATORS

Figure 2 identifies the risk factors of which intercultural educators must be aware when selecting and sequencing learning activities. Each activity should be evaluated in terms of these factors. Activities that involve more than one kind of risk are more threatening for the learner and, thus, more challenging for the educator to facilitate.

Figure 2: Risk Factors in Intercultural Education

Risk of personal disclosure

Risk of failure

Risk of embarrassment

Risk of threat to one's cultural identity

Risk of becoming culturally marginal and culturally alienated

Risk of self-awareness

Risk of Personal Disclosure

All cultures have private and public domains in which the self operates (Barnlund 1975). We may be very willing to talk about (or do) some things, for they are a part of conventional public discourse. Others, however, may be considered much more private and personal, in particular our deeply held attitudes, values, and beliefs. Moreover, there may be elements in our life history we may not wish to disclose to others. Learning activities which focus on controversial issues such as prejudice, religious and other beliefs, or value orientations go to the core of our being and can be very threatening if we are required to explore them publicly.

Experiential learning methods such as role plays and simulations that require learners to go public verbally and behaviorally are among the most challenging activities. Those which require a considerable degree of personal disclosure should come later in the sequence, after less challenging activities have been used and when an atmosphere of trust and comfort has been established in the learning group.

Risk of Failure

In intercultural education, certain activities are more likely to be construed in terms of success or failure by the learners. This will most often occur when the educational program itself is part of an evaluation process where performance influences job promotion or final selection decisions. It is also more likely with groups of high achievers and professionals who are used to competing, being in control, and performing at a high level. The more focused they are on achievement, the less used they are to failure, and the more absolute their performance standards, the more sensitive they will be to the possibility of failure. Activities which require individuals to make presentations or perform in front of the group, in role plays for instance, involve high stakes for these learners. If they don't perform well, they will consider themselves to have failed. They may end up being quite upset with themselves and/or with the program and its instructors.

Intercultural educators can reduce the risk of this kind of failure by defining mistakes not as failures but as a natural part of the cultural adaptation process. Learners who are tolerant of themselves and their cultural errors will have an easier time adapting and will be more likely to participate actively in the culture. They won't be immobilized by fear of failure.

A supportive, cooperative learning environment can also help by removing the sense that every learning activity is a win-lose situation for the learner. In a competitive, judgmental atmosphere, learners will be more prone to hide rather than make mistakes they can learn from or confront their own biases.

Risk of Embarrassment

Almost all learning activities have the potential to embarrass participants. The poorly informed question or statement, culturally inappropriate behavior, incorrect use of the target language, wrong nonverbal gesture, lack of culturally specific knowledge, or overly emotional reaction can cause personal discomfort because the learner has been embarrassed in front of his or her peers. Here, it is appropriate to remind learners that intercultural experiences themselves are at times going to embarrass them as they attempt to act in new and unfamiliar ways, interpret (and often misinterpret) the new culture, encounter puzzling cultural differences, and adapt to the new setting. It is also useful to encourage learners to have a sense of humor about themselves. Misunderstandings and embarrassment are part of the human condition; they are not limited to intercultural situations and they cannot be avoided.

Risk of Threat to One's Cultural Identity

The initial exploration of cultural differences and intercultural sensitivity can threaten one's sense of cultural identity. This is very much the case when learning activities present contrasting value orientations, promote less judgmental and more relativistic thinking about them, and suggest to the learners the necessity of understanding them as meaningful constructs for members of the other culture. Through discussion of these issues, learners will raise many critical questions about what it really means to function effectively in another culture. Will they have to suspend judgment altogether? Will they have to accept uncritically all aspects of the new culture? Will it be necessary for them to give up their own values and beliefs? How will they be able to adapt to those new ways of thinking and behaving which are quite alien, even unacceptable, to them? Will they have to "go native" in order to survive? Shouldn't they just "be themselves" as the more authentic way to approach the intercultural experience? How can they maintain their commitments, for example, to equality or women's rights, in societies that do not honor these in the same way? These are profoundly provocative questions to which there are no easy answers. Consequently, many intercultural educators prefer to move very gradually toward those learning activities that challenge the participants' sense of cultural identity.

When conceptualizing the issues surrounding cultural identity, it is useful to remind learners that the cultural immersion will itself be an assault on their worldview. Cultures were not invented to satisfy the outsider; consequently, the responsibility to adapt falls much more on the sojourner than on the hosts. Indeed, the pressures to conform can be extremely powerful, as any international student, immigrant, or long-term sojourner can attest. At the same time, culture groups generally do not expect or even want the outsider to go totally native since that is intuitively seen as insincere, a form of alienation from one's own cultural roots.

Risk of Becoming Culturally Marginal and Culturally Alienated

Closely related to the previous risk factor is the possibility that intercultural education moves learners toward becoming culturally marginal and alienated. At the more advanced stage of the program, learners come to realize that intercultural effectiveness means becoming multicultural; it involves what Milton Bennett (this volume) refers to as ethnorelativism: the acceptance of, adaptation to, and integration of cultural differences. This can be a disturbing prospect; it is not easy for learners to envision how they can adapt to or adopt alternative, even contradictory, cultural patterns yet maintain cultural authenticity in their own eyes as well as in the eyes of others. They may fear the negative psychological consequences of the intercultural experience identified originally by Adler (1976): personal disorientation, alienation from their own culture, lack of cultural authenticity, and marginalization. They may anticipate that the very capacity to adapt successfully to another culture may distance, even alienate, them from their own without necessarily guaranteeing them full acceptance or membership in the other. They may recognize an apparent paradox, that the more interculturally sensitive they are, the more marginal they become.

Janet Bennett's work (this volume) is invaluable for intercultural educators seeking to address these concerns, for she makes an important conceptual distinction between encapsulated marginality (a dysfunctional state) and constructive marginality (an empowered state). It is imperative for the intercultural educator to be aware of how certain learning activities, most notably those dealing with the concepts of intercultural effectiveness, sensitivity, and multiculturalism, can provoke such questions. The more in-depth discussions of these issues should be sequenced into the later stages of the program.

Risk of Self-Awareness

By and large, human beings seem to need the security of having a sense of certainty and comfort about how they go about their lives. They seem little inclined to reflect consciously and critically on their own culture or alternatives to it. And they do not routinely test their assumptions about the personal qualities they feel they possess. It takes a jarring life transition (J. Bennett 1977) such as an intense intercultural experience to force self-reflectiveness and self-awareness. Such confrontations with the self can be challenging and painful. As learners realize that their cultural reality may not be central to the perceptions of culturally different others and is definitely not seen as superior, they will begin to question their own assumptions. As learning activities begin to test the learners' flexibility, openness, tolerance, and other qualities, they may come to view themselves differently and not necessarily in such previously naive or positive terms. They may, in fact, learn things about themselves they would rather not know. It behooves intercultural educators to create a climate which encourages self-discovery and to inoculate learners against the inevitable stresses of self-awareness.

Activities most likely to challenge or threaten the learners' sense of self are those which require them to confront their own prejudices and biases as well as those which are designed to move them into the ethnorelative stages of intercultural development. Many conceptual foundations must be in place and the supportive learning environment must have been established before these more self-confrontational activities are introduced.

CONCLUSION

In closing, let us refer back to Paige and Martin's (1983) observation that intercultural education is inherently transformative. It is preparing learners for a major transition in their lives and it is, in fact, a part of that transition. As such, it poses serious risks for the learner. Competent intercultural educators will recognize these risks, systematically assess learning activities in light of them, and sequence those activities accordingly. They will know when the time is right to confront and challenge the learners. They recognize that it is *not* the purpose of intercultural education to so overwhelm the learners initially that they are turned off to further learning and hesitant to engage in intercultural interactions. Rather, the well-crafted intercultural education program will motivate learners and heighten their enthusiasm for the intercultural adventures ahead.

REFERENCES

Adler, Peter S. (1976). "Beyond cultural identity: Reflections upon cultural and multicultural man." In Larry A. Samovar and Richard E. Porter (Eds.), *Intercultural communication: A reader* (2d ed.). Belmont, CA: Wadsworth.

Barnlund, Dean (1982). *Public and private self in Japan and the United States.* Yarmouth, ME: Intercultural Press.

Bennett, Janet (1977). "Transition shock: Putting culture shock in perspective." *International and Intercultural Communication Annual* 4: 45-52.

Bennett, Milton (1986). "A developmental approach to training for intercultural sensitivity." *International Journal of Intercultural Relations* 10, no. 2: 176-96.

Berger, Peter, and T. Luckmann (1967). *The social construction of reality.* Garden City, NY: Doubleday.

Brislin, Richard, Kenneth Cushner, Craig Cherrie, and Mahealani Yong (1986). *Intercultural interactions: A practical guide.* Beverly Hills, CA: Sage.

Grove, Cornelius (1994). "A New Conceptualization of Intercultural Adjustment and the Goals of Training." In R. Michael Paige (Ed.), *Education for the intercultural experience.* Yarmouth, ME: Intercultural Press.

Hughes-Weiner, Gail (1986). "The 'learning-how-to-learn' approach to cross-cultural orientation," *International Journal of Intercultural Relations* 10, no. 4: 485-505.

Oberg, Kalvero (1960). "Cultural shock: Adjustment to new cultural environments." *Practical Anthropology* 7: 177-82.

Paige, R. Michael, and Judith N. Martin (1983). "Ethical issues and ethics in cross-cultural training." In Dan Landis and Richard W. Brislin (Eds.), *Handbook of intercultural training* 1. New York: Pergamon.

Singer, Marshall R. (1987). *Intercultural communication: A perceptual approach.* Englewood Cliffs, NJ: Prentice-Hall.

Torbiörn, Ingemar (1994). "A New Conceptualization of Intercultural Adjustment and the Goals of Training." In R. Michael Paige (Ed.), *Education for the intercultural experience.* Yarmouth, ME: Intercultural Press.

2

Towards Ethnorelativism:
A Developmental Model
of Intercultural Sensitivity

Milton J. Bennett

INTRODUCTION

Intercultural sensitivity is not natural. It is not part of our primate past, nor has it characterized most of human history. Cross-cultural contact usually has been accompanied by bloodshed, oppression, or genocide. The continuation of this pattern in today's world of unimagined interdependence is not just immoral or unprofitable—it is self-destructive. Yet in seeking a different way, we inherit no model from history to guide us.

Education and training in intercultural communication is an approach to changing our "natural" behavior. With the concepts and skills developed in this field, we ask learners to transcend traditional ethnocentrism and to explore new relationships across cultural boundaries. This attempt at change must be approached with the greatest possible care. We should understand why people behave as they normally do in the face of cultural difference, how they are likely to change in response to education, and what the ultimate goal is toward which our efforts are expended. In short, we should be operating with a clear model of how intercultural sensitivity is developed.

In this chapter, intercultural sensitivity will be defined in terms of stages of personal growth. This developmental model posits a continuum of increasing sophistication in dealing with cultural difference, moving from ethnocentrism through stages of greater recognition and acceptance of difference, here termed "ethnorelativism."

Developmental or personal-growth models ideally are based upon key organizing concepts. In the case of intercultural sensitivity, this concept is *differentiation*, taken in two senses: first, that people differentiate phenomena in a variety of ways and, second, that cultures differ fundamentally from one another in the way they maintain patterns of differentiation, or worldviews. If a learner accepts this basic premise of ethnorelativism and interprets events according to it, then intercultural sensitivity and general intercultural communication effectiveness seem to increase. However, the concept of fundamental difference in cultural worldview is the most problematic and threatening idea that many of us ever encounter. Learners (and teachers) employ a wide range of strategies to avoid confronting the implications of such difference.

A developmental model, then, should both describe how cultural difference is comprehended and identify the strategies that impede such comprehension. To accomplish these purposes, the model should be phenomenological in the sense that it describes a learner's subjective *experience* of cultural difference, not just the objective behavior of either learner or trainer.

A developmental model need not, of itself, suggest particular teaching methods or subject matter. Effective teaching and training strategies already exist for the presentation of basic intercultural concepts (see J. Bennett 1984; Paige and Martin 1983; Pusch 1981). Experiential techniques for the classroom are reviewed by several authors, including Asuncion-Lande (1979), Kohls and Ax (1979), Hoopes and Ventura (1979), and Mumford-Fowler (1994), and intercultural group development processes are listed by Gudykunst (1976). The basic learning goals of intercultural communication are also generally agreed upon, encompassing cultural self-awareness, other-culture awareness, and various skills in intercultural perception and communication (Gudykunst and Hammer 1983; Paige and Martin 1983).

The need addressed here is for a straightforward developmental model that can guide the sequencing of concepts and techniques to match some typical progression of development in learners. Samovar (1979) has noted that our field is "sorely lacking" in research to support such a model. Nevertheless, some models of development have been proposed.

For instance, Brislin, Landis, and Brandt (1983, 3) suggested a developmental sequence in response to the question, "What are the antecedents of intercultural behavior?" This model seems well suited to guide the research called for by Samovar but, in its present form, does not offer clear guidance to a classroom or workshop educator.

Paige and Martin (1983, 55) suggest a training model in response to their slightly different question, "How should different types of training activities be sequenced to produce the most effective learning?" They organize typical training elements into a sequence of increasing complexity and difficulty within three dimensions: behavior requirements (active/passive), risk of failure and/or self-disclosure (low/high), and culture-learning focus (cognitive/affective/behavioral). This model represents a considerable refinement of earlier, nonsequenced lists of activities and adds a phenomenological dimension, but it still leaves implicit the basic assumption about where participants are "starting" and where they should "end up," in terms of their subjective experience. Thus it is limited in its ability to diagnose the needs of a particular group or individual. Gudykunst and Hammer (1983) offer a model which suggests the sequencing of three stages: perspective training, interaction training, and context-specific training. These authors have a clear subjective goal in mind—the development of "third-culture perspective"—but their model again refers to types of training activities, not to the nature of a participant's developmental experience.

Hoopes (1981) comes closest to proposing a phenomenological model when he states:

> The critical element in the expansion of intercultural learning is not the fullness with which one knows each culture, but the degree to which the process of cross-cultural learning, communication and human relations [has] been mastered (20).

With this focus, Hoopes lists the following categories of a "spectrum"of intercultural learning: ethnocentrism; awareness; understanding; acceptance/respect; appreciation/valuing; selective adoption; and, in the end, assimilation, adaptation, biculturalism, multiculturalism.

This approach to learning, and that of the model described below, do not stress cultural literacy so much as they emphasize intercultural competence.

The following pages present a formal developmental model built upon prevailing concepts in the field of intercultural communication, a model which goes beyond earlier attempts to conceptualize underlying assumptions and delineate stages. This greater specificity will allow trainers and educators to diagnose stages of development for individuals or groups, to develop curriculum relevant to particular stages, and to sequence activities in ways that facilitate development toward more sensitive stages.

ASSUMPTIONS OF THE MODEL

The developmental model described in the following pages is phenomenological in the sense that it takes as paramount the meaning which is attached by people to phenomena (Pilotta 1983). Experience, in this view, is a function of the relationship a person forms with phenomena—a relationship which is the product (or manifestation) of the attribution of meaning. In the words of George Kelly (1963):

> A person can be a witness to a tremendous parade of episodes and yet, if he fails to keep making something out of them..., he gains little in the way of experience from having been around when they happened. It is not what happens around him that makes a man experienced; it is the successive construing and reconstruing of what happens, as it happens, that enriches the experience of his life (73).

Specifically, we are interested in the way people construe cultural difference and in the varying kinds of experience that accompany different constructions. This experience is termed "intercultural sensitivity," and it is assumed that such sensitivity can be described in developmental terms better than as a collection of specific behaviors. In other words, *it is the construction of reality as increasingly capable of accommodating cultural difference that constitutes development;* behaviors such as negative stereotyping will be treated as simply manifestations of a certain stage of construction.

The importance of "difference" is so widely accepted in the field of intercultural communication that it is sometimes overlooked as the major factor in a learner's successful acquisition of the intercultural perspective. Classic statements of the importance of difference have been made by Whorf (1956), Hall (1973), Stewart (1972), and Singer (1975). All these authors hold the view, essentially, that the reality which we experience is constructed according to variable cultural patterns and that these differences are the crucial factors in our attempts to understand and communicate experience cross-culturally.

It is possible to find authors in the field who also stress the importance of perceiving cultural similarity, such as Brislin's (1981, 60) observation: "Perceiving similarities leads to a basis for interaction; perceiving
differences leads to a basis for out-group rejection." Or, as a statement in
another intercultural textbook puts it, "It is our likenesses that enable us
to find common ground and establish rapport." (Samovar, Porter, and
Jain 1981, 210). As a counter to the virulent defensiveness of ethnocentrism, the recognition of basic cross-cultural similarity may be effective.
For instance, when Americans began traveling to Russia in greater
numbers, many of them noted that their former enemies were "pretty
much like us." Nevertheless, I observe in most classroom and workshop
environments that difficulties in learning the concepts and skills of
intercultural communication are nearly always attributable to a disavowal of cultural difference, not to a lack of appreciating similarity.
Barnlund supports this contention more generally when he states, "People
have consistently shielded themselves, segregated themselves, even
fortified themselves, against wide differences in modes of perception or
expression" (1982a, 11). For this reason, the experience of cultural difference is taken as basic to the developmental continuum.

Cultural difference can be experienced at several levels. In the initial
stage of development, the mere existence of cultural differences may
have eluded one's attention. At this level, intercultural sensitivity increases when differences in modes of perception or expression are
construed as cultural factors, rather than as examples of physical or
moral defects. For instance, the construing of male/female differences in
expression as cross-cultural contrasts represents an increase in sensitivity over the interpretation of these differences as, say, weakness or
bellicosity. Here, intercultural sensitivity can be understood as a kind of
cognitive complexity, where greater sensitivity is represented in the
creation and increasing differentiation of cultural categories.

At the next level, one's own culture is experienced as but one of a
variety of worldviews. As noted earlier, the idea of culture itself refers to
patterns of differentiation. These patterns form the constructs that provide us with interpretations of phenomena. To become aware of one's
own worldview is to realize that one *is* construing in a particular cultural
way. It is to find one's own "meaning-making" meaningful, an activity
that exists on a metalevel, above the basic differentiation of cultural
categories. At this level, intercultural sensitivity increases as people
experience themselves as members of more than one culture. For instance, while recognizing the influences of their national culture, Ameri-

cans might also feel identity with African-American, Asian-American, or European-American ethnicity, with male or female culture, and with a regional culture. At later stages of development, intercultural sensitivity may increase as more than one contrasting worldview is experienced, as is the case with people who are biculturally Japanese and American.

At yet another level, one may experience the construction of one's own identity. One's self is both a cultural product and a producer of the meanings that constitute cultural patterns (Stewart and Bennett 1991). We can experience ourselves as constructs of ourselves. At this level, intercultural sensitivity increases as people consciously select and integrate culturally disparate aspects of their identities. Sensitivity at this level is more dynamic than at the basic level of cultural discrimination or the metalevel of pattern appreciation. Here, sensitivity involves turning the attribution of meaning back onto the meaning-maker—a self-reflectivity that is the essence of consciousness. Development of intercultural sensitivity is ultimately the development of consciousness and, through consciousness, developing a new "natural" approach to cultural difference.

It is also useful to consider intercultural development as it moves through cognitive, affective, and behavioral dimensions. The separation of these dimensions is not always clear for each stage, nor should it be, since development is multidimensional. Nevertheless, a tentative sequence can be suggested. Initial development is cognitive—the generation of relevant categories for cultural difference. The reaction to this development is affective—a feeling of threat to the stability of one's worldview. The developmental treatment for a threat response is behavioral—joint activity toward a common goal—and the response to this treatment is cognitive—consolidation of differences into universal categories. Subsequent appreciation of cultural difference is affective and is combined with increased cognitive knowedge of differences. This change is followed by behavioral applications involving the building of intercultural communication skills. Finally, all three dimensions are integrated in the operation of "constructive marginality."

The model described here is developmental in the sense referred to by Dinges (1983) as "dynamic learning." It includes the elements of increasing awareness and expanded understanding mentioned by Dinges, elements which are also consistent with a phenomenological perspective. There is a linear assumption built into the model that beginning, intermediate, and end stages can be described and that development between and within each stage can also be described. It is not assumed that progression through the stages is one-way or permanent. Several examples of possible "retreat" will be mentioned.

Even though progression through stages can be reversed, care should be taken not to neglect the developmental aspect of this model. Each stage is meant to characterize a treatment of cultural difference that is fairly consistent for a particular individual at a particular point of development. New cultural differences, *once they are defined as cultural*, will be treated in more or less the same way as familiar differences. For example, differences in religion or sexual orientation may not initially be defined as cultural, and they may not be experienced in the same way as national or ethnic cultural differences. But once those areas are given a cultural cast, one's treatment of them should match that accorded other cultural differences.

In general, the early stages of the model correspond with varieties of ethnocentrism discussed widely in intercultural literature, and the latter stages include concepts such as Adler's (1977) "multicultural man," Bochner's (1979) "mediating person," Heath's (1977) "maturity," and the concept of "intercultural competence" as discussed by many authors (e.g., Dinges 1983; Brislin, Landis, and Brandt 1983). In the model described here, the latter stages are termed ethnorelativism, with the intention of coining this single term as an appropriate complement to ethnocentrism.

The choice and sequencing of stages in this model are based on the theoretical considerations discussed above and on twenty years of teaching and training experience in intercultural communication with a wide range of learners. Varieties of this model have been presented to many groups of intercultural educators and discussed in advanced intercultural communication seminars over a period of eight years. In addition, the model has been used successfully to design curricula for courses and workshops in intercultural communication (e.g., Bennett, Bennett, and Stillings 1979), to guide student-services programming in colleges (e.g., Clifford 1990), and to provide a framework for research in health care communication (Culhane-Pera 1987), expatriate adaptation (Turner 1990), peace-organization rhetoric (Rosenberg 1989), and dozens of organizational case studies. As much as possible, it represents the real-life observations of educators and trainers in this field and the actual reported experiences of learners.

In the five years since this material was originally published (M. Bennett 1986a; 1986b), several developments have encouraged me to expand somewhat on the formulation. Most notably, many people have begun thinking in developmental terms about domestic cultural diversity. In some cases, it appears that sensitivity toward ethnic, regional, and other domestic cultural differences may follow the general pattern of sensitivity development. However, when the difference involves people who have been oppressed for reasons of race, ethnicity, class, gender, or sexual orientation, there may be some variation in the forms of ethnocentrism exhibited. There are, in my belief, two major factors in this variation: (1) the cultural identities of oppressed people are devalued in the media and in other institutions controlled by a dominant cultural group and (2) the dominant cultural group demands conformity or segregation, which forces minorities who desire both inclusion and unique identity into fight or flight. For these and possibly other reasons, oppressed people may navigate the development of intercultural sensitivity differently from those in dominant groups. I will include speculation on these differences in the discussion of each model stage.

A DEVELOPMENTAL MODEL OF INTERCULTURAL SENSITIVITY

THE ETHNOCENTRIC STAGES

I. DENIAL
   A. Isolation
   B. Separation

II. DEFENSE
   A. Denigration
   B. Superiority
   C. Reversal

III. MINIMIZATION
   A. Physical Universalism
   B. Transcendent Universalism

THE ETHNORELATIVE STAGES

IV. ACCEPTANCE
   A. Respect for Behavioral Difference
   B. Respect for Value Difference

V. ADAPTATION
   A. Empathy
   B. Pluralism

VI. INTEGRATION
   A. Contextual Evaluation
   B. Constructive Marginality

THE ETHNOCENTRIC STAGES

The term "ethnocentric" is here defined in the simplest possible way as "assuming that the worldview of one's own culture is central to all reality." As such, ethnocentrism parallels "egocentrism," wherein an individual assumes that his or her existence is necessarily central to the reality perceived by all others. All the various functions commonly attributed to ethnocentrism, such as racism, other negative evaluation of dissimilar cultures, and the construction of in-group/out-group distinctions, can be seen as derivative of the "centrality" assumption.

Operating from an ethnocentric assumptive base, the meaning a learner attaches to cultural difference will vary from total denial of its existence to the minimization of its importance. These positions are explicated in the following sections.

I. DENIAL

A denial of difference is the purest form of ethnocentrism. Just as an egocentric person may attend little to the concerns of other people, so a purely ethnocentric person simply does not consider the existence of cultural difference. Even in the face of seemingly obvious differences in human behavior associated with world affairs or domestic multicultural issues, a person at this stage of development believes that cultural diversity only occurs elsewhere. While this pure form of ethnocentrism might seem rare in a heterogeneous and intercommunicating world, semblances of the position can be maintained through either the isolation of physical circumstance or by the separation created by intentional physical and social barriers.

A. Isolation

The circumstance of physical isolation can foster the denial of the existence of difference. Perhaps certain tribes in the forests of the Philippines or Amazon Basin are (or were until recently) purely ethnocentric. If a group simply has not confronted cultural difference in any way, then it is unlikely to entertain the existence of alien realities.

Nowadays, physical isolation is more likely to be relative, such as that of a small town with a homogeneous population in a country where more cosmopolitan cities exist. In these cases, the term "parochial" may be applied. Even a city of half a million people can be called parochial if it has a homogeneous population and is relatively isolated, such as some cities in the U.S. Pacific Northwest. Collective attention in such places often is lavished on keeping the local area "nice," which in many cases means excluding cultural diversity.

From a position of relatively pure isolation, cultural difference is not experienced at all; it simply has no meaning. This condition of *no categories for cultural difference* implies that if such a difference is confronted, it is probably overlooked through processes of selective perception. An example of this phenomenon is the experience of a high school foreign exchange student posted to a small U.S. town. She reported that at no time during her stay did anyone seem genuinely interested in how she was culturally different. Rather, she felt she was expected to be "nice" in American cultural terms, and that was all anyone wanted to (or could) see. Similarly, the one African-American student in an otherwise European-American school is, as proudly reported by whites, "not noticed."

Isolation can also be taken abroad, as indicated by innumerable reports by Americans of how, say, Tokyo is "just like home." When I ask how this is so, the reply is usually, "Well, there are lots of cars, big buildings, and McDonald's." This statement betrays the lack of categories for relevant cultural differences, so only that which is already familiar is perceived.

The partial isolation of parochialism may lead people to maintain *wide categories for cultural difference*. For instance, many people recognize cultural differences between Asians and Westerners, but more parochial people are less likely to recognize differences among Chinese, Japanese, Vietnamese, etc. In one embarrassing case of parochialism in a U.S. city, a parade float honoring the Japanese sister city included both Japanese and Chinese women as riders. When informed that high-ranking Japanese visitors to the parade were disturbed by the inclusion of Chinese women, the parade coordinator reportedly said, "Chinese, Japanese...close enough."

Another example of broad categories for difference is the often reported "stupid question" posed by well-meaning but uninformed hosts. In Japan, people from Oregon are sometimes asked if they ride horses every day. Americans direct questions about wild animals to African visitors, and everyone asks people from Chicago about the Mafia. These questions arise from broad, poorly differentiated categories. If one's category for Africa, for instance, includes only the elements "black people live there" and "wild animals live there," then no other question but the one about animals is likely. I have termed these manifestations of broad categories *benign stereotypes*. It is useful to distinguish benign stereotypes from the more virulent type used for intentionally derogatory purposes, since they indicate different stages of development.

Other reactions to difference at this stage include nonhostile embarrassment (such as giggling—common with children) or studious politeness (more common with adults). Movement toward greater sensitivity within this stage of development is facilitated by simple exposure to difference, combined with attention being drawn to it. Movement is inhibited if difference is downplayed, either to mitigate embarrassment or to maintain a facade of politeness. Development is indicated if the symptoms of isolation give way to the more overt manifestations of separation.

B. Separation

While cases of complete isolation and extreme parochialism are now quite rare in the U.S., it is not difficult at all to find incidences of the separation form of denial. Separation is here defined as the intentional erection of physical or social barriers to create distance from cultural difference as a means of maintaining a state of denial. Racially distinct neighborhoods and ethnically selective clubs are examples of such separation. Religious, economic, political, and other types of groups or cults also create strong social (and sometimes physical) barriers. Even intense nationalism is a form of separation, since it is often associated with keeping our distance from foreigners. Isolation and separation are potentially interactive. For instance, the social barriers of racial discrimination may eventuate in the physical barriers of a ghetto. These forms of separation create the conditions for people born into and outside of the ghetto to be in circumstantial isolation from one another. Many European-Americans living in cities with African-American populations have never met or talked with a black person. These people may not intend to maintain barriers, but they have been placed in isolation by an earlier separation. Conversely, being in isolation apparently makes one more inclined to separate oneself from difference when confronted with it (Rich 1974). Apartheid, townships, homelands, and other devices of separation practiced in South Africa offer eloquent evidence for this syndrome (Malan 1990).

The domestic syndrome described above is mirrored in the international arena. More separation from foreign influence seems to eventuate in greater isolation, which breeds more separation. Rather than easing tensions, nationalistic separation creates the conditions for more international tension; neighbors in the global village come calling more aggressively. It was the U.S. who forced pre-Meiji Japan to end its international separatism. Some would say that modern Japan is now reciprocating. Other examples abound: Stalinist Russia, revolutionary China, Iran, Burma. Perhaps nations, like people, are easily entangled in denial.

On the surface, denial may appear to be a benign stage. People in denial do not actively seek any quarrel, as long as the others keep their distance and hold their peace. The stereotypes of those in denial are based more on naivete than negativity. However, the dangerous underside of denial is its implicit relegation of others to subhuman status. When others are mere objects in the environment, they may seem like a subhuman force to be reckoned with or a vermin to be controlled. Efforts in the U.S. to control homeless people and violent reactions in some European countries to guest workers may have this quality. In the extreme case, when control fails, "subhumans" can be eliminated. An example in the U.S. might be the early white settlers' treatment of American Indians, behavior currently paralleled in the genocide occurring among some Central American Indian groups. The Nazi extermination of Jews and other "undesirables" and the Khmer Rouge elimination of educated Cambodians have come to define this extreme.

People of oppressed groups tend not to experience the stage of denial, partially for the reasons set out just above. When it is *your* difference that is being denied, it's hard to deny that there's a difference! Additionally, media in both social and educational contexts dwell on the doings of the dominant group, so that, except in the case of oppressed people believing themselves to be part of the dominant group (termed "ethnic psychological captivity" by Banks 1988, 23), the nondominant groups are inundated with reminders that they are different. In the context of domestic multicultural relations, denial can be thought of as a luxury of the dominant group. Generally it is only members of that group who can afford both financially and psychologically to remain oblivious to cultural differences.

Separation necessitates the temporary acknowledgment of some kind of difference, and therefore it represents a slight development in intercultural sensitivity beyond isolation. Developmental movement from denial to the next stage, defense, is inhibited by two major factors. One is an oscillation which may have become established between isolation and separation. This oscillation can take the form of a negative spiral, trapping one in intensification of the denial, or it may simply become a homeostatic system from which escape is difficult. The second factor is that the stage of denial may, in some cases, appear as a more sensitive position than the following stage. In terms of the incidence of overt negative evaluation, this is true. People in denial are more superficially polite than people in the stage of defense, where outright denigration of difference occurs more frequently.

Developmental Strategies

At the denial stage of sensitivity (and only at this stage), the best technique for development seems to be "cultural awareness" activities. These generally take the form of International Night, Multicultural Week, or similar functions, where music, dance, food, and costumes are exhibited. In terms of this model, the purpose served by these activities is to create more differentiation among general categories of cultural difference. It should be noted that not much more than this can be expected from such functions, even though they are sometimes touted as great contributions to intercultural sensitivity.

For more sophisticated (but not more sensitive) audiences, history lectures, discussion of political topics, or other such presentations may serve the same purpose as the cultural-awareness activity. Again, that purpose is not so much improving communication as it is facilitating simple recognition of difference.

Overall, the strategy of development here is to avoid premature discussion of really significant cultural differences. Such discussion will either be ignored or, more detrimentally, be used as a rationale for maintaining the comfort of denial. At the same time, cultural awareness should be facilitated in such a way that depth is slowly and inexorably developed. Unfacilitated intercultural contact tends to be more entertaining (or destructive) than developmental. Movement toward more cultural sensitivity can be best assured by providing intercultural facilitators to monitor and push discussion a little in these situations. This is often accomplished by forcing cross-cultural contact across the separation barriers with exchanges, simulations, or other structured activities. These activities should only be undertaken by skilled practitioners, since the first reaction to encountering difference is likely to be increased tension associated with the next developmental stage—defense.

II. DEFENSE

The term "defense" refers to a posture intended to counter the impact of specific cultural differences perceived as threatening. The threat is to one's sense of reality and thus to one's identity, which at this point is a function of that one cultural reality. In the denial stage, the threat was amorphous: culture could be ignored, thus denying it meaning, or it might be eliminated like some environmental irritant. While this kind of denial is certainly a form of psychological defense against threat, it differs from defense in the way cultural differences are perceived. Rather than simply denying difference in general, people in defense recognize specific cultural differences and create specific defenses against them. Because difference is overtly acknowledged, defense represents a development in intercultural sensitivity beyond denial. Nevertheless, the difference is still threatening, and strategies are now sought to fight the differences directly in an effort to preserve the absoluteness of one's own worldview.

The defense battle against difference progresses through three forms: denigration, superiority, and reversal. The first two forms are highly interactive, each reinforcing the other. The last form, reversal, is a strategy that occurs only in certain cases, which will be described below.

A. Denigration

The most common strategy to counter the threat of difference is to evaluate it negatively. This derogatory attitude toward difference is generally called "negative stereotyping," wherein undesirable characteristics are attributed to every member of a distinct group. The denigration may be fundamentally attached to race, religion, age, gender, or any other assumed indicator of difference (see Berger, Cohen, and Zelditch 1966, on status characteristics and expectation-states theory).

Denigration is easy to recognize in individuals and, occasionally, entire groups. Overt statements of hostility toward any one culture should be taken as indicative of a defense level of sensitivity. As predicted by the model, defense should be expected in people who have just come out of denial. In a typical intercultural workshop or classroom setting, statements of hostility may be masked by requests for objective confirmation that one particular group really is troublesome. It is not uncommon to find a mix of denial and denigrative defense, where one culture is targeted as bad and other cultures are simply ignored. Group pressure may exacerbate the denigration and discourage more sensitive individuals from participating in the discussion.

A more tenacious form of denigration combines negative stereotyping of different groups with a rationale for their inherent inferiority. Nazis and the Ku Klux Klan, for instance, provide their members with a philosophy that makes denigration of certain groups inevitable. Some organizations teach that certain cultures or philosophies are evil. Notable in this regard are some fundamentalist religious sects and extremist political groups. In terms of the model, such organizations institutionalize the denigration form of development and make further development difficult or even dangerous for their members.

Denigration is here considered a manifestation of a stage of development, not an isolated act. This has dramatic implications for education and training, since it may be relatively worthless to address the inaccurate assumptions that underlie a given negative stereotype without also addressing the general process of denigration that is characteristic of this stage of development. The culprit in defense is ethnocentrism, not misinformation.

Movement beyond denigration is impeded both by the institutionalization of hatred mentioned above and by the tendency to retreat to denial. For example, a notable movement from denial to defense was evident in the cross-racial busing of schoolchildren. This attempt to move beyond denial eventuated in *increased* negative stereotyping and other overt acts of denigration, as predicted by this model. Two erroneous assumptions contributed to the general failure of busing as a developmental activity. One was the naive ideal that busing would, in itself, solve problems. Instead, it created different problems. The other assumption was that estranged people, if they just came into contact, would like each other. Sometimes this happened; more often, hostilities were exacerbated. The outcome of cross-cultural contact is not so simple, particularly when politically charged cultural differences are involved (Brislin 1981, 118, 171-93). Had defensive behavior been seen as a normal stage of intercultural development, more effort might have been put into weathering the storm in anticipation of smoother sailing ahead. As it was, many people retreated from defense back into denial, opting for the relative peace of separation over what was mistakenly seen as the unending friction of contact. The retreat to denial lessened rancor, but it also diminished the potential for developing intercultural sensitivity.

The tendency to retreat is also evident in individual development, when a person is shocked by his or her own negative evaluating of others and concludes that it would be better for everyone if further contact were restricted. Some isolation of expatriates and foreign students may be due to this kind of retreat. Development is facilitated by an awareness of the inevitability of denigration and by framing it as a temporary phenomenon. Rather than retreating from defense or institutionalizing it with a denigrative rationale, threat can be countered by a movement toward building cultural self-esteem in the face of difference.

B. Superiority

This form of defense emphasizes the positive evaluation of one's own cultural status, not necessarily the overt denigration of other groups. Black pride, feminism, and some manifestations of nationalism might be examples of superiority, if the emphasis is mainly on the positive characteristics of the group. Cultural difference perceived as threatening is countered at this stage by implicitly relegating it to a lower-status position.

The idea of modernization, for example, often embodies the assumption of superiority. Eisenstadt (1966, 1) begins his treatment of the topic with the observation that "modernization is the process of change towards those types of social, economic, and political systems that have developed in Western Europe and North America...." Later, he explicates this change as "the development of a new outlook...characterized by an emphasis on progress and improvement, on happiness and the spontaneous expression of abilities and feeling, on individuality as a moral value, and concomitant stress on the dignity of the individual and, last, on efficiency" (5). A better list of Western cultural values would be difficult to find, and clearly they are treated as superior.

The notion that one worldview represents an acme of development is associated with an evolutionary perspective. Rhodes (1970, 1) suggests that "adherents of the evolutionary perspective picture a transition in terms of stages through which all societies (with perhaps minor variations) evolve." Any contact between traditional and modern societies will naturally lead the former to evolve toward the latter. It seems apparent that the United States Agency for International Development (USAID) takes such an evolutionary perspective. The term "developing" in the phrase "aid to developing countries" implies some direction and destination inherent in progress. Not surprisingly, the destination looks a lot like U.S. society. Of course, other societies may consider themselves at the top of the ladder, using precisely the same evolutionary rationale.

The perspective of cultural evolution treats difference as an inferior, possibly temporary, state that interferes with social development. As such, cultural difference needs to be overcome for the construction or maintenance of superiority. Individuals who hold this view are protected from confronting difference as a viable worldview alternative.

Superiority represents a developmental step beyond denigration because difference is less negatively evaluated, even though it is still something to be overcome. Being less denigrated, difference is more likely to be tolerated and thus to be recognized. However, the recognized cultural difference is not perceived as particularly viable, and so the perspective is still ethnocentric.

The defense forms of superiority and denigration are interactive. At that point of intercultural development, any assumption of cultural superiority carries with it an implied denigration of cultural difference. The more superior one feels about one's own group, the more inferior other groups must become. Likewise, overt denigration of cultural difference is likely to be accompanied by feelings of cultural superiority, as one can easily see in the previously mentioned examples of the Ku Klux Klan and other groups specializing in denigration. A self-reinforcing oscillation between denigration and superiority is institutionalized by such groups, and further intercultural development may be sidetracked into a spiral of hatred and self-aggrandizement.

A more subtle and perhaps more severe impediment to intercultural development is the relative desirability of attitudes of superiority compared to the previous form of denigration. Positive evaluation of one's own group seems healthy, perhaps as a parallel to the assumed benefits of positive self-esteem to an individual. While this form of defense is indeed more interculturally sensitive, there is a danger that cultural pride may become an end in itself. Such a goal may well be psychologically healthy and politically expedient, but it may impede further intercultural development if it is not treated as simply a stage of ethnocentrism.

People who have been oppressed may spend more time in the superiority form of defense. If identifying with a minority culture has been discouraged or demeaned by a dominant culture, then additional effort may be needed to buttress the positive value of an ethnic identity. In support of this idea and the irrelevance of denial for oppressed people, one model of ethnic identity development begins with Phase 1, "Preoccupation with Self, or the Preservation of Ethnic Self-Identity" (Smith 1991). This same model continues with Phase 2, "Preoccupation with the Ethnic Conflict and with the Salient Ethnic Outer-Boundary Group." Phase 2 of this model may correspond to some degree with the denigration form of defense in the Intercultural Sensitivity model. Oppressed people may be more derogatory of other cultures (particularly the dominant one) *after* they have solidified a beleaguered identity through superiority. In any case, defense may serve oppressed people more as a vehicle for challenging rather than preserving the status quo and the cultural prejudice it manifests toward them.

Development beyond superiority is facilitated by allowing, but not overemphasizing, the benefits of cultural pride. An example of how this can be accomplished is afforded by predeparture orientations for study abroad. Students in these programs sometimes lament, "So what's wrong with just being an American?" This can be interpreted as a defensive statement of superiority elicited by the imminent exposure to cultural differences that will be encountered on the sojourn. An appropriate response aimed at facilitating development of the students is to first affirm the positive qualities of American culture, discussing, for instance, the virtues of a culture that encourages cross-cultural contact. These assertions should be followed immediately by a discussion of the equally good, but perhaps different attributes of the host culture. Ideally, students will be drawn toward the next stage of development, wherein all cultures are seen as having valid ways of viewing the world.

It is tempting at this stage to introduce the idea of cultural relativity as an antidote to bigotry and aggrandizement. However, excessive discussion of cultural differences in behavior or values may backfire, leading people toward more intense superiority or into a retreat to denigration. The final state of ethnocentrism, minimization, must be passed before a strong emphasis on cultural difference will be effective.

C. Reversal

Although the phenomenon here termed "reversal" is not an inevitable stage of intercultural development, it is a common enough occurrence to deserve mention. Frequently encountered in Peace Corps volunteers (PCVs) and other long-term sojourners, reversal involves a denigration of one's own culture and an attendant assumption of the superiority of a different culture. A fellow PCV in Micronesia, for instance, maintained that Micronesian culture was really superior to all others and that North American culture was particularly bad in comparison. Others given to this view include culturally rebellious groups such as neo-hippie "new agers," who seemingly embrace the superiority of Eastern over Western cultural values, some environmentalists who pit idealized American Indian values against the evils of European-American society, or Black Muslims, who disparage integrated American black culture, believing African/Moslem values to be superior (Jones 1972, 45).

When it occurs, reversal may appear to be a more interculturally enlightened position than other defense stages. A typical progression of development for a PCV is to move from negative evaluation of the host culture (denigration), to an effort to "help" that culture progress toward an American ideal (superiority), to a disavowal of all American values and an embracing of unchanging host-culture values (reversal). In this context, the reversal form may appear most sensitive, but it is actually only changing the center of ethnocentrism. The subjective meaning attached to difference is the same, although for the PCV, the culture that is "different" has changed.

Because of the perceived credibility of the source, strongly reversed denigrative statements are difficult to combat in training. For instance, if a well-traveled American has begun denigrating the behavior of "typical" American tourists, a shift to emphasizing the superiority of these tourists is ill-advised. One technique which has worked in this circumstance is to spread around the denigration by noting that tourists from other cultures also exhibit insensitivity and then shift emphasis to positive aspects of tourists in general (e.g., curiosity, benefits of simple cross-cultural contact, etc.). The best treatment of reversal, however, is the inoculation. This technique involves noting the possible existence of reversal attitudes before any statement of them comes from the group. Participants in reversal are less likely to make such comments after an inoculation, and if they do, their disruptive credibility is lessened.

In the domestic multicultural context, reversal may be associated with the very beginning of ethnic identity development. Banks (1988) calls Stage 1 of his typology of ethnic identity "Ethnic Psychological Captivity," which is where an individual "absorbs the negative ideologies and beliefs about his or her ethnic group that are institutionalized within the society." People of oppressed groups (including many immigrants) experience subtle and sometimes overt pressure to disavow their cultural roots in favor of becoming a "real" American. Of course, the model for such a successful product of the melting pot is usually the dominant European-American, who is neither more nor less real than Americans with other heritages.

The developmental implication of the reversal form of defense is that positive valuing of a culture not one's own is not necessarily ethnorelative. If such positive attitudes are accompanied by denigration of one's own culture, it is likely that more development through ethnocentric stages is necessary before work on ethnorelativism can be undertaken.

Developmental Strategies

Overall, developmental movement out of defense is facilitated by emphasizing the commonality of cultures, particularly in terms of what is generally good in all cultures. While this seems antithetical to the cultural relativity called for in successful intercultural communication, it is a necessary stage of development that must precede a subsequent emphasis on difference. A failure to allow the next stage, minimization, to follow defense by "skipping ahead" to "acceptance" or "adaptation" may eventuate in a strengthening of the defense stage and rejection of further development. One technique for stressing commonality is the "ropes course" or some other challenging group activity that necessitates cooperation for safety or success. If organized and facilitated properly, such activities allow people in defense to discover the vulnerability and value that all human beings share. In other words, the antidote to defense is the discovery that everyone is, after all, just human.

III. MINIMIZATION

The last attempt to preserve the centrality of one's own worldview involves an effort to bury difference under the weight of cultural similarities. The stage of minimization represents a development beyond defense because, at this stage, cultural difference is overtly acknowledged and is not negatively evaluated, either explicitly as in the denigration form of defense or implicitly as in the superiority form. Rather, cultural difference is trivialized. While differences are seen to exist, they are defined as relatively unimportant compared to the far more powerful dictates of cultural similarity.

The strength of this position is in its ability to counter the threat reaction to difference that occurs in the defense stage. In minimization, human similarity seems more profound than cultural difference, and so we can stand on the common ground of our shared humanity and put aside our differences. In constructivist terms, one finds superordinate constructs that place previously polarized elements onto one side of a larger construct. The clearest example of this phenomenon occurs during intense competition, when internal frictions are subordinated to pulling together against the common enemy. Another example occurs when a woman in a largely male work force comes to be perceived as "one of the guys." (I have not heard of males surrounded by female workers becoming "one of the gals," but it ought to be reciprocal.)

Minimization is an alluring position, because adherents to it manifest an orientation that is associated with human sensitivity. For instance, most cross-cultural applications of the Golden Rule—do unto others as you would have them do unto you—derive from an assumption of underlying intercultural similarity (M. Bennett 1979). Many models of sensitive interpersonal communication are also based on the discovery or creation of similarity between people (e.g., Crable 1981, 45; DeVito 1980, 12). These parallels may lead people—even intercultural educators—to posit this position as an ideal end state of intercultural sensitivity—a kind of "one world, one people" notion. Many world peace organizations, for example, seem to operate from the minimization stage of development (Rosenberg 1989).

What makes minimization an ethnocentric state is the naive assertion that, despite differences, all people share some basic characteristics, such as individual motivation for achievement. These assumed universal characteristics are almost always derived from the native culture of the person making the assertion, who is usually a member of the dominant culture of a society. For this reason, people of oppressed cultures tend not to remain in this stage. Once they are beyond the stage of Banks's "ethnic psychological captivity," described earlier as similar to the reversal form of defense, oppressed people are likely to attain and maintain the idea that they are culturally different. Of course there are exceptions to this, as is sometimes alleged of the American black, upper-middle class. But in general, people who have experienced cultural oppression are wary of the "liberal" assumption of common humanity. Too often, the assumption has meant "be like me."

Forms of minimization may be categorized under "physical universalism" and "transcendent universalism."

A. Physical Universalism

A typical statement of this position is that all people must eat, procreate, and die. That is, human beings in all cultures have physical characteristics in common that dictate behavior which is basically understandable to any other human being. With the further assumption that all cultures are merely elaborations of fundamental biology, cultural difference is relegated to the relatively unimportant position of permutation.

The field of ethology exemplifies this view. In his book based on the innatist assumptions of Lorentz (1977), Eibl-Eibesfeldt (1979) states: "We humans conduct ourselves according to norms so universally distributed that we can assume that their basic rules are inborn" (18). Morris's popularization of this field in The Naked Ape (1967) notes that much, if not all, human behavior can be understood as elaborations of instinctual behavior like territoriality and sex. Similarly, Eckman and Friesen (1969) suggest that physical displays of human emotions are universally recognized because they are representative of a limited number of categories into which humans organize affective reactions.

While some of the assertions of ethology and physical universalism in general may be accurate, for intercultural communication they are trivial. They fail to address the culturally unique social context of physical behavior that enmeshes such behavior in a particular worldview. Failure to consider this context leads people to assume that knowledge of the physical universals of behavior is sufficient for understanding all other people. But, since no human behavior exists outside some social context (by most definitions of "human"), it is likely that people at this stage of development will unconsciously use their own cultural worldview to interpret behavior they perceive. The result is ethnocentrism—less evaluative than defensive ethnocentrism, but ethnocentrism nonetheless. Physical universalism is a position taken most often by people oriented toward the discovery of empirical truth. The physical science bias of people at this stage can be used to facilitate development. Presentation of anthropological, psychological, sociological, and communication studies which demonstrate the necessarily social context of human behavior is most effective, since these perspectives throw into question the comprehensiveness of purely biological approaches to intercultural communication.

B. Transcendent Universalism

In a kind of abstract parallel to the concrete behavioral assumptions of physical universalism, transcendent universalism suggests that all human beings, whether they know it or not, are products of some single transcendent principle, law, or imperative. The obvious example of this view is any religion which holds that all people are creations of a particular supernatural entity or force. The statement, "We are all God's children," is indicative of this religious form of universalism, particularly when the "children" include people who don't subscribe to the same god.

Other forms of transcendent universalism include the Marxist notion of historical imperative, wherein all people are subject to the same historical forces; economic and political laws that are thought to affect all people in the same way, such as the capitalist concept of individual achievement; and psychological principles, such as archetypes or needs that are assumed to be invariably valid cross-culturally.

Among all the ethnocentric stages, this stage of development allows for the greatest acknowledgment of cultural difference. Such difference is usually not trivialized, as it is in the previous stage of physical universalism. Rather, cultural difference may be seen as "part of the plan"—an intrinsic element of the universal principle. People at this stage of development may find differences interesting and worth learning about as curiosities or as important factors in communication. The ethnocentrism of transcendent universalism is nevertheless evident. The principle or supernatural force assumed to overlie cultural difference is invariably derived from one's own worldview. I have yet to hear anyone at this stage say, "There is a single truth in the universe, and it is *not* what I believe."

A more pernicious manifestation of ethnocentrism based on transcendent universalism is derived from any of a variety of aggressive conversion activities. Whether the conversion sought in another culture is religious, political, or economic, it rests on the assumption that there is a single truth, or best way, and that with sufficient education all people will discover this truth within themselves. These overtly ethnocentric conversion efforts may be accompanied by a high degree of interest in cultural difference, perhaps with the rationale that knowledge of difference is necessary to implement the conversion effectively.

Intercultural communication in the state of minimization is often based on the assumption that one need only be truly one's self to ensure successful interaction. This belief seems to be derived from the idea that deep down everyone is the same and that this commonality can be tapped for communication by avoiding any artifice. Of course, it is ethnocentric to think that one's natural self is automatically understandable, since it assumes that one's own culture is central to everyone's worldview. This form of ethnocentrism is particularly appealing to Americans, given their cultural valuing of "genuineness."

As I have noted elsewhere (M. Bennett 1979), both forms of universalism can degenerate quickly into the earlier defense stage. This occurs when expectations of successful interaction based on assumed commonality are not met, that is, being yourself doesn't get you anywhere. The conclusion drawn from this disappointment is not, apparently, that the original assumption of universalism was incorrect, but that there must be something terribly obtuse about one's interactional partners. It is but a short step backwards from this position to either superiority or derogation.

The major impediment to development beyond this stage is the belief that one can get by with minimization behavior in many intercultural situations. An experienced travel/study group leader once suggested to me that intercultural sensitivity "might not be so important." She described a person in her last group who was so aggressively "himself" that he accosted total strangers on the street (in an Asian country) to solicit their phone numbers and behaved in other culturally inappropriate ways that he defended as natural for himself. At first the leader and other group members were embarrassed by this behavior, but the leader later concluded that the participant "got a lot out of the trip" and that his hosts found him "interesting" and "amusing."

I have heard renditions of the above story often from professors, students, and businesspersons returning from sojourns. But in no case has this position been taken by someone highly trained in intercultural communication, such as professionals in the field or Peace Corps volunteers. I conclude from this informal observation that people who have not dedicated themselves in some way to intercultural development may find it preferable to maintain a familiar identity abroad and that the maintenance of that identity is easily rationalized with the assumption that everyone likes people who are "themselves" (however that is). This assumption, of course, may protect one from incorporating cultural difference into one's behavior and may help maintain a fairly comfortable state of ethnocentrism.

Developmental Strategies

Between this stage and the next stage, acceptance, is a "paradigmatic barrier." Movement to the next stage represents a major conceptual shift from reliance on absolute, dualistic principles of some sort to an acknowledgment of nonabsolute relativity. For Westerners, this shift seems best approached inductively. First, cultural self-awareness should be generated through discussion, exercises, and other methods of discovery. For many people in minimization, lack of awareness of their own culture underlies the assumption of cultural similarity. When they can place more of their own behavior in a cultural context, they are less inclined to assume that the behavior is universal.

Simulations, reports of personal experience, and other methods of illustrating substantial cultural differences in the interpretation of behavior are effective at this point. Awareness of these differences must be shown to have definite practical significance for intercultural communication to overcome the stasis of minimization. Even if this is done effectively, learners are still likely to experience a degree of disorientation and confusion as they struggle with the implications of relativity. Care should be taken that this confusion is simply acknowledged and not prematurely eased by retreating to earlier ethnocentric states.

It is particularly effective at this stage to use members of other cultures as resource persons. These people work best in a small facilitated discussion group (as opposed to the overused and largely useless panel). Resource persons should be selected and, if possible, trained, since being from another culture does not preclude ethnocentrism. In particular, having a resource person in his or her own state of minimization is worse than none at all. If resource persons are selected carefully and placed in facilitated situations, they can provide credibility for the concept of cultural difference that would otherwise forever elude the trainer. Participants in minimization are unlikely to face someone from another culture, as they do in this kind of training session, and deny the cultural differences claimed by that person.

THE ETHNORELATIVE STAGES

Fundamental to ethnorelativism is the assumption that cultures can only be understood relative to one another and that particular behavior can only be understood within a cultural context. There is no absolute standard of rightness or "goodness" that can be applied to cultural behavior. Cultural difference is neither good nor bad, it is just different, although some cultural behaviors may be more adaptive than others to particular environmental conditions. One's own culture is not any more central to reality than any other culture, although it may be preferable to a particular individual or group.

The shift away from ethnocentric absolute standards may raise an ethical concern. Does ethnorelativism imply moral acquiescence to each and every cultural value, no matter how personally repugnant? Ethnorelativism is here taken as a contrast to ethnocentrism, not as a philosophical or ethical position in its own right. In other words, a state of ethnorelativism does not imply an ethical agreement with all difference nor a disavowal of stating (and acting upon) a preference for one worldview over another. The position does imply, however, that ethical choices will be made on grounds other than the ethnocentric protection of one's own worldview or in the name of absolute principles. The ethical implications of relativism will be discussed further in the "contextual evaluation" section of the integration stage.

For the development of intercultural sensitivity, ethnorelativism represents a major change in the meaning attributed to difference. In phenomenological terms, the experience of difference is substantially altered. In the ethnocentric stages, difference is experienced as threatening, either explicitly (as in the stages of denial and defense) or implicitly (as in minimization), and actions taken from these stages are meant to counter the threat in various ways. The ethnorelative experience of difference is nonthreatening, since attempts are made to elaborate new categories rather than simply to preserve existing ones. Cultural difference is more likely to be enjoyable and actually sought after in these stages.

The contrast in the ways of experiencing difference is illustrated in the reports of two study-abroad students who had just returned from a homestay in France. One student stated, "My homestay mother was always yelling at me in French, which I didn't understand well. I felt like I was always doing something wrong. It was a bad situation, and I was happy when I got changed to a different home where the mother spoke some English." The second student reported a similar situation but a different reaction: "My homestay mother would burst into my room in the morning, throw open the window, and yell things in French I didn't understand. It was just wonderful—so French!" In the first case, what may be a cultural difference is seen as problematic or threatening, and an attempt is made to eliminate it. In the second case, there is more attention given to the possibility that the mother's behavior was cultural, and it is experienced as exciting.

While the experience of a dominant culture for members of oppressed groups is unlikely to carry the excitement of study abroad, it may at this stage be interpreted as more developmental than debasing. People are likely to recognize the need to live together in a multicultural society, and they are willing to accord respect as well as demand it. Emphasis in intercultural relations may expand from an exclusive concern with countering the negative effects of racism, sexism, and other forms of prejudice to include building positive channels for understanding cultural differences.

Stages of ethnorelativism begin with the acceptance of cultural difference as inevitable and enjoyable, through adaptation to cultural differences with intercultural communication skills, to the final stage of integration in which ethnorelativism may be synthesized into a coherent and workable new identity.

IV. ACCEPTANCE

In this stage, cultural difference is both acknowledged and respected. Rather than being evaluated negatively or positively as part of a defensive strategy, the existence of difference is accepted as a necessary and preferable human condition.

While the state of acceptance itself represents "crossing the barrier" from ethnocentrism to ethnorelativism, two forms of development within this stage seem common. First comes respect for cultural differences in behavior, followed by respect for cultural differences in values.

A. Respect for Behavioral Difference

The easier of the two ideas to accept is that verbal and nonverbal behavior varies across cultures and that all forms of such behavior are worthy of respect (if not personal support). While superficial differences in verbal and nonverbal behavior may have been recognized in earlier stages, here the recognition and acceptance are at the deeper level of cultural relativity. People begin to see alien behavior as indicative of profound cultural differences, not just as permutations of universal (and probably ethnocentric) laws.

The most obvious of behavioral differences is language. The existence of foreign language requirements and university departments for this subject attests to its acceptability as a legitimate cultural difference that commands respect. Nevertheless, the naive view of foreign languages as simply different codes with which to communicate similar ideas continues to exist. This view, supported to some extent by the universalist assumptions of transformational grammar (Chomsky 1965), is supplanted at this stage by the hypothesis of linguistic relativity (Whorf 1956), that is, languages are seen as shapers of realities rather than simply as tools with which to represent an a priori universe.

In addition to the acceptance of linguistic relativity, people at this stage begin to recognize differences in communication style. Phatic communication, such as greeting rituals, may vary in content, length, and purpose. Description may be more linear or more circular, argument more inductive or deductive, or expression of feeling more implicit or explicit. These differences now begin to elicit curiosity rather than animosity.

One of the most dramatic discoveries in acceptance is recognizing the cultural relativity of nonverbal behavior. Cultural variation in paralinguistics, kinesics, proxemics, haptics, and other categories of behavior is the subject of both classic and contemporary literature in intercultural communication (e.g., Hall 1973; Barnlund 1982; Jensen 1985). Yet the topic continues to seem new and surprising to many students, teachers, and even some intercultural professionals. Perhaps this is because, at least for Americans, nonverbal behavior is more out of awareness than is verbal behavior. When we are unconscious of the cultural context of our behavior, it may seem more natural and central to reality (Stewart and Bennett 1991).

Development into ethnorelativism is first established by stressing recognition and nonevaluative respect for variation in verbal behavior and communication style, since such behavior is most generally recognized as appropriately different. Using verbal language as a parallel, body language (kinesics) and other categories of nonverbal behavior differences can be acknowledged and accorded the same respect. For less sophisticated audiences, reversing the order may be more effective. By introducing nonverbal differences first, examples can be made more concrete and immediately recognizable. The approach to exploring nonverbal difference can then be applied to the more abstract concepts of communication style.

Failure to move fairly quickly beyond this stage of development opens the possibility that verbal and nonverbal difference will be incorporated into the previous stage of transcendent universalism. As noted earlier, transcendent universalism usually includes substantial recognition of behavioral difference. Unless respect for value differences associated with behavior is established, efforts at this stage may serve simply to elaborate details within an ethnocentric frame.

On the other hand, moving prematurely to an ethnorelative discussion of values without sufficiently establishing behavioral relativity may create a threat that encourages retreat to a defensive state. For instance, in a training program some years ago, I skipped the behavioral stage and attempted a presentation on American values as contrasted to those of some European cultures. Vociferous and hostile argument came from the trainees, whose reactions were scattered across the ethnocentric stages. Some claimed that no generalizations about values were possible (denial), others accused me of berating American culture (defense), and most held that there weren't significant differences between Americans and Europeans anyway (minimization). In later programs, I carefully noted behavior differences before broaching the associated values, and there has been no repetition of that particular reaction.

B. Respect for Value Difference

Relativity of cultural values is central to intercultural sensitivity. At this stage of development, there is acceptance of the different worldview assumptions that underlie cultural variation in behavior. Alternative beliefs about both what exists in reality and the value which may be attached to those phenomena are respected as viable, at least as they are expressed in a cultural context. In addition, at this stage one acknowledges one's own worldview as a relative cultural construct (cultural self-awareness).

Intrinsic to this stage of development is a sense of *process*. Values and assumptions are not seen as things so much as they are perceived as manifestations of human creativity. Consistent with this process approach is the idea that assumptions are not something we *have* —instead we actively *assume* things about the world that allow it to be organized in particular ways. This is, of course, a general parallel to Whorf's (1956) well-known statement of linguistic relativity:

> The categories and types that we isolate from the world of phenomena we do not find there because they stare every observer in the face; on the contrary, the world is presented in a kaleidoscopic flux of impressions which has to be organized by our minds—and this means largely by the linguistic systems in our minds (213).

Similarly, we do not *have* values. Instead we value or assume relative goodness or rightness about the phenomena which emerge from our organization of the world. It is this active assignment of worth to a given organizational pattern that perpetuates its existence as part of an ongoing process (Berger and Luckmann 1967). Failure to recognize our dynamic participation in the perpetuation of process is what Hall (1976) terms extension transference: "...the common intellectual maneuver in which the extension is confused with or takes the place of the process extended" (25). In this case, the process of valuing may be extended into values. When the results of valuing become things, they may take on an apparent life of their own and eventually become the absolutes of ethnocentrism.

Avoiding extension transference ("reification" in the terminology of Berger and Luckmann) is what differentiates the ethnorelative experience of acceptance from the ethnocentric experience of earlier stages. If the *act of valuing* is reified into *having values*, then those values are more likely to be defined as intrinsic to one's identity, and competing values become threats that must be countered. In acceptance, valuing remains a process which can be pursued in various ways. Other cultures' different valuing is worthy of understanding and respect, but not necessarily agreement.

The main impediment to development from this stage is the possibility that value difference is not understood as a process. Eventually, someone else's cultural assumption or value will be personally offensive.

A likely candidate is some form of valuing men over women, although the culprit may also be the valuing of different sexual orientations, health care procedures, or treatment of children. If the particular difference is perceived as a static value held by members of that culture, those who find it offensive may retreat to superiority, denigration, or possibly minimization (they don't *really* feel that way). To preserve the sensitivity of this stage, difference that might be personally devalued must be seen as part of a culture's overall organization of the world. As such, the offending difference becomes a way to organize reality, rather than a distasteful trait. It should be stressed that this view of cultural difference does not disallow one's having a personal opinion about the difference—it simply precludes that opinion from becoming an ethnocentric evaluation. (The ethical implications of this stance will be discussed more fully later.)

Developmental Strategies

Movement into the next stage of intercultural sensitivity, "adaptation," is encouraged by emphasizing the practical application of ethnorelative acceptance to intercultural communication. In actual education or training contexts, this move must be made fairly quickly to add personal relevance and usefulness to the necessarily anecdotal treatment of behavioral difference and the theoretical treatment of values. In some cases, communication applications can be combined effectively with discussions of values to facilitate the development. For instance, in one training program a discussion of American/European value difference was accompanied by immediate applications to improving relations with prospective homestay families. At this point of transition, cross-cultural simulations can be particularly effective in educational and training programs. The goal of these kinds of activities is to put ethnorelativism into action.

V. ADAPTATION

The essence of ethnorelativism is respect for the integrity of cultures, including one's own. In acceptance, the framework for appreciating cultural difference was established. At this stage, adaptation, skills for relating to and communicating with people of other cultures are enhanced.

The term "adaptation" is meant to exclude the connotations of "assimilation," wherein one's identity is absorbed by a new culture (Prosser 1978). While culturally appropriate communication skills probably are enhanced by assimilation, they may be gained at the cost of achieving ethnorelativism. Assimilation often seems most closely related to the reversal form of defense, where, for instance, immigrants may be encouraged to denigrate their native cultures and embrace the superiority of their adopted one. At best, assimilation yields minimization, where cultural diversity is dissipated in the dominant culture's melting pot. In both cases, a *substitutive* process promotes replacement of one worldview with a new one. Bicultural and multicultural assimilation into two or more different cultures are special cases and are discussed under "pluralism" below.

In adaptation, new skills appropriate to a different worldview are acquired in an *additive* process. Maintenance of one's original worldview is encouraged, so the adaptations necessary for effective communication in other cultures extend, rather than replace, one's native skills. The key to this additive principle is the assumption that culture is a process, not a thing. One does not have culture; one engages in it. Consequently, that one might temporarily behave or value in a way appropriate to a different culture does not threaten the integrity or existence of one's own cultural identity. Rather, the new ways of being are added to one's repertoire of cultural alternatives.

A major concern in the adaptation stage is developing alternative communication skills. Communication may be defined in general as the "creation of common meaning." Within a single culture, common meaning can be approached by displaying verbal and nonverbal behavior that elicits similar "constructs" in the overlapping worldviews of the communicants (Kelly 1963). In other words, people of the same culture more or less understand the language and actions of each other. No such assumption can be made cross-culturally without recourse to an ethnocentric stage, such as the transcendent universalism form of minimization. Thus, ethnorelative intercultural communication must posit an approach to common meaning that includes variable worldviews. One way to do this is to allow shifting of cultural frames of reference by the people communicating.

The stage of adaptation suggested in this model posits two phases of development one goes through in shifting one's cultural frame of reference for the purpose of communication. The first is *empathy*, where such shifts are intentional and temporary, and the second is *pluralism*, where the shifts may be more unintentional and tied to multiple permanent frames of reference.

A. Empathy

Central to any intercultural communication skill is the ability to experience some aspect of reality differently from what is "given" by one's own culture. Anything less than this shift in experience risks the perpetuation of ethnocentrism. Though some kinds of information may be exchanged adequately across cultural boundaries while maintaining one's own worldview, such exchanges fall short of the creation of common meaning intrinsic to forming relationships.

The ability to experience differently in a communication context is here termed "empathy." Elsewhere (M. Bennett 1979), I have contrasted empathy to "sympathy," where one attempts to understand another by imagining how one would feel in another's *position*. Sympathy is ethnocentric in that its practice demands only a shift in assumed circumstance (position), not a shift in the frame of reference one brings to that circumstance; it is based on an assumption of similarity, implying other people will feel similar to one in similar circumstances. Empathy, by contrast, describes an attempt to understand by imagining or comprehending the other's *perspective*. Empathy is ethnorelative in that it demands a shift in frame of reference; it is based on an assumption of difference, and implies respect for that difference and a readiness to give up temporarily one's own worldview in order to imaginatively participate in the other's. The contrast between sympathy and empathy usually is quite clear in expression, and it can thus be used to diagnose achievement of this stage of development. For instance, the statement, "What I'd do in his position..." is nearly always indicative of a sympathetic approach. Statements such as "I know she has a different view of this, so..." or "I feel different about this when I imagine him viewing it" are more likely indicative of empathy. Recently I observed this contrast illustrated by two American reactions to an Arab student's weekend flight to London. The sympathetic (and ethnocentric) comment was, "Boy, it must be great to have so much money you could just do anything you wanted." The empathic response was, "Maybe airplanes are like modern camels—conveyances you use to fulfill obligations to friends across some ocean-desert." The sympathetic response projected an individualistic American worldview into the perceived situation, while the empathic response assumed that the Arab's experience of an airplane trip was probably different than an American's would be. It is not so important that the empathic statement was correct; what is important is that it acknowledged and respected possible cultural difference.

The ability to make the temporary shift in perspective represented by empathy indicates a relatively high level of intercultural development. Upon this base, most people can engage in reasonably satisfactory intercultural communication. Development within this stage may go on for some time (perhaps years), taking the form of increased knowledge of other cultures, facility in foreign languages, understanding of communication styles and nonverbal patterns, and heightened sensitivity to how situations "feel different" when alternative cultural values are applied. Such development can be encouraged by constantly coupling knowledge of other cultures with the practice of ethnorelative empathy.

Yet the empathy form of adaptation has limitations in terms of intercultural sensitivity. People at this stage may not be able to handle respectful disagreement with different cultural views. They may think all cultural difference is "good" and be frustrated when people of other cultures evaluate their own or some other culture negatively. This is similar to the stage of "multiplicity" suggested by Perry (1970) in his model of ethical development, wherein judgment is paralyzed by a plethora of equally valuable alternatives.

Another possibility at this stage is the problem of mutual empathy. What happens when one person attempts to shift to another cultural perspective at the same time the other person is doing the same thing? My wife and I once tried to order sushi the "correct" way in Japan by indicating we wanted seven (seven fingers) orders of the fish and rice preparation. In Japan, sushi always comes in pairs, so we expected fourteen pieces. An unusually long wait was filled with animated voices from behind the counter, accompanied by many looks in our direction. Finally, we were presented with what was, for the Japanese, impossible—an unlucky seven pieces of sushi. Apparently, our hosts had decided on empathizing with us. We contemplated how to solve this problem of mutual consideration gone awry, ate our seven sushi, and finished the meal elsewhere with an ice-cream cone.

Empathy is limited in both time and breadth. Because one is shifting temporarily into portions of different worldviews, a long-term experience of a complete alternative worldview is not necessarily encountered. This more comprehensive experience of another culture characterizes the next form of adaptation.

B. Pluralism

The term "pluralism" is here used to indicate two aspects of the adaptation stage of intercultural sensitivity. One is a philosophical

commitment to the existence of a "multitude of irreducible and equivalent ultimate wholes, ideas, values and value scales, as well as experiences in which they are tested" (Fairchild 1970). In terms of the meaning
attributed to difference, this definition suggests that cultures are not only
different, but that such difference must always be understood totally
within the context of the relevant culture. Implied by this philosophical
stance is the requirement that understanding of difference must derive
from actual experience *within* that complete cultural frame. Therefore,
the second meaning of pluralism as it is used here is the existence of two
or more internalized cultural frames of reference. Pluralism can thus be
considered the general category which contains "biculturalism" and
"multiculturalism."

The development of multiple cultural frames of reference usually
involves some significant living experience in another culture. This form
of development is sometimes achieved naturally by children of expatriates or by others who have grown up in two or more cultures (Useem,
Donoghue, and Useem 1963). The minimum time spent in a different
culture needed to develop rudimentary pluralism seems to be around
two years, judging from the experience of some Peace Corps volunteers,
but this apparently depends heavily on the intensity of the living experience. (I once met an armed services family stationed on Guam who had
only been off the base twice in two years). Pluralism is also exhibited by
many people of color and others who routinely deal with European-
American culture, including women who work in largely male cultural
contexts. To a lesser extent, European-Americans who are routinely
exposed to other ethnic groups, such as inhabitants of culturally heterogeneous urban neighborhoods, may have developed pluralism. Occasionally even men attain female frames of reference.

Characteristic of all pluralism is the internalization by one individual
of two or more fairly complete cultural frames of reference. Because
people in this form of adaptation are identified with different worldviews,
they experience cultural difference as part of their normal selves. The
question of "respect for difference" that was a major factor in earlier
stages here becomes synonymous with "respect for self." In other words,
pluralistic people are not ethnocentric, at least in regard to the cultures
they have internalized.

In most cases, pluralism represents a development in intercultural
sensitivity beyond empathy. In the pluralism form, cultural difference is
respected as highly as one's self, since it is intrinsic to that self. As such,
difference may be experienced more completely than it is in the empathy

form, where a different worldview is still "outside" the self, before and after the act of empathy. It could be construed that pluralistic people have a kind of natural empathy for differences included in their multiple worldviews and that this natural empathy is a more powerful tool for intercultural communication than is the intentional empathy described in the previous form of adaptation.

For people who have been oppressed by a dominant culture, adaptation is the stage at which bicultural identity can be solidified. Banks (1988) and Smith (1991) suggest stages in their models of ethnic-identity development that seem to match the adaptation stage. Members of oppressed minority groups who maintain their own culture and who can also operate successfully in the dominant culture are pluralistic, since they demonstrate a command of at least one alternative worldview. If they have dealt with the issues of acceptance, they are likely to be interculturally sensitive. However, as with others noted below, the simple fact of pluralism may not indicate ethnorelativism. If adaptation to the dominant group is unconscious or based only on survival, then the skills involved may not indicate general intercultural sensitivity.

In addition, people who have experienced cultural oppression may be caught in the dilemma of betrayal. If they sometimes adapt their behavior to the dominant culture, they risk being perceived as betraying their own cultural roots. If they restrict their behavior to only that acceptable to the minority culture, they betray their own intercultural abilities. Various terms—such as Oreo cookie, coconut, apple—that indicate white on the inside and some other color on the outside are applied by less developed observers to denigrate those who dare act biculturally. People dealing with identity issues in defense are likely to see every act as political, and their evaluation of people in adaptation can be devastating.

In the case of oppressed minority group members and others, pluralism may be *accidental* if it was achieved without systematic movement through earlier stages of development. This is most likely to occur when living experience in another culture is undertaken without preparation or previous experience with ethnorelative stages, such as might be the case with young children raised abroad, with untrained personnel posted to long overseas assignments, or with members of minority groups who are forced to live in the dominant culture. In these situations, people may understand and even respect the differences with which they are familiar, but they may be unable to recognize or use this sensitivity as part of a generalized skill in adapting to cultural difference. For example, I have observed Americans who were bicultural with Japanese be very insensitive to Arabs, and I have seen Arabs who were perfectly bicultural with Americans not have the slightest inclination to relate respectfully to a Japanese. In the U.S., I have observed people who seem to be multicultural in relation to several domestic ethnic groups, but who are unable to generalize intercultural sensitivity to different national cultures.

This type of accidental pluralism seems to be what Lum (1977) refers to as "cultural pluralism": the ability to shift into a variety of cultural frames of reference. Lum implies that cultural pluralism is a less sensitive condition than that claimed by Adler (1977) for multicultural persons, who have more qualities of "marginality" (associated with the next stage of integration).

Pluralism, then, has two faces. One is the increase in general intercultural sensitivity allowed by internalization of different cultural worldviews. The other is a simple increase in the number of cultures with which one identifies, which is not necessarily adaptive to difference in general. The former case is accompanied by a conscious assumption of ethnorelativism, such as might be developed by experience in earlier stages of intercultural sensitivity. In the latter case, pluralism describes a nondevelopmental state in which general ethnorelativism is missing.

An additional drawback of accidental pluralism is that it may be accompanied by neutrality or negativity toward intercultural communication education. For instance, one bicultural manager of an international marketing division rejected a personnel training proposal with the rationale, "They need to sink or swim." These and other similar reactions (e.g., "You can't train this kind of knowledge") seem to betray an orientation antithetical to the idea that cross-cultural effectiveness improves as part of a developmental process. That is, pluralism is seen by these people as simply extended knowledge of another culture and not as a stage of development. Consequently, they do not believe that sensitivity will be enhanced by any general approach to cultural difference. It may also be that some at this stage develop the "French Foreign Legion Syndrome," wherein they think, "Things were tough for me— why should you get off easy?"

In some programs run by accidental pluralists which I have observed, education or training provided for prospective sojourners is oriented heavily to historical and sociological data on the host culture. This manifestation of bias against a personal-development approach to intercultural experience seems common in international education, where purely logistic and academic predeparture programs are usual. In other cases, any prior knowledge at all of cultural factors is seen as superfluous. This actively negative attitude is more often found, in my experience, in some government contexts. In relationship to intercultural sensitivity, it is notable that these attitudes are held by some people who qualify as bicultural or multicultural, in the common use of those terms.

The key to pluralism's being representative of a high level of intercultural sensitivity development is the generalizability of a positive attitude toward cultural difference. If the pluralistic experience is interpreted by an individual as representative of essential ethnorelativism, then that person is likely to support efforts toward general development of intercultural sensitivity in others. Certainly many bicultural people, and perhaps most multicultural people, support that position. This is supported by Adler, who includes in his description of the ethnorelative multicultural person many of the qualities associated with adaptation. The possible limitations of this stage—inability to generalize cultural adaptation or to accept personal development as part of intercultural learning—simply offer warning that pluralism in itself is not necessarily interculturally sensitive, nor is it automatically useful in education toward intercultural development. Bochner (1981, 12) also notes this limitation when he states: "knowing more than one culture is a necessary but not sufficient condition for cultural mediation."

Movement beyond the adaptive stages is impeded by the high credibility claimed by and accorded to people at this point of development. There may be little motivation for these people to attempt further intercultural development. And, more importantly, pluralistic people often are hired to work in the field of intercultural education, such as international student exchange or foreign language teaching, on the basis of their "obvious" personal qualifications. If the pluralism of people in these positions is not accompanied by conscious ethnorelativism, they may actually impede the development of others.

Developmental Strategies

Participants moving out of acceptance are eager to apply their knowledge of cultural difference to actual face-to-face communication. Thus, now is the time to provide opportunities for interaction. These activities might include dyads with other-culture partners, facilitated multicultural group discussions, or outside assignments involving interviewing of people from other cultures. Training in the practice of empathy is also appropriate. As much as possible, activities should be related to real-life communication situations. For instance, in the case of Americans anticipating study abroad, communication practice could refer to homestays or developing friendships in the other culture. In the case of international students and visitors, practice could include communicating with faculty and with others in everyday situations. There is less need for facilitation of discussion at this stage, unlike earlier stages when knowledgeable intervention was crucial. Generally, people in the later phase of adaptation know how to orchestrate their own learning.

These same real-life situations seem to be effective for pluralists who are less ethnorelative. However, the reason for their success may be different. In these cases, it may be that the limitations of culture-specific adaptation become evident and create a motivation for the pluralists to generalize their abilities through more use of ethnorelative principles.

While the state of adaptation is "good enough" in most contexts of personal intercultural communication and professional intercultural education, there is still ethnorelative territory beyond adaptation. An identity crisis may be brought on by the "internal culture shock" generated by multiple worldviews. This may fuel a desire for a holistic, coherent sense of self that somehow integrates multiple frames of reference.

VI. INTEGRATION

A new type of person whose orientation and view of the world profoundly transcends his indigenous culture is developing from the complex of social, political, economic, and educational interactions of our time.

With these words, Adler (1977, 25) begins his description of the multicultural person. (Adler uses the label "multicultural" to refer to aspects of both adaptation and integration, as they are defined in this model.) The multicultural person is one whose "essential identity is inclusive of life patterns different from his own and who has psychologically and socially come to grips with a multiplicity of realities" (25). But this person is not simply sensitive to a variety of cultures, as I have described people in adaptation. Rather, this person is "always in the process of becoming *a part of* and *apart from* a given cultural context" (26). This additional act of defining one's relationship to cultural context is the key identifier of the integration stage of development.

In adaptation, it is sufficient for one's identity to be defined in pluralistic terms; that is, to see one's self existing within a collection of various cultural and personal frames of reference. It is likely that one will maintain a primary cultural affiliation. For some people, however, the primary cultural affiliation is lost or discarded. The multiple internalized frames of reference clash with one another and create what might be described as *internal cultural shock*. The subsequent disintegration of identity leads toward *cultural marginality*—existence on the periphery of two or more cultures (Stonequist 1937; Bochner 1981).

The integration stage describes the attempt to integrate disparate aspects of one's identity into a new whole while remaining culturally marginal. The goal of this new definition of identity is not to reaffiliate with one culture, nor is it simply to reestablish comfort with a multiplicity of worldviews. Rather, the integrated person understands that his or her identity emerges from the act of defining identity itself. This self-reflective loop shows identity to be one act of constructing reality, similar to other acts that together yield concepts and cultures. By being conscious of this dynamic process, people can function in relationship to cultures while staying outside the constraints of any particular one.

Students in my intercultural communication courses typically react to Adler's portrayal of the multicultural person with the statement, "So how can this person ever choose to do anything, if everything's always changing?" It may be useful to take Adler's concept as a starting point for integration—an identification with ethnorelativism that is necessary but not sufficient for actually living outside of normal cultural boundaries.

The first form of integration, contextual evaluation, describes mechanisms which allow for ethical choice and action in the profoundly relativistic world implied by an ethnorelative identity. The second form, constructive marginality, suggests an end state of development wherein marginality becomes a constructive force for intercultural communication and coexistence.

A. Contextual Evaluation

All the stages of ethnorelativism to this point have emphasized nonevaluation of difference. Suspension of evaluation was necessary to overcome the earlier ethnocentric states and to allow full development of adaptive skills. But the flexibility of cultural adaptation may have a price—the paralysis of commitment. Partially developed ethnorelativism may lead individuals into a multiplistic quagmire where all possible choices among alternative perspectives seem equally good. Long-term experience of this debilitating ambiguity may eventuate in a retreat to the surer ground of ethnocentrism or into the mentally unstable conditions of what Adler calls "multiphrenia" or "detachment." Contextual evaluation is a development beyond adaptation where one attains the ability to analyze and evaluate situations from one or more chosen cultural perspectives. Implied by this ability is both the skill to shift cultural context and the concomitant self-awareness necessary to exercise choice. The outcome of this action is a judgment of relative goodness that is specific to some identified context. This notion is virtually identical to Perry's (1970) stage of "contextual relativism" in his model of cognitive and ethical development, which offers an extremely useful ethical perspective for interculturalists.

The simplest example of contextual evaluation is to posit the question, "Is it good to take off my clothes?" The answer will almost certainly be contextual: "It depends on the circumstances." In the context of a bath, most people think it's good. In the context of a classroom, most people think it's bad. This is not situational ethics, which connotes peer pressure as a determiner of "goodness." Even if all the others in the classroom took off their clothes, I still must evaluate my action relative to the context (classroom) and not just in terms of others' choices.

This kind of example extends easily into intercultural situations. For example, is it good to refer directly to a mistake made by yourself or someone else? In most American contexts, it is good. In most Japanese contexts, it is bad. However, it might be good in some cases to use an American style in Japan, and vice versa. The ability to use both styles is part of adaptation. The ethical consideration of context in making a choice is part of integration.

A more complex type of intercultural contextual evaluation involves assessing a different culture's conflicting evaluation of some phenomena. For instance, when I first arrived in Truk, I was approached by a man who offered to help build a house for me. I accepted gladly, and I was not at all disturbed when he asked me for a few little favors in return (mostly Scotch whiskey). However, as I internalized Trukese culture, it became evident that this man's behavior was bad by Trukese standards. He was not the person who, according to clan affiliation, should have been helping me. Because he was "out of place" in the scheme of reciprocal helping, I shouldn't have been buying him whiskey either, although it was fine to buy liquor for the right people. (Another lesson from this situation, which has been confirmed often since, is that outsiders are usually first approached by people perceived as deviant in their own culture.) My ability to feel his behavior as bad, even though it was good by American standards, was an exercise of empathy or rudimentary biculturalism. I may approach integration by later calling these contexts to mind as I seek ethical behavior that is neither purely Trukese nor purely American.

The more sophisticated type of contextual evaluation is one in which one consciously chooses to subject a phenomenon to two or more cultural frames for the purpose of evaluation. An example of this is a college teacher who faced the challenge of designing appropriate individual assignments for a group of Arab students in an American school. She knew that in an Arab context working jointly on projects was normal. She also recognized that by American standards the method of producing this work might be considered cheating. Considering both evaluations, she devised an assignment which included some initial group work followed by individual commentaries on the project. In terms of this stage of intercultural development, she chose an action that took into account differences in contextual evaluation. She might also have chosen to act in concert with only one or the other of the evaluations; the important point is that multiple evaluations were considered.

Among people who seem to be operating in the contextual-evaluation form of integration, I often hear statements such as "I think I'll approach this situation Japanese" (resulting in an unusually subtle style, by American standards) or "I'm trying to decide if I should treat this as evasion or Nigerian" (which considers whether the operant context is linear or circular). These people see their identities as including many cultural options, any of which can be exercised in any context, by choice. They are not so much bound by what is right for a given culture (although they are aware of that) as they are committed to using good judgment in choosing the best treatment of a particular situation. Disagreement about what is best is not threatening to people at this stage; it is even encouraged. They are conscious of themselves as choosers of alternatives, so they feel no need to defend the rightness of their actions (although they might argue their "bestness").

Contextual evaluation is a particularly powerful form for people who have experienced cultural oppression. They are able to evaluate those aspects of the dominant culture that lead to oppression without rejecting the entire culture. They are able to see the strengths and limits of their own cultures without embracing them entirely. For the first time in ethnorelative development, members of oppressed minority groups may feel released from the dilemma of betrayal. By defining the context in which evaluation of their actions occurs, people under political pressure can separate the reactive forces of defense identity maintenance from integration commitments to constructive action. The politics are still difficult, but the issue of identity is much clearer.

In this form of integration, we see the first application of a difference-based identity—the natural use of contextual evaluation for the purpose of determining action. For many people, particularly those whose pluralism is tentative, this will be the last stage of intercultural development. Movement beyond this point is unnecessary for most nonprofessional purposes, and even much professional intercultural activity can be undertaken satisfactorily from this form of sensitivity.

However, for people with more intensive living experience in different cultures, with great commitment to principles of internationalism and multiculturalism, or with an exceptionally strong desire for coherence, development beyond this form may occur. If it does, the problems and potentials of cultural marginality must be faced squarely.

B. Constructive Marginality

Much effort has been expended in seeking an alternative to the term "marginality" to describe the position of someone who operates outside of normal cultural boundaries. Adler uses "multicultural person," as already noted. Bochner (1981) and Taft (1981) both juxtapose "the mediating person" to the marginal person, emphasizing the more useful aspects of the former and the relative debilitation associated with the latter. Yoshikawa (1987) coins the evocative term "dynamic in-between-ness" to capture many of the aspects of both multicultural and mediating persons. In all these cases, the effort seems to be to avoid the connotations of marginality that indicate an unhealthy outsider status. Colin Wilson (1956) actually uses the term "outsider" to describe people who are marginal within their own culture (but who are not necessarily pluralistic). It is likely that the negative associations of marginality can be traced to Park's (1926) original description of "marginal man," wherein he itemized the difficulties and strains faced by this kind of person.

Against this semantic tide, I will argue here that marginality describes exactly the subjective experience of people who are struggling with the total integration of ethnorelativism. They are outside all cultural frames of reference by virtue of their ability to consciously raise any assumption to a metalevel (level of self-reference). In other words, there is no natural cultural identity for a marginal person. There are no unquestioned assumptions, no intrinsically absolute right behaviors, nor any necessary reference group. And it is certainly true that many marginal people experience great discomfort and dysfunction as a result of their status.

Yet marginality—the real outsider kind—can be a constructive stage of intercultural sensitivity. When marginality is preceded by other stages of ethnorelative development (or when those stages are added to marginality), the elements of adaptation and choice come into play. These two skills allow a marginal person to construct appropriate frames of reference for particular purposes. In the previous form of contextual evaluation, we saw this kind of construction operating relative to particular situations. At this stage, it is not simply different contexts that are being consciously developed; it is total frames of reference. In other words, constructive marginality is the experience of one's self as a constant creator of one's own reality.

When marginality is not a development from preceding stages of sensitivity, the stresses and tensions noted by Adler for multicultural man become more likely. Vulnerability, diffuse identity, inauthenticity, and anomie are dangers that loom beyond an unprepared departure from cultural boundaries. One common form taken by these stresses is a cycle first noted by Stonequist (1937): (1) assimilation (of new cultural frames), (2) recognition (of marginality), (3) instability (of identity), and (4) attempt to reconcile. This destruction/reintegration process may be indicative of a marginal person's attempt to "catch up" to his or her stage by dipping back into earlier stages of development for relevant skills. Lacking awareness of which stage to emphasize (or even that there are stages, including marginality), these people may experience a kind of void where they cannot feel a part of any culture, nor can they clearly feel themselves as constructive actors outside of culture.

Janet Bennett (this volume) uses the term "encapsulated marginality" to indicate this state of being stuck on the margins of two or more cultures without conscious choice. She associates encapsulated marginality with the ethical position of multiplicity (Perry 1970), which was mentioned earlier as a danger in the empathy form of adaptation. In Yoshikawa's (1987) terms, encapsulated marginals are in-between but not dynamic.

A treatment for some of the stresses of marginality may be as simple as labeling the stage as both marginal and constructive. For example, in a workshop I conducted with Indochinese caseworkers, many of the above symptoms of encapsulated marginality were verbalized by the participants. Predominant among them was the expressed feeling that the caseworkers were accepted by neither their fellow Indochinese clients nor their North American professional colleagues. My cofacilitator and I suggested that they were experiencing marginality and that such a position could be used constructively for the job they had undertaken. Subsequent discussion and feedback, well after the workshop, indicated that this was a new idea for these people and that the label itself was helpful in their more comfortable acceptance of a culturally marginal mediating role. Ideally, given enough training time, people such as these caseworkers should go through an abbreviated course on the development of intercultural sensitivity. This would enable them to construe their experience of personal "differentness" as a natural outgrowth of highly developed sensitivity to cultural relativity.

Most generally, the problems associated with this final stage of ethnorelativism can be attributed to the fact that cultures do not encourage self-reflectiveness. Intercultural communication is one of the few disciplines that promote systematic contrastive analysis of one's own cultural assumptions. Perhaps if such mechanisms were common, the unconscious cultural conditioning we currently observe wouldn't exist for long. (This is not meant as a universalist vision—if cultures didn't exist, neither would human beings, as we currently understand them.) Lacking experience in applying consciousness to culture, we are woefully unprepared to experience total responsibility for our own reality. Without the prior development of ethnorelativism, we are likely to reject this responsibility; or, if marginality is somehow thrust upon us, we are likely to experience debilitating alienation.

With preparation, however, constructive marginality can be the most powerful position from which to exercise intercultural sensitivity. Cultural mediation could be accomplished best by someone who was not enmeshed in any reference group, yet who could construct each appropriate worldview as needed. International negotiation could be facilitated most effectively by professionals who were not identified with either party to the dispute, yet who could choose to operate in either cultural context. And, if there is ever to be a "meta-ethic" (Barnlund 1979) that can restrain the worst excesses of cultural-value conflict and guide respectful dialogue, it must come from those whose allegiance is only to life itself.

Lest this final stage of intercultural sensitivity development be considered some sort of arrival, it should be noted that this is simply the end of a continuum, not the end of learning. The next task for people who have mastered these stages is to construct new continua that stretch in directions beyond our current vision.

CONCLUSION

To the educators and learners who wish to employ this model, three assumptions about the development of intercultural sensitivity should now be clear. First, the phenomenology of difference is the key to intercultural sensitivity. Intercultural communication behavior is treated as a manifestation of this subjective experience. The evidence presented for this position is that people in similar circumstances of sojourning or other cross-cultural contact behave differently, depending on their construing of events.

The second assumption is that the construing of difference necessary for intercultural sensitivity is that of ethnorelativism, whereby different cultures are perceived as variable and viable constructions of reality. The key to ethnorelativism is the idea of *process*. Perceiving behavior, values, and identity itself as a process of constructing reality overcomes ethnocentrism by reducing reification and the assumptions of absoluteness, centrality, and universalism that usually accompany reification.

The third assumption of this model is that ethical choices can and must be made for intercultural sensitivity to develop. However, these choices cannot be based on either absolute or universal principles. Rather, ethical behavior must be chosen with awareness that different viable actions are possible. The incorporation of this kind of ethnorelative ethic into one's identity forms the basis of the last stage of this model—integration. And it is this last stage which makes the model both one of intercultural sensitivity development and of personal growth.

A final consideration is that of the appropriate level of intercultural sensitivity of a trainer or educator. In general, it is my experience that operating one stage beyond that which is being trained for is sufficient. Thus, teachers of a beginning intercultural communication class whose goal for students is acceptance could operate effectively from adaptation. The facilitator of a predeparture program aiming at adaptation should be at least at contextual evaluation in the integration stage.

Facilitating development to a level prior to one's own reminds trainers and educators that they are guides on a journey, not imparters of final truth, and that further growth is always possible. This reminder is especially necessary for instructing learners in integration. In this case, the required position may be beyond the model itself. The instructor must see clearly that this and other models are themselves only constructions of reality.

REFERENCES

Adler, Peter (1977). "Beyond cultural identity: Reflections upon cultural and multicultural man." In Richard W. Brislin (Ed.), *Culture learning: Concepts, application and research*. Honolulu: University Press of Hawaii.

Asuncion-Lande, Nobleza C. (1979). "Experiential learning in intercultural communication." In William G. Davey (Ed.), *Intercultural theory and practice: Perspectives on education, training and research*. Washington, DC: Society for Intercultural Education, Training and Research.

Banks, James A. (1988). *Multiethnic education: Theory and practice* (2d ed.). Newton, MA: Allyn and Bacon.

Barnlund, Dean (1979). "The cross-cultural arena: An ethical void." In Nobleza C. Asuncion-Lande (Ed.), *Ethical perspectives and critical issues in intercultural communication*. Falls Church, VA: Speech Communication Association.

_____ (1982a). "Communication in a global village." In Larry A. Samovar and Richard E. Porter (Eds.), *Intercultural communication: A reader* (3d ed.). Belmont, CA: Wadsworth.

_____ (1982b). *Public and private self in Japan and the United States*. Yarmouth, ME: Intercultural Press.

Bennett, Janet M. (1984). "Intercultural communication training in cultural self-awareness for study abroad." Doctoral dissertation, University of Minnesota.

Bennett, Janet M., Milton J. Bennett, and Kathryn Stillings (1979). "Intercultural communication workshop: Facilitators guide." (rev. ed.). Portland, OR: Portland State University.

Bennett, Milton J. (1979). "Overcoming the golden rule: Sympathy and empathy." In D. Nimmo (Ed.), *Communication Yearbook* 3. Washington, DC: International Communication Association.

_____ (1986a). "Towards ethnorelativism: A developmental model of intercultural sensitivity." In R. Michael Paige (Ed.), *Cross-cultural orientation: New conceptualizations and applications*. New York: University Press of America.

_____ (1986b). "A developmental approach to training for intercultural sensitivity." *International Journal of Intercultural Relations* 10, no. 2: 179-95.

Berger, J., B. P. Cohen, and M. J. Zelditch (1966). "Status characteristics and expectation states." In J. Berger, M. Zelditch, and B. Anderson (Eds.), *Sociological theories in progress* 1. Boston: Houghton Mifflin.

Berger, Peter, and T. Luckmann (1967). *The social construction of reality.* Garden City, NY: Doubleday.

Bochner, Stephen (1979). "The mediating man and cultural diversity." In Richard W. Brislin (Ed.), *Culture learning: Concepts, application and research.* Honolulu: University Press of Hawaii.

_____ (1981). "The social psychology of cultural mediation." In S. Bochner (Ed.), *The mediating person: Bridges between cultures.* Cambridge, MA: Schenkman.

Bostain, James (1977). *How to read a foreigner* (videotape). Portland, OR: Portland State University.

Brislin, Richard W. (1981). *Cross-cultural encounters: Face-to-face interaction.* Elmsford, NY: Pergamon.

Brislin, Richard W., Dan Landis, and Mary Ellen Brandt (1983). "Conceptualizations of intercultural behavior and training." In Dan Landis and Richard W. Brislin (Eds.), *Handbook of intercultural training* 1. Elmsford, NY: Pergamon.

Chomsky, Noam (1965). *Aspects of the theory of syntax.* Cambridge, MA: MIT Press.

Clifford, Kay (1990). Personal correspondence. Office of International Programs, Ann Arbor: University of Michigan.

Crable, R. E. (1981). *One to another: A guidebook for interpersonal communication.* New York: Harper and Row.

Culhane-Pera, K. (1987). Personal correspondence. Department of Family Practice, St. Paul Ramsey Medical Center, St. Paul, MN.

DeVito, J. A. (1980). *The interpersonal communication book* (2d ed.). New York: Harper and Row.

Dinges, Norman (1983). "Intercultural competence." In Dan Landis and Richard W. Brislin (Eds.), *Handbook of intercultural training* 1. Elmsford, NY: Pergamon.

Eckman, Paul, and Wallace V. Friesen (1969). "The repertoire of nonverbal behavior: Categories, origins, usage, and coding." *Semiotica* 1: 49-98.

Eibl-Eibesfeldt, Irenaus (1979). *The biology of peace and war.* New York: Viking.

Eisenstadt, S. N. (1966). *Modernization: Protest and change.* Englewood Cliffs, NJ: Prentice-Hall.

Fairchild, H. P. (Ed.) (1970). *Dictionary of sociology.* Totowa, NJ: Littlefield, Adams.

Fiedler, Frederick, Terence Mitchell, and Harry Triandis (1971). "The culture assimilator: An approach to cross-cultural training." *Journal of Applied Psychology* 55, no. 2 (April): 95-102.

Gudykunst, William B. (1976). "A model of group development for intercultural communication workshops." *International and Intercultural Communication Annual* 3: 86-93.

Gudykunst, William, and M. R. Hammer (1983). "Basic training design: Approaches to intercultural training." In Dan Landis and Richard W. Brislin (Eds.), *Handbook of intercultural training* 1. Elmsford, NY: Pergamon.

Hall, Edward T. (1973). *The silent language.* New York: Doubleday.

_____ (1976). *Beyond culture.* New York: Doubleday.

Heath, D. H. (1977). *Maturity and competence: A transcultural view.* New York: Gardner Press.

Hoopes, David S. (1981). "Intercultural communication concepts and the psychology of intercultural experience." In Margaret D. Pusch (Ed.), *Multicultural education: A cross-cultural training approach.* Yarmouth, ME: Intercultural Press.

Hoopes, David S., and Paul Ventura (1979). *Intercultural sourcebook: Cross-cultural training methodologies.* La Grange Park, IL: Intercultural Network.

Jensen, J. V. (1985). "Perspective on nonverbal intercultural communication." In Larry A. Samovar and Richard E. Porter (Eds.), *Intercultural communication: A reader* (4th ed.). Belmont, CA: Wadsworth.

Jones, James M. (1972). *Prejudice and racism.* Reading, MA: Addison-Wesley.

Kelly, George (1963). *A theory of personality.* New York: Norton.

Kohls, L. Robert, and Elizabeth Ax (1979). *Methodologies for trainers: A compendium of learning strategies.* Washington, DC: Future Life Press.

Lorentz, Konrad (1977). *Behind the mirror: A search for a natural history of knowledge.* New York: Harcourt, Brace, Jovanovitch.

Lum, J. (1977). "Marginality and multiculturalism: Another look at bilingual/bicultural education." *Culture Learning Institute Report* 5, no. 1.

Malan, R. (1990). *My traitor's heart.* New York: Vintage Press.

Morris, Desmond (1967). *The naked ape.* New York: McGraw-Hill.

Mumford-Fowler, Sandra (1994). *Intercultural sourcebook* 1. (rev. ed.). Yarmouth, ME: Intercultural Press.

Paige, R. Michael, and Judith N. Martin (1983). "Ethical issues and ethics in cross-cultural training." In Dan Landis and Richard W. Brislin (Eds.), *Handbook of intercultural training* 1. Elmsford, NY: Pergamon.

Park, Robert E. (May 1926). "Human migration and the marginal man." *American Journal of Sociology:* 881-93.

Perry, William G., Jr. (1970). *Forms of intellectual and ethical development in the college years.* New York: Holt, Rinehart and Winston.

Pilotta, Joseph J. (1983). "The phenomenological approach." In William B. Gudykunst (Ed.), "Intercultural communication theory: Current perspectives." *International and Intercultural Communication Annual 7.* Beverly Hills, CA: Sage.

Prosser, Michael (1978). *The cultural dialogue.* Boston: Houghton Mifflin.

Pusch, Margaret D. (Ed.) (1981). *Multicultural education: A cross-cultural training approach.* Yarmouth, ME: Intercultural Press.

Rhodes, Robert I. (Ed.) (1970). *Imperialism and underdevelopment: A reader.* New York: Monthly Review Press.

Rich, Andrea L. (1974). *Interracial communication.* New York: Harper and Row.

Rosenberg, H. (1989). "U.S.-Soviet interchange: An evaluation of the underlying assumptions of U.S. peace organizations sponsoring contact with Soviet citizens." M.A. thesis, Portland State University, Portland, OR.

Samovar, Larry A. (1979). "Intercultural communication research: Some myths, some questions." In W. G. Davey (Ed.), *Intercultural theory and practice: Perspectives on education, training and research.* Washington, DC: Society for Intercultural Education, Training and Research.

Samovar, Larry A., Richard E. Porter, and Nemi C. Jain (1981). *Understanding intercultural communication.* Belmont, CA: Wadsworth.

Singer, Marshall R. (1975). "Culture: A perceptual approach." In David S. Hoopes (Ed.), Intercultural communication workshop. *Readings in intercultural communication* 1. Pittsburgh, PA: Intercultural Communications Network.

Smith, Elsie (1991). "Ethnic identity development: Toward the development of a theory within the context of majority/minority status." *Journal of Counseling and Development* 70. September/October.

Stewart, Edward C. (1972). *American cultural patterns: A cross-cultural perspective.* Pittsburgh, PA: Intercultural Communications Network.

Stewart, Edward C., and Milton J. Bennett (1991). *American cultural patterns: A cross-cultural perspective* (rev. ed). Yarmouth, ME: Intercultural Press.

Stonequist, Everett V. (1937). *The marginal man: A study in personality and culture conflict.* New York: Russell & Russell.

Taft, Ronald (1981). "The role and personality of the mediator." In S. Bochner (Ed.), *The mediating person.* Cambridge, MA: Schenkman.

Towers, K. (1990). "Intercultural sensitivity survey: Construction and initial validation." Doctoral dissertation, University of Iowa, Iowa City.

Turner, Deborah A. (1990). "Assessing intercultural sensitivity of American expatriates in Kuwait." M.S. thesis, Portland State University, Portland, OR.

Useem, John, John D. Donoghue, and Ruth H. Useem (1963). "Men in the middle of the third culture." *Human Organization* 22: 169-79.

Walsh, John E. (1973). *Intercultural education in the community of man.* Honolulu: East-West Center, University Press of Hawaii.

Whorf, Benjamin L. (1956). *Language, thought and reality: Selected writings of B. L. Whorf.* J. B. Carroll (Ed.) New York: John Wiley.

Wilson, Colin (1956). *The outsider.* Cambridge, MA: Riverside Press.

Yoshikawa, Muneo J. (1987). "The double-swing model of intercultural communication between the East and the West." In D. Lawrence Kincaid (Ed.), *Communication Theory: Eastern and Western perspectives.* San Diego: Academic Press.

3

A New Conceptualization of Intercultural Adjustment and the Goals of Training

Cornelius Grove and Ingemar Torbiörn

Our purpose in this chapter is first to reconceptualize what happens to someone who relocates to an unfamiliar environment and then to use that new conceptualization to better understand the goals of intercultural training. One of us is responsible for developing the essential features of a new theory of the adjustment process (Torbiörn 1982) and has been considering also its relevance to training. The other has been grappling with practical training issues (Grove 1982) and was impressed by the potential of the new theory of the adjustment process for informing the pedagogy of training. In seeking to apply that theory he has made some modest alterations in the way the models are described and illustrated.

In a thorough review of the literature, Church (1982) states that "concepts and theory remain underdeveloped in the sojourner adjustment literature" and that "the development of theories of sojourner adjustment has probably been inhibited by the frequent emphasis...on identification of adjustment problems and sojourn outcomes rather than on the dynamics of the process of adjustment." Church also states that "there has been a minimal attempt to apply theoretical concepts already existing in the sociopsychological literature to the dynamics of adjustment" (Church 1982, 562-63). In this chapter we will attempt to address these concerns by going beyond the symptom level to look for consistent explanations regarding the adjusting person's "inner world" of basic cognitive and emotional processes and by applying those explanations to the practice of training. The hypothesis presented here offers an explanation of adjustment from a perspective of cognitive and motivational psychology; it has gained empirical support in some crucial aspects (Torbiörn 1982). However, our objective here is not primarily to offer validation of the hypothesis but rather to illustrate its content and to discuss its implications with respect to current models of cross-cultural training.

A NEW CONCEPTUALIZATION OF INTERCULTURAL ADJUSTMENT

The Person in His or Her Accustomed Environment

Well-adjusted and socially adept people operating within the environment in which they were enculturated might be described as people whose behavior, that is, habitual pattern of activity, is not only socially acceptable but also interpersonally effective in that it very often yields the outcomes desired in interactions with others similarly enculturated. The *applicability* of their behavior is high—considerably higher than some merely adequate level that would enable them to get by with minimal effectiveness. Their associates recognize that the behavior is highly acceptable and effective within their common environment. They themselves also recognize this, a fact significant for our purposes.

These well-adjusted and socially adept people also feel confident that their understanding of the way the world works is accurate, complete, clearly perceived, and positively useful in guiding their behavior. They recognize (perhaps implicitly) that their habitual pattern of activity is consistent with their mental model of the functioning of society. The *clarity* of their mental frame of reference is high—considerably higher than some merely adequate level that would enable them to simply get by with minimal confidence in their understanding of the way the world works.

Figure 1 (see p. 99) illustrates graphically the quality of functioning they experience in their accustomed environment. Figure 1 employs the standard format in which the vertical axis indicates the quantitative or qualitative measure and the horizontal axis indicates the passage of time. On this chart, the vertical axis starts at zero, which means that someone is utterly dysfunctional, and proceeds upward to a high point that represents the highest attainable extent of applicability and/or clarity. Both *applicability of behavior* and *clarity of the mental frame of reference* are depicted in figure 1 as being steadily high, illustrating the consistently high level of functioning of the person described in the previous two paragraphs. *Level(s) of mere adequacy* appears as a horizontal line proceeding from the midpoint of the vertical axis; it indicates the minimum extent of applicability and (separately) of clarity that people must attain in order to experience their situation or some aspect of it as barely adequate or minimally satisfactory. To the extent that a person's applicability or clarity rises and remains above that level (the case illustrated in figure 1), the situation will be explained as being better than merely adequate. If that applicability or clarity falls below the mere adequacy level, the situation will be experienced as less than satisfactory, the person's behavior or actions as less than functional, or, perhaps, him- or herself as less than appropriately enculturated (or acculturated). We presume that many people, probably most, aspire to function in their daily lives at levels that are somewhat above those that they perceive to be merely adequate. We further presume that many people, perhaps most, are in fact able to function at more or less elevated levels so long as their lives are proceeding smoothly within an environment to which they are accustomed.

Further Consideration of the Psychological Constructs

As noted above, our new theory of the adjustment process employs three psychological constructs: *applicability of behavior, clarity of the mental frame of reference*, and *level of mere adequacy*. Let us now look at the first two of these in more detail. Figure 2 (see p. 100) shows the relationships among a person's frame of reference, behavior, and environment. Behavior occupies the central position. On one side, behavior is linked with environment, that is, with the state of things surrounding the person and especially the habitual patterns of activity of other people, particularly those in the person's circle of acquaintances (by which we designate all those with whom he or she interacts at least sporadically). The degree to which a person's own behavior is consistent with his or her environment in this sense is what we term *applicability of behavior*. Although applicability may be judged objectively by anyone else who witnesses the behavior of the person, it is important to keep in mind that the person exhibiting the behavior also is observing and judging it for him- or herself; it is his or her own subjective evaluation of applicability that is important for our purposes. On the other side (as shown in figure 2), behavior also is linked with frame of reference, that is, with all the values, attitudes, opinions, ideas, and knowledge that the person has accumulated as a result of his or her experiences. The frame of reference embraces a number of cognitive elements that, in a given situation, recommend or advise against a certain type of behavior. The advice given by these disparate elements may or may not be unanimous. The extent to which the elements are unanimous in recommending behavior—that is, the extent to which manifest behavior is consistent with the recommendations of the many elements—is what we term *clarity*. Clarity is not readily judged by anyone else who witnesses the person's behavior (although inferences may be possible). In any case, the person's subjective evaluation of clarity is what is important for our purposes.

Behavior occupies the central position in figure 2, but it must not be conceived as some sort of barrier between the environment and the frame of reference. The environment is affected by a person's frame of reference because the frame recommends behaviors; these, in turn, directly and immediately affect what is occurring in the environment. *More importantly for our purposes is the fact that the environment affects the frame of reference.* As people notice what is occurring in their environment and the degree to which their behavior is in harmony with that of others, the facts and evaluations thus acquired are fed back into their frame of reference to become part of their total accumulation of values, attitudes, opinions, ideas, knowledge, and so forth. To the extent that these incoming facts and evaluations are different from those already stored there, the frame of reference may be slowly transformed, in whole or in part. At the same time, we assume that a person's frame of reference is not monolithic, but rather composed of numerous disparate elements; an incoming fact or evaluation may have an effect on one or two elements, but not on any of the others. Since some elements undergo transformation more than others, the recommendation regarding behavior given by the various elements gradually may become mutually contradictory, thus reducing the person's confidence or (as we have termed it) clarity.

Let us underscore a key point. When considered at any given moment in their lives, the subjective evaluation people have of their own applicability is separate and distinct from their subjective evaluation of their own clarity. Over time, however, the low evaluation people have of their applicability gradually will depress their evaluation of their clarity. In common parlance, we would say that if people notice that their behavior is consistently out of step with that of their acquaintances, their confidence in their understanding of the way the world works will be progressively undermined.

Let us now explore further the concept level of mere adequacy. This level is an internal standard or benchmark against which people evaluate, implicitly or explicitly, their levels of applicability and (separately) of clarity. We suspect that it is most accurate to speak in terms of people using this subjective standard (or set of standards) to evaluate their momentary situation vis-à-vis other people or things in their environment. An unsatisfactory situation—one in which someone, something, or some event fails to attain the standard—often may be experienced, at least initially, not as a failure or abnormality of the self but rather as a failure or abnormality of an (external) person or thing. The tendency of people to view unsatisfactory situations initially as due to inadequacies within themselves or within other people or things may be dependent on their level of self-confidence or self-esteem, their commitment to objectivity in thinking, and/or to other factors. More important for our immediate purposes is the fact that different people have differing levels of mere adequacy with respect to both applicability and clarity. For instance, Person A may not feel that a situation is basically satisfactory unless her behavior is highly congruent with that of others, and with the expectations of others, in her environment. Such a person might be described as a perfectionist. Person B may be much less preoccupied with the maintaining of environmentally congruent behavior at all times. B's level of mere adequacy with respect to applicability is therefore lower than A's. Person C may not feel that a situation is basically satisfactory unless her behavior is uniformly congruent with the recommendations being offered by the many disparate elements within her frame of reference. Such a person might be described as being intolerant of ambiguity. Person D may be much less concerned about maintaining behavior that is fully consistent with her frame of reference. D's level of mere adequacy with respect to clarity is therefore lower than C's. Equally important is the question of the extent to which levels of mere adequacy can vary over time. Our opinion is that these levels can vary only within a restricted range, that is, a range much narrower than those possible in the cases of applicability and clarity. We believe that *some* variation is possible because, after all, these levels are not arbitrarily imposed by an external authority; rather, they are internally developed by the individual over a lifetime. (This is not to argue that the standards commonly accepted by others similarly enculturated are not taken into account by the individual in setting personal standards.) Nevertheless, we believe that variation is possible only within a restricted range because the levels are, in effect, personality traits. People with relatively low levels of mere adequacy resist the idea of significantly raising their minimum standards because doing so would make their lives unacceptably difficult. People with relatively high levels of mere adequacy resist the idea of significantly lowering their minimum standards because doing so would require them to compromise their ideals. (How does one persuade a perfectionist to be content with performing in a mediocre fashion?) Whatever the levels adopted, they are bound up with an understanding of what is basically reasonable and normal. But if the conception of what constitutes fundamentally reasonable and normal behavior in a given set of circumstances can be changed, then the levels of mere adequacy for applicability and/or clarity can be changed.

The Person in an Unaccustomed Environment

The same well-adjusted and socially adept people to whom we referred earlier now enter an unaccustomed environment. For purposes of illustration, let us assume that this new environment contrasts very sharply with their previous home environment. Let us further assume that these people are continuously in contact with host nationals and do not isolate themselves in an expatriate ghetto. Note that a sharply contrasting environment need not necessarily be found on the opposite side of the world. We are attempting to understand psychological mechanisms that appear to operate whenever a person is abruptly transplanted for a fairly long period of time into any sort of new and unknown setting. A similar situation occurs when a person enters an institution that constitutes a total environment (such as a prison or the military), or when a person's circumstances are suddenly and radically changed (such as becoming unemployed, handicapped, or widowed).

Figure 3 (see p. 101) illustrates our conception of how the three psychological constructs vary over time beginning at the moment when people find themselves confronting a new total environment. We assume in the case of figure 3 that the newcomers have received no orientation or training of any kind prior to arrival and that they receive none during their sojourn. Note first of all that *level of mere adequacy* shows no variation whatsoever; it remains at the same steady level as in figure 1 (which illustrated the person in his or her accustomed environment). Earlier we postulated that level of mere adequacy with respect to both applicability and clarity is, in effect, a personality trait and therefore resistant to change. It is possible, of course, that the level's steady course could be disturbed by the shock of entering a new total environment. But we believe that most people in such a situation would be far more concerned about maintaining a sense of their own basic reasonableness and normality than about altering the fundamental standards against which they judge their reasonableness and normality or that of the situations in which they find themselves. Indeed, some might even struggle to preserve those standards intact at all costs; in their view, allowing their standards to slip would undermine their self-esteem by presaging their ultimate personal degradation under the influence of the hostile values in the new environment.

Look next at *applicability of behavior* in figure 3. At the moment the person arrives in the new environment, his or her habitual pattern of activity is both socially unacceptable and interpersonally ineffective. To the extent that the person is consciously aware of this deficiency, the line representing applicability in figure 3 will be below the level of mere adequacy. We assume that most people lose little time in perceiving that their usual behaviors are not in harmony with those of host nationals, and so we have started the applicability line at a very low point. (It does not begin at zero, however, because zero applicability seems to indicate that the person would have insufficient ability to survive socially and perhaps even physically.) The applicability line then rises over time, slowly at first, but then more rapidly as more and more time in the new environment is accumulated. The gradually increasing slope of the line over time suggests that the person is able to assimilate new and more subtle patterns of activity at a more and more rapid rate after the basic patterns have been haltingly noticed and laboriously acquired early in the sojourn experience.

Now consider the line for *clarity of the mental frame of reference*, which has an entirely different appearance. Our newcomers are naive and untrained, and therefore they confront the new environment with all their implicit and explicit assumptions about how the world works intact. Their behavior may be unlike that of host nationals, and they may notice this immediately (as presumed in the case of the applicability line); but at first their confidence in the correctness of their frame of reference is not shaken. From their ethnocentric point of view, it is "they" (the host nationals) who are acting strangely or even unnaturally, not "us" (the newcomers). As time in the new environment begins to accumulate, however, the extreme disharmony between their own behavior and that of host nationals is manifested in every encounter. As these facts and evaluations are fed back into their frame of reference, their confidence in its correctness drops precipitously and before long is below the level that they consider merely adequate. It continues to decline but bottoms out before reaching zero, as illustrated in figure 3. (It does not drop to zero because zero clarity seems to indicate that people would be too confused and uncertain to be able to guide their own behavior to any extent at all.) The reason why the clarity line first declines sharply, then slows its rate of decline, then levels off and gradually turns upward has to do with the balance (or lack of balance) existing in the frame of reference between the cognitive elements derived from home-culture experience and those derived from host-culture experience. At first, home-culture elements completely dominate the frame of reference. But as experiences in the host culture are accumulated and applicability improves, host-culture elements enter the frame at an increasing rate. In most cases, the home- and host-based elements are mutually contradictory, so that the frame increasingly becomes a repository of cognitive elements that give conflicting advice regarding behavior, thus reducing the person's confidence or—as we have termed it—clarity. Clarity decreases, then, until that point in time when the two sets of contradictory elements attain a rough balance. This is the point of maximum internal confusion about the way the world works, that is, of minimum clarity. But even at this time the person is continuing to accumulate experiences in the host culture and is continuing to improve his or her applicability, so that host-culture elements are continuing to enter the frame. As the balance begins to tip in favor of the host-based elements, clarity begins to increase. The increase is slow at first because home-based elements remaining in the frame continue to contradict elements derived from the host culture. Eventually, however, host-based cognitive elements come to more or less dominate the frame of reference, and clarity climbs past the level of mere adequacy.

In figure 3, both applicability and clarity are illustrated as regaining levels similar to where the person had been able to maintain them in his or her own home environment (figure 1). Note, however, that figure 3 and subsequent figures represent idealized theoretical constructs and have been drawn as simply as possible to facilitate both illustration and understanding. We regard as open the question of whether and at what point in time applicability and clarity can attain the highest possible levels through acculturation (as opposed to enculturation). We suspect that, in most cases, a sojourn of a year or two in a completely unfamiliar environment would not be sufficient to enable applicability and/or clarity to regain the levels maintained in the home environment. In cases where they eventually attain the highest possible levels, the person very well may have undergone a change of identity, something more profound than passing through a cycle of adjustment, which is what is being described here.

Stages of Adjustment Cycle

In figure 3, there appear three lines of demarcation that descend to the horizontal axis from the points where the lines of applicability and clarity intersect the level of mere adequacy. Together with the sides of figure 3, these lines mark off four sequential stages in time; these stages of the adjustment cycle are labeled I, II, III, and IV. The character of these four stages is as follows:

Stage I: applicability *less* than adequate, clarity *more* than adequate

Stage II: applicability *less* than adequate, clarity *less* than adequate

Stage III: applicability *more* than adequate, clarity *less* than adequate

Stage IV: applicability *more* than adequate, clarity *more* than adequate

Stage I is characterized by the period of euphoria often experienced by people immediately after they enter a completely new culture. The key to understanding Stage I lies in the fact that the newcomer's clarity remains above its level of mere adequacy. So long as one can remain confident about the correctness of one's mental frame of reference, the obviously different behavior patterns of host nationals can be viewed with detachment as "fascinating," "quaint," "exotic," and so forth. Tourists and short-term sojourners very often do not progress beyond Stage I because they know that there will be no sustained expectation on anyone's part for them to adjust to any significant extent. Such people usually have relatively fleeting and superficial contacts with host nationals, with the result that their frames of reference remain very largely intact. Unless the elements in one's frame of reference are shaken up and their reliability seriously challenged, contact with an unfamiliar environment is unlikely to have a lasting effect on one's values, perspectives, and behaviors.

Stage II, during which clarity and applicability are inadequate, is characterized by culture shock. Culture shock is a type of mental and physiological stress resulting from overstimulation and overuse of the body's coping mechanisms due to a high degree of novelty in the environment (Barna 1983). Stage II is associated with culture shock because the disturbing effect of low applicability is no longer counteracted by high confidence in one's mental frame of reference. Detachment is not possible, for the newcomers can no longer preserve the notion that they are merely fascinated observers of the natives' exotic behavior. They are thoroughly involved and deeply confused. They *must* respond to and make sense of the novelty and the nuances in their environment; this necessity is why their coping mechanisms are overtaxed. Of particular interest in figure 3 is the fact that Stage II is by far the longest of the four stages; using the arbitrary units of measurement along the horizontal axis, Stage II is shown to be 7.9 out of 12.0 units of time in length. The length of Stage II will be of special interest in the second part of this chapter which deals with training.

Stage III is characterized by progressive recovery from culture shock. For the first time since arriving in the unfamiliar environment, people notice a significant degree of consonance between their behavior and that of the host nationals. With applicability surfacing through its level of mere adequacy and continuing to improve, and with clarity bottoming out and starting to rise, the person is beginning to feel less and less overwhelmed. Note that clarity continues below its level of mere adequacy, which is why we cannot say that culture shock has ended in Stage III.

Stage IV is characterized by completion of the process of adjustment. The applicability of the person's behavior is quite good, and the clarity of his or her mental frame of reference is just beginning to be better than merely adequate. Applicability and clarity may continue to improve toward optimum levels, and at the point in time when both are above their levels of mere adequacy, a person can be regarded as reasonably well-adjusted to the environment that formerly was completely new and different.

THE NEW CONCEPTUALIZATION OF THE GOALS OF TRAINING

Further Consideration of Stage II of the Adjustment Cycle

It is well known that Stage II of the adjustment cycle is very painful for many sojourners—so painful for so long that some of them never get through it at all. Some adopt an extremely hostile and critical stance vis-à-vis host nationals ("fight"), others retreat to the safety of an expatriate ghetto or even return home prematurely ("flight"), and still others rapidly and uncritically abandon their former identities and attempt to ape host nationals in every possible way ("going native"). These general patterns of coping as well as the various specific psychological symptoms of newcomers (rationalization, projection, withdrawal, overidentifying, and other defensive mechanisms) should not be viewed as irredeemably bad. Although they involve distortions of reality, they may be functional for newcomers in that they enable them temporarily to continue to *experience* clarity instead of overwhelming confusion in their mental frame of reference. These coping mechanisms slow down the entry of cognitive elements from the host culture and bolster the strength of cognitive elements brought from the home culture, thus preventing a precipitous collapse of the frame of reference. (All of this defensive coping requires tremendous mental effort, which is one reason why culture shock should be understood, in part, as a form of exhaustion.) From a clinical psychological perspective, the various coping mechanisms become a severe mental health problem only when, in terms of both strength and duration, they come to dominate the person's interaction with the environment, or when they completely collapse and leave the person vulnerable to extreme anxiety, psychosomatic disorders, alcoholism, drug abuse, and so forth.

Advocates of intercultural training have been consistent in pointing to the benefits of a gradual process of adaptation in which the intellect gains in awareness and understanding while the emotions are prevented from welling up to the point where the newcomer loses self-control. Gradual adaptation enables the newcomers to maintain their sense of personal identity while judiciously adjusting certain of their assumptions, values, attitudes, opinions, ideas, styles of reasoning, and patterns of behavior to bring them more nearly into line with those prevailing in the new environment. In short, gradual adaptation occurs when the newcomer negotiates Stage II without being overwhelmed.

We are not implying that Stage II can or should be eliminated or skipped in any fashion. Given a newcomer in a completely unfamiliar environment, we take it as axiomatic that Stage II cannot be eliminated, not even through the intervention of skilled intercultural trainers. But trainers should not even think of trying to eliminate Stage II because it is the disturbance of the mental frame of reference during the stage that makes intercultural learning possible during Stages III and IV. The gradual but profound change in one's assumptions, values, attitudes, opinions, ideas, and so forth that is necessary to attain Stage IV is possible *only to the degree that one's frame of reference has had its tightly integrated and monolithic character disturbed.* Adaptation is not possible unless and until the clarity line in figure 3 has fallen below its level of mere adequacy. Adaptation may be seen as the process of reconstructing one's mental frame of reference in the wake of a period during which one has lost confidence in its previous structure and quality.

Earlier we associated the well-known term "culture shock" with Stage II. Guthrie (1975) proposed the term "culture *fatigue*," which is useful to reintroduce at this point because it does not include the heavily negative connotations of "shock." In speaking of negotiating Stage II without being overwhelmed, we suggest that it is desirable to avoid culture *shock*, an incapacitating breakdown in the neural and endocrinal systems of the body that is known to physiologists as a consequence of extreme stress (Barna 1983; Keller 1981). Fatigue, on the other hand, is an unavoidable consequence of heavy and continuous (but not over-whelming) demands made on the neural and endocrinal systems in stressful situations such as when one's applicability and clarity are both below their levels of mere adequacy—but not so far below as to be bordering on zero. Culture fatigue is a necessary prerequisite to effective adjustment because intercultural learning cannot occur to any significant extent in the absence of a partial breakdown of the mental frame of reference that originally was constructed in one's home culture. Although our terminology may be different, we are not the first to point out this necessity; Peter Adler noted it in 1975. (See also a recapitulation by Brislin 1983, 157-58.)

The appropriate context now exists in which we can assert our conviction that *the principal goal of intercultural training is to reduce the severity and shorten the duration of the newcomer's passage through Stage II of the adjustment cycle.* Notice that this principal goal refers to alterations that are desirable in Stage II, not in Stages I, III, or IV. There may be those who would reason that the principal goal of training is to improve the quality (or, in terms of the chart in figure 3, the "height") of both applicability and clarity as the newcomer finally attains the end of his or her adjustment cycle in Stage IV. Such a goal has much to recommend it. Our view, however, is that training can do relatively little to raise the levels of applicability or clarity that a sojourner ultimately is able to attain. Intercultural training is not a scheme for helping to reconstruct a person's mental frame of reference in all its breadth and complexity, nor for teaching every nuance and detail of appropriate behaviors in the myriad social settings found in the new culture. It is possible for frames of reference to be reconstructed and for different behaviors to be learned, but these tasks must be accomplished by the sojourner through acculturation and assimilation as he or she interacts moment by moment with host nationals over a long period of time. Indeed, there are numerous people around the world who have relocated, temporarily or permanently, in unfamiliar cultures and who have managed, without benefit of intercultural training, to achieve personal satisfaction and social acceptance in those cultures. Yet we know that some of these ultimately successful adapters experienced a long and bitter struggle to pull themselves through Stage II. We know, too, that there are people who never manage to negotiate Stage II, but who settle instead for fight, flight, or going native. The principal value of intercultural training, then, is that it helps to prevent the worst excesses of severity and duration that Stage II potentially holds in store for the naive newcomer. And it helps newcomers, who otherwise might not do so, to be able to negotiate Stage II and move on to Stages III and IV.

Theoretically Desirable Changes in the Adjustment Cycle

In terms of the theory that has been presented so far in this paper, three means are potentially available for reducing the severity and duration of Stage II. These are through manipulation of the three psychological constructs: applicability, clarity, and level of mere adequacy. In the following paragraphs we will deal with each of these theoretical terms, leaving for the next section consideration of the practical issues that are necessarily involved.

Figure 4 (see p. 102) illustrates what the adjustment cycle might look like if only *applicability* were manipulated in a desirable fashion by means of intercultural training. In relation to figure 3, notice that the applicability line in figure 4 is different in two ways.

1. At the moment of arrival, applicability is higher than was the case for the untrained newcomer. It still begins below the level of mere adequacy, of course, for no training program can teach more than a small fraction of the behaviors that are socially acceptable and interpersonally effective in an unfamiliar culture.

2. The slope of the applicability line is steeper during the early stages of the adjustment cycle, illustrating that intercultural training has managed to increase the rate at which the newcomer learns new behaviors through his or her observation of and participation with host nationals in their daily lives. Overall, the curvature of the applicability line is less pronounced than it was in figure 3.

In Stage II, these two changes in applicability may not have made a change in the severity of culture fatigue (since clarity and level of mere adequacy are unchanged from figure 3), but the duration of Stage II has been shortened significantly from 7.9 units of time down to 5.8 units.

Figure 5 (see p. 103) illustrates what the adjustment cycle might look like if only *clarity* were manipulated in a desirable fashion. In relation to figure 3, this clarity line is different in three ways.

1. At the moment of arrival, clarity is lower than was the case for the naive newcomer. This drop indicates that intercultural training is—or should be—able to reduce the confident ethnocentrism of the monocultural person, that is, should be able to disturb and challenge his or her explicit and implicit assumptions about how human beings relate to one another. Notice, however, that clarity still begins well above the level of mere adequacy, for it is highly unlikely that any type of training could begin with trainees who are mentally secure and reduce them to the point where they do not even feel minimally confident about their understanding of the way the world works. (We are ignoring the question of whether brainwashing or similar heavy-handed techniques could break down a person's mental frame of reference; ethical considerations prevent intercultural trainers from considering the use of such techniques.)

2. The lowest point reached by clarity is not as close to zero as was the case for the naive newcomer, although it is still significantly below the level of mere adequacy. The reduced depth of the low point illustrates that intercultural training should be able to prevent culture shock, as discussed in the preceding section.

3. The lowest point reached by clarity occurs earlier in time than was the case in figure 3, illustrating that intercultural training is likely to accelerate the process whereby the newcomer loses confidence in his or her original frame of reference, restructures it, and regains confidence. Though not illustrated in figure 5, intercultural training should be improving applicability (as shown in figure 4) at the same time that it is dealing with clarity; since clarity is dependent upon applicability, it is not unreasonable to expect the clarity curve to bottom out sooner in a situation in which applicability is improving relatively rapidly.

In Stage II, these three changes in clarity indicate a reduction in the severity of culture fatigue (since clarity is less depressed in absolute terms as well as less distant from its level of mere adequacy). Furthermore, the duration of Stage II has been shortened from 7.9 units of time down to 6.5 units.

Figure 6 (see p. 104) illustrates what the adjustment cycle might look like if only the *level of mere adequacy* were manipulated in a desirable fashion. (For purposes of discussion, we are treating the level as a unity, but as noted earlier, applicability and clarity have separate levels of mere adequacy.) Whether the level of mere adequacy is amenable to change through training is open to question, of course; earlier we described it as, in effect, a personality trait and therefore resistant to change. For the moment, however, let us assume that training can bring about some small and temporary change in the level. In order to be beneficial to the newcomer, that change would have to move downward from its previous location (as illustrated in figures 1 and 3). People would have to lower temporarily their standards of self-evaluation; for example, they would have to become less perfectionist and more tolerant of ambiguity. Figure 6 shows the level of mere adequacy lowered slightly during the early portion of the sojourn, then gradually returning to its usual level; a change of this type is probably the best that training can hope to accomplish.

In Stage II, this change reduces the severity of culture fatigue (since distance between the level and the lowest point in the clarity line is decreased). The change also shortens the duration of Stage II from 7.9 units of time down to 6.8 units.

Practical Considerations in Changing the Adjustment Cycle

A good program of intercultural training attempts to bring about the theoretically desirable changes in all three psychological constructs. Certain methods and procedures of training may be able to bring about changes in two or even all three constructs simultaneously. But for expository purposes it seems wise to continue to address each psychological construct—and indeed each change—as though it were a separate entity. It is not our purpose to recommend a completely integrated training design; a training program can be designed only in relation to specific trainees in a specific context. By focusing here on methods and procedures for addressing each change, we are offering considerations that may prove useful to those who are designing specific training programs.

With respect to each of these changes, two basic questions must be raised: *How* can that change be brought about? *When* is that intervention best attempted?

How is one to examine the arsenal of methods and procedures that trainers potentially have at their disposal in order to determine which type of intervention appears most likely to bring about a specific desirable change? We will confine ourselves to thinking about *types* of intervention in order not to become bogged down in the details of specific training approaches. The six principal types to which we will refer are those outlined by Brislin, Landis, and Brandt (1983):

1. FACT-ORIENTED TRAINING—In this relatively traditional approach, the trainees are presented with facts about the host country and culture through lectures, panels, videotapes, films, readings, workbooks, case studies, critical incidents, community descriptions, culture capsules, dramatizations, question-answering sessions, and discussions.

2. ATTRIBUTION TRAINING—Most closely associated with the culture-assimilator technique (but not limited to it), this approach helps the trainees learn to explain events and behaviors from the point of view of host nationals. The objective is for the trainees to internalize values and standards of the host culture so that their attributions will become increasingly similar (isomorphic) to those of their hosts.

3. CULTURAL-AWARENESS TRAINING—With philosophical underpinnings in cultural relativism, this approach introduces trainees to the culture concept and the nature of cultural differences; often the

vehicle for accomplishing these ends is study of the trainees' own home culture in anthropological perspective. Specific techniques include value-orientation checklists, value-ranking charts, self-awareness building, and the contrast-culture technique (best known in the form of the contrast-American technique). Similar objectives may be attained by culture-general approaches such as communication and nonverbal activities, perceptual exercises, simulation games, and studies of the nature of cross-cultural adjustment.

4. COGNITIVE-BEHAVIOR MODIFICATION—This little-used approach applies certain principles of learning to the special problems of cross-cultural adjustment. For instance, trainees are asked to list what kinds of activities they find rewarding (or punishing) in their home environment; then they carry out a guided study of the host culture to determine how they can duplicate (or avoid) those activities there. Trainers may attempt to help the trainees feel positively challenged by those features of the host culture that the trainees fear the most.

5. EXPERIENTIAL LEARNING—For our purposes, this type of intervention will be limited to activities focused on learning about a specific host culture. (Other activities that are experiential in nature, but that are not host-culture specific, are listed above under "Cultural-Awareness Training.") Experiential techniques are those that involve the trainees emotionally and physically as well as intellectually; the trainees learn through actual experience. Role plays, situation exercises, community investigations, field trips, and total immersion are examples of host-culture-specific experiential learning.

6. INTERACTIONAL LEARNING—This type of training involves structured or unstructured interaction between the trainees, on the one hand, and host nationals and/or "old hands" (experienced expatriates), on the other. The objective is for the trainees to feel more and more comfortable with the host nationals and to learn details about life in the host country from them and/or the old hands.

Besides considering these six principal types of intervention, we also will keep in mind the need of trainees for a balance among three kinds of personal development and learning: greater *awareness*, more extensive *knowledge*, and improved or newly learned *skills* (Pedersen 1983). We are aware of other critical issues in training design—for example, the importance of consonance between the trainees' preferred learning style and the trainer's teaching style (Grove 1981; Smart 1983)—but believe that these concerns are beyond the scope of this chapter.

When is one to consider the timing of any potentially worthwhile training method or procedure? It seems natural to assume that training precedes the sojourners' arrival in the host country, but some writers have been saying for years that certain types of training are significantly more effective when carried out after the sojourners' arrival (Textor 1966; Chaffee 1978; Gudykunst and Hammer 1983). Furthermore, this postarrival training need not necessarily occur immediately upon the sojourners' arrival; some training has maximum impact when intentionally delayed until the sojourners are attempting to cope with Stage II of the adjustment cycle. Another issue related to timing involves the sequencing of different methods and procedures in order to take advantage of the possibility that the learning accomplished in one may be a useful background or even a prerequisite for the learning to be accomplished in another. This issue has received almost no attention in the literature; in the discussion that follows, we will be able to take it into consideration only occasionally.

Two theoretically desirable changes were suggested for *applicability of behavior* (figure 4). The first was to raise its initial level, which primarily requires the trainee to develop new skills in order to be able to behave more nearly acceptably in the new culture. Fact-oriented training is a necessary beginning; much can be told and demonstrated about characteristic behaviors of one group that may be misinterpreted by the other group. But because mere knowledge of the inappropriateness of certain behaviors is unlikely to enable one to make sweeping modifications in his or her habitual patterns of activity, fact-oriented training by itself is not sufficient. Cognitive-behavior modification may be useful if it assists trainees to focus their attention on certain appropriate, agreeable, and well-practiced activities that can be adapted to the new environment. Interactional learning also may be useful, but only to the extent that the interactions involve guided learning and the practice of applicable behaviors. Most promising is experiential learning, for its emphasis on learning through actual experience carries the greatest potential for perfecting and/or developing needed skills.

As for timing, fact-oriented training can be delivered equally well before or after the sojourners arrive in the host country, as can cognitive-behavior modification. The interactional-learning approach seems to imply home-country (that is, prearrival) training, but could be even more effective after the sojourners have arrived in the new culture and are becoming more fully aware that they need help in recognizing and learning applicable behaviors. Most experiential-learning techniques are appropriate for implementation after the sojourners have arrived in the host country because of the need for indigenous physical settings and authentic social contexts. Note that the fact-oriented training and experiential-learning techniques can be mutually supportive if they are carefully planned in advance; the factual presentations can elucidate certain details of the practical experiences, and the practical experiences can motivate the trainees to receive the factual presentations more attentively than otherwise might be the case.

The second desirable change suggested for applicability was to increase the rate at which the newcomers learn new behaviors. This is a change that can only be achieved through intervention during the trainees' stay in the host country. In addition, it seems obvious that the training cannot be confined to the time immediately following arrival, but must occur intermittently at least through Stage II. The four types of training discussed in the previous two paragraphs are well suited to achieve the desired end so long as training does not cease after the newcomers leave the postarrival orientation site.

Three desirable changes were suggested for *clarity of the mental frame of reference* (figure 5). The first was to lower its initial level, which primarily requires the trainees to be deprived of their confident ethnocentrism. Cultural-awareness training is specifically designed for this purpose. To the extent that it focuses on building knowledge and awareness of the home culture, it has the added advantage of better enabling the trainees to explain themselves to host nationals. Attribution training also can help to lower the trainees' initial level of clarity because of its focus on specific discrepancies between the attributions made by trainees and host nationals. Both of these types of training are primarily suitable for implementation prior to the trainees' arrival in the host country. Note especially that attribution training is a host-culture-specific approach that is perfectly usable during the weeks and months prior to the trainees' travel to the host country.

The second desirable change suggested for clarity was to raise the lowest level to which it falls during Stage II. No other theoretically desirable change addresses so directly the key objective of preventing culture fatigue from becoming culture shock. Let us further examine, therefore, exactly what seems to be required to keep clarity from sinking too far. Above we have described the mental frame of reference as composed of a number of disparate elements whose advice regarding potential behavior may or may not be unanimous. It is to be expected that during Stage II, one of the problems newcomers will experience will be that their frame of reference is simultaneously recommending incompatible behaviors. This situation corresponds more or less to what Newcomb (1963) labeled "cognitive inconsistency" and Ball-Rokeach (1973) termed "focused ambiguity." Equally likely during Stage II is the predicament in which the newcomers are unable to find any guidance for their actions among the elements of their frame of reference because they simply are unprepared to understand or define the social context in which they find themselves. This situation is similar to what Newcomb termed "cognitive ambiguity" and Ball-Rokeach called "pervasive ambiguity." We will use Ball-Rokeach's terminology in the discussion that follows.

It is important to recognize at the outset that training can do relatively little to *prevent* the occurrence of focused and pervasive ambiguity. The total social milieu of any host culture is far too rich, complex, and full of subtle nuances to lend itself to analysis and categorization at a level that can be readily transmitted through a comparatively brief training program. The trainees themselves also are virtually always unprepared by previous experience or education to grasp and to recall later all that could be said about a completely unfamiliar culture. We are not taking the position here that any attempt to reduce ambiguity is bound to be futile. Rather, we are making a point about timing: *training that ceases before ambiguity sets in is training that missed its golden opportunity to reduce the severity and shorten the duration of the newcomer's passage through Stage II of the adjustment cycle.* The complexity and the idiosyncratic nature of any given sojourner's experience in the host culture are bound to be so great that training primarily aimed at the prevention of focused or pervasive ambiguity is bound to be only marginally successful. (We are not the first to suggest that the benefits of preventive preparatory training may be severely limited; in 1975, Guthrie pursued this point of view in an insightful article.) If the problems of Stage II are going to be substantially lessened, the intervention must occur *during* Stage II.

What types of intervention may be appropriate? In the case of focused ambiguity, cultural-awareness training may be useful if its underlying philosophy of cultural relativism can help to deaden the moral overtones surrounding the newcomer's dilemma of having to choose between incompatible behaviors. On the other hand, there are certain ethical implications to be considered if trainers advocate cultural relativism too openly. Focused ambiguity is another way of referring to the partial breakdown of the mental frame of reference—a breakdown that we view as inevitable as well as indispensable to intercultural learning. Consequently, we believe that the role of trainers should be confined to the provision of individualized support for sojourners whose extreme degree of focused ambiguity is threatening to reduce their clarity to zero.

Intercultural training is far better equipped to deal with pervasive ambiguity. Any type of training that deals specifically with the host culture is potentially a step toward reducing the pervasive ambiguity of one or more trainees. The efficiency and effectiveness of such culture-specific training will be increased if the trainees actually have experienced the ambiguity that comes from not understanding or not being able to define the social contexts in which they find themselves. In short, the trainees need to know that they don't know. The principal responsibility of the trainers, then, is *to be responsive to the specific needs of individual trainees* as they proceed with any or all of the types of training that focus on aspects of the host culture. Individualized support for especially distressed trainees is also highly appropriate. In sum, training and support during Stage II needs to focus on the acquisition of knowledge and the development of skills at the same time as it offers emotional solace and encouragement. Training during Stage II needs to be more reactive than proactive.

The third and final desirable change suggested for clarity was to move forward in time to the point at which the clarity line dips to its lowest point. To a considerable extent this change is an expected outcome of all the other changes that have been discussed so far in this section. In terms of the model we have been using (figures 3 and 5), lowering clarity's initial level and raising its trough seems likely to result in a forward displacement of the trough. In more practical terms, the types of training recommended so far for applicability as well as clarity should have the desired effect. Keep in mind that clarity is dependent upon applicability in the long run.

Let us turn finally to the *level of mere adequacy* (figure 6). The theoretically desirable change was to lower the level as much as possible and for as long as possible, the implication being that the level will always tend to return to its customary position. Up to this point the level had been treated as though it were a unity, but now it is necessary to discuss separately its two components: the level for applicability and the level for clarity. In addition, a new parameter needs to be introduced at this point: *strength*.

The levels of mere adequacy are internal standards against which the person evaluates the applicability and clarity of his or her behavior. But

there are many types of behavior, many patterns and organizing concepts around which behavior is structured. Some of these are bound to
be more important than others from the point of view of the individual.
Referring to figure 2, we can say that the parameter of strength indicates
the relative importance, subjectively, to the individual, of any behavior's
being consistent with that of (selected) acquaintances in the environment, and of that behavior's being fully consonant with all the elements
in his or her mental frame of reference. For purposes of intercultural
training, it is too burdensome to focus exclusively on what is subjectively
most important to each individual; practical considerations dictate an
alternative focus on the average person (or perhaps the average person
of a certain type) from the native culture of the trainees. Making a
judgment about relative strengths in this way requires a sophisticated
knowledge of the native culture of one's trainees, but intercultural
trainers should have or know how to acquire such knowledge. Two
examples: If one is training U.S. businesspeople, one needs to know
about their culturally determined expectations regarding individualism.
If one is training Japanese adolescents, knowledge of behaviors relating
to amae (dependency relationships) is of central importance. Within their
respective cultural contexts, individualism and amae are very strongly
held organizing concepts for behavior, and training that attempts to
lower the level of mere adequacy must address them directly in addition
to anything else it might do.

Lowering the level of mere adequacy for applicability means in
practice that each trainee becomes less determined that his or her
behavior be consistent with that of others in the new environment.
Training to this end should stress the impossibility of behaving in ways
that are socially acceptable and interpersonally effective; the expectations of the trainee regarding the quality of his or her own public
"performances" should be lowered. Kohls (1979) has suggested that the
most important skills for sojourners to develop are "sense of humor,"
"low goal/task orientation," and "the ability to fail," in that order. With
the proviso that "sense of humor" is misleading, we believe that Kohls's
advice is appropriate because it is directed precisely at lowering the level
of mere adequacy for applicability. What needs to be added is the notion
that, for any given group of trainees, expectations regarding certain
specific patterns of behavior must be explicitly dealt with because of their
relative strength, the objective being to enable the trainees to attach less
importance to those patterns.

How to lower the level of mere adequacy for applicability through training is a challenging question. We suspect that the question of how is closely associated with the question of when because of the resiliency of the level of mere adequacy. Whether or not appropriate training occurs prior to the sojourner's arrival in the host country, it certainly should occur during the early stages of the sojourn so that assistance and encouragement can be provided at times when the level of mere adequacy needs to be maintained. Fact-oriented training is the most straightforward approach and ought not to be overlooked; pointing out to trainees the advantages of lowering their self-expectations and increasing their tolerance for failure is a necessary beginning even if it is not sufficient to complete the job. Cultural-awareness training, especially self-awareness building and certain simulation games, may be helpful in underscoring for trainees their heavy emotional investment in certain patterns of behavior as well as the advantages for them of calmly accepting inevitable discrepancies between their patterns and those of host nationals. Attribution training may be particularly valuable, for in its most recent manifestation it is teaching people to attribute the behaviors of others less to personal traits and more to situational factors (Ross 1977; Brislin 1983, 91-105; Detweiler, Brislin, and McCormack 1983). This message can be applied to oneself as well. The situational factors present in an unfamiliar cultural context are powerful and complex, and to the extent that the newcomer can attribute his or her behavioral inadequacies to these rather than to supposed personal deficiencies, the objective of lowering the level of mere adequacy for applicability will have been significantly realized. No doubt the culture assimilator is one technique for accomplishing this objective; there may be others as well.

Lowering the level of mere adequacy for clarity means in practice that each trainee becomes less disturbed by the occurrence of ambiguity in his or her mental frame of reference. In short, successful training is that which better enables the trainee to tolerate ambiguity—both focused and pervasive. Training should define the two types of ambiguity and stress that they are a normal, indeed an inevitable concomitant of taking up life in a completely unfamiliar environment. Trainees must be taught to expect and to recognize both types of ambiguity during the early stages of their sojourn. Whether the ability to tolerate ambiguity is a trainable skill is open to question. We suspect that it is a personality trait, but one that can be improved through appropriate training. Such training needs to consider the parameter of strength. The frame of reference is composed of many diverse elements that may advise for or against any given behavior. Strength takes into account that unanimity is more important for some types of behavior than for others, depending on the person's cultural background. For example, maintenance of a correct structure in male-female roles and relationships is more important in some cultures than in others where roles are more fluid and relationships more casual. Ambiguity in relations with the opposite sex could be highly disturbing to a newcomer from the former type of cultural background. One way of helping trainees deal with such ambiguity is to explain in detail how female-male roles and relationships are structured in the unfamiliar culture, but, conceptually speaking, this approach does not belong here. (It belongs under the desirable changes for applicability and clarity, per se.) Here the conception is for the trainer to say, in effect, something like this: "You trainees are going to have an exceptionally difficult adjustment concerning male-female relationships in the new culture. Adhering to a certain structure of roles and relationships has been very important to you. You've got to expect that you'll be confused and disturbed by the differences in the new culture, and that in some cases you simply won't know how to act. It's normal to feel this way; it's inevitable for people like yourselves because of the way you learned to behave in your home culture. You must accept that you'll be miserable for a while. Just about everyone from your culture goes through this, and just about everyone who goes through it gets over it sooner or later. The secret is not to allow yourself to get too anxious and distraught about the confusion you'll feel. Accept the confusion as part of the adjustment process and expect that it'll pass in time."

In that little scenario lies, perhaps, a plan for the overall "how" of training that is addressed to the level of mere adequacy for clarity. The trainees should be given explicit information regarding the nature and the normalcy of ambiguity. They should be led to expect that it will occur and that it will be deeply disturbing when it does occur. They should be assured that it is a temporary condition that they can weather if they will only not take their distress too seriously. Thus, training should present a "worst case" regarding the decline of clarity so that the trainees will be more likely to evaluate themselves against a standard—their level of mere adequacy for clarity—that has been lowered somewhat from the previous level. And this message should be repeated and reinforced throughout the early stages of the sojourn so that the level of mere adequacy for clarity is continually held down during the period when clarity is at its lowest ebb. In terms of the six categories of training, then, this approach seems to fall under both fact-oriented and cultural-awareness training. As far as the latter is concerned, it could be especially useful during the prearrival phase to include simulation games or other exercises that artificially create ambiguous situations so that people can learn to recognize both focused and pervasive ambiguity and can think more clearly about lowering their self-expectations regarding clarity.

It may be that some readers will view the approach just recommended as scare tactics and will question the ethics of training that emphasizes how difficult and disturbing an intercultural experience can be. Debate on this issue would be useful. Meanwhile, one of us (Torbiörn) wishes to relate briefly the methods and results of an actual training situation. A Swedish firm was planning to send a number of employees on assignment to Saudi Arabia. Prearrival training was conducted, in part, in the manner suggested above; that is, the trainers emphasized the negative sides of expatriate life in Saudi Arabia, saying how dreadful everything would be to achieve, sustain, and so forth. Now that the period of assignment is over, the company reports great success in terms of there being very few premature returns and very few complaints from their employees who were trained in this manner. It is fair to add that there were some very good arrangements for this group in Saudi Arabia; these in conjunction with the method of training probably account for the fine results experienced with this group of sojourners.

The Importance of Training during the Sojourn

Throughout the previous section we have stressed the point that intercultural training is most effective when it is begun prior to the trainees' departure from their home culture and continued periodically during their sojourn in the host culture, ideally through Stage II of our theoretical model. Figures 7 and 8 will help to reinforce this point; they should be viewed in comparison with figure 3 as well as with each other.

Figure 7 (see p. 105) illustrates a hypothetical newcomer's progress through the four stages of the adjustment cycle after receiving a thorough training program, but only prior to his or her arrival in the new environment. Figure 8 (see p. 106) illustrates the sojourner's progress through the stages when the same prearrival training is reinforced and supplemented by periodic training during the first two stages of the experience. Note that the starting point for the three psychological constructs is the same in figures 7 and 8, indicating equally valuable training prior to the newcomer's arrival in the host culture. However, when training continues through Stage II, as depicted in figure 8, the following differences may be expected: (1) the slope of the applicability line is steeper than in figure 7 during the early stages of the adjustment cycle, indicating that continued training enables the newcomer to learn new behaviors at a more rapid rate; (2) the lowest point reached by the clarity line is both higher above zero and earlier in time than in figure 7, indicating that continued training enables the newcomer to reduce more successfully the confusion and ambiguity of his or her mental frame of reference; and (3) the level of mere adequacy remains depressed longer than in figure 7, indicating that continued training encourages and assists the newcomer to judge himself or herself against lowered standards for a longer period of time.

With prearrival training only, the duration of Stage II is shortened from 7.9 units of time (figure 3) down to 5.8 units (figure 7). With training both before arrival and periodically after arrival in the new culture, the duration of Stage II is shortened from 7.9 units of time (figure 3) down to only 3.8 units (figure 8).

Figure 1:   The Well-Adjusted and Socially Adept Person in His or Her Accustomed Environment

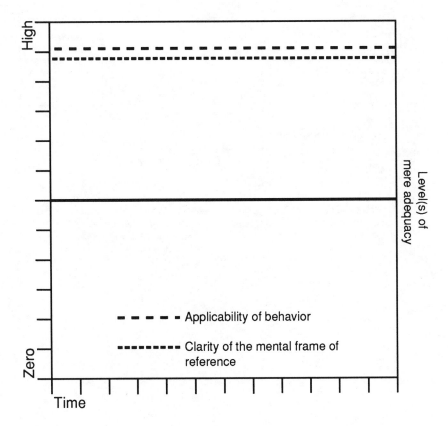

Figure 2:   The Relationships among a Person's Frame of Reference, Behavior, and Environment

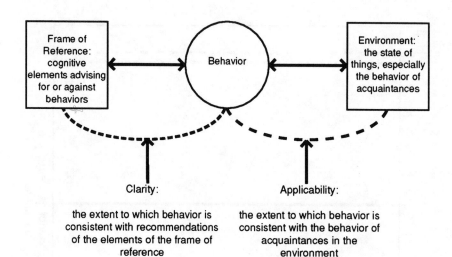

Figure 3: The Person in a Highly Unfamiliar Environment without Benefit of Intercultural Training

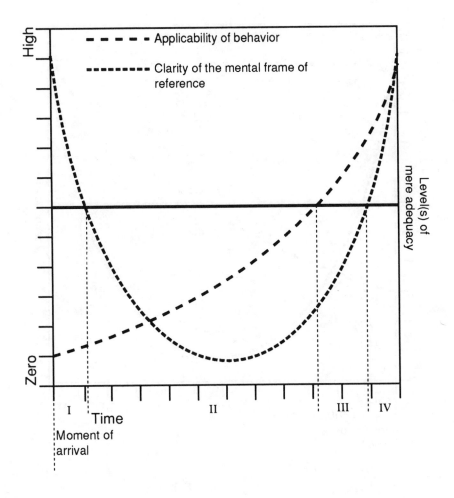

**Figure 4: The Person in a Highly Unfamiliar Environment
with His or Her Applicability Markedly Improved
through Intercultural Training**

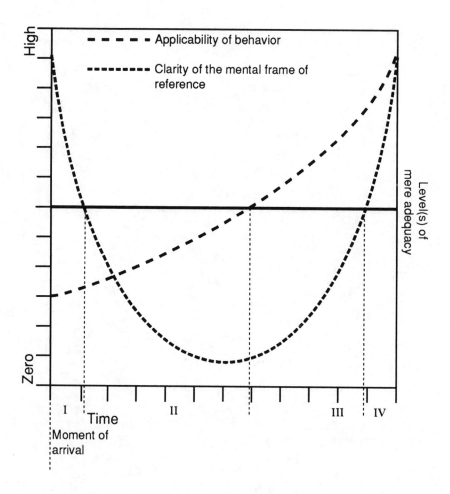

Figure 5: The Person in a Highly Unfamiliar Environment with His or Her Clarity Markedly Improved through Intercultural Training

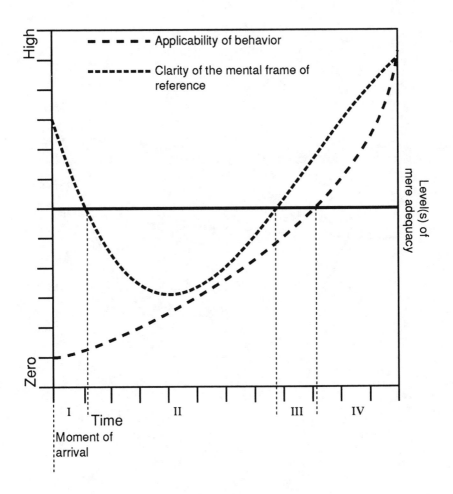

**Figure 6:   The Person in a Highly Unfamiliar Environment
with His or Her Level(s) of Mere Adequacy
Slightly Lowered through Intercultural Training**

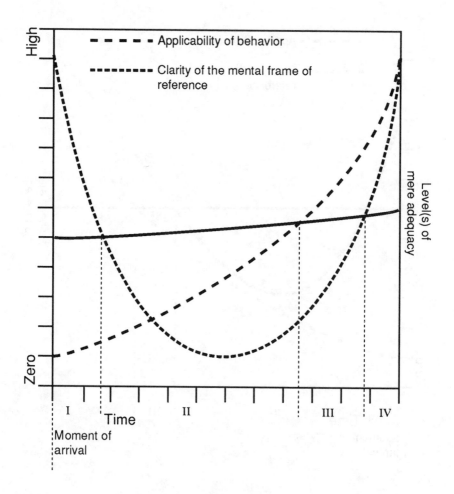

**Figure 7:   The Person in a Highly Unfamiliar Environment
with the Benefit of a Comprehensive Intercultural
Training Program Prior to Arrival**

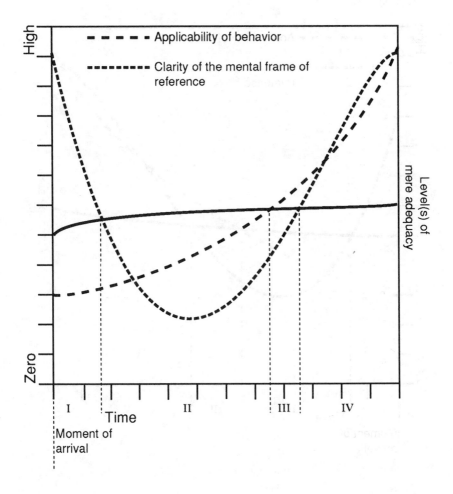

Figure 8: **The Person in a Highly Unfamiliar Environment with the Benefit of a Comprehensive Intercultural Training Program Both Prior to Arrival and during Stages I and II of the Adjustment Cycle**

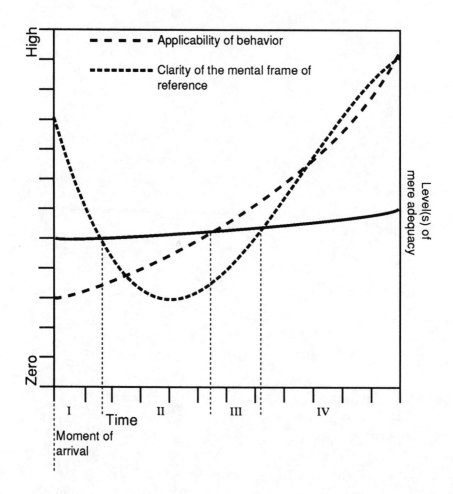

REFERENCES

Adler, Peter S. (1975). "The transitional experience: An alternative view of culture shock." *Journal of Humanistic Psychology* 15, no. 4.

Ball-Rokeach, S. J. (1973). "From pervasive ambiguity to a definition of the situation." *Sociometry* 36, no. 3.

Barna, LaRay M. (1983). "The stress factor in intercultural relations." In Dan Landis and Richard W. Brislin (Eds.), *Handbook of intercultural training* 2. Elmsford, NY: Pergamon Press.

Brislin, Richard W. (1983). *Cross-cultural encounters: Face-to-face interaction.* Elmsford, NY: Pergamon Press.

Brislin, Richard W., Dan Landis, and Mary Ellen Brandt (1983). "Conceptualizations of intercultural behavior and training." In Dan Landis and Richard W. Brislin (Eds.), *Handbook of intercultural training* 1. Elmsford, NY: Pergamon Press.

Chaffee, Clarence (1978). "Cross-cultural training for Peace Corps volunteers." In David S. Hoopes, Paul B. Pedersen, and George W. Renwick (Eds.), *Overview of intercultural education, training, and research* 2. Washington, DC: Society for Intercultural Education, Training and Research.

Church, Austin T. (1982). "Sojourner adjustment." *Psychological Bulletin* 91, no. 3.

Detweiler, R. A., Richard W. Brislin, and W. McCormack (1983). "Situational analysis." In Dan Landis and Richard W. Brislin (Eds.), *Handbook of intercultural training* 2. Elmsford, NY: Pergamon Press.

Grove, Cornelius L. (1981). Book Review of *Training for the cross-cultural mind*, Pierre Casse. *International Journal of Intercultural Relations* 5, no. 4.

_____ (1982). "Improving intercultural learning through the orientation of sojourners." *Occasional papers in intercultural learning* 1. New York: AFS International/Intercultural Learning Programs.

Gudykunst, William B., and Mitchell R. Hammer (1983). "Basic training design: Approach to intercultural training." In Dan Landis and Richard W. Brislin (Eds.), *Handbook of intercultural training* 1. Elmsford, NY: Pergamon Press.

Guthrie, George M. (1975). "A behavioral analysis of culture learning." In Richard W. Brislin, Stephen Bochner, and Walter J. Lonner (Eds.), *Cross-cultural perspectives on learning.* Beverly Hills, CA: Sage.

Keller, S. E. (1981). "Suppression of immunity by stress: Effect of a graded series of stressors on lymphocyte stimulation in the rat." *Science* 213 (September).

Kohls, L. Robert (1979). *Survival kit for overseas living*. Yarmouth ME: Intercultural Press.

Newcomb, T. (1963). "Individual systems of orientation." In S. Koch (Ed.), *Psychology: A study of science* 3. New York: McGraw-Hill.

Pedersen, Paul (1983). "The transfer of intercultural training skills." *International Journal of Psychology* 18.

Ross, Lee (1977). "The intuitive psychologist and his shortcomings: Distortion in the attribution process." In L. Berkowitz (Ed.), *Advances in experimental social psychology* 10. New York: Academic Press.

Smart, Reginald (1983). "Using a Western learning model in Asia: A case study." *Occasional papers in intercultural learning* 4. New York: AFS International/Intercultural Learning Programs.

Textor, Robert (Ed.) (1966). *Cultural frontiers of the Peace Corps*. Cambridge: MIT Press.

Torbiörn, Ingemar (1982). *Living abroad: Personal adjustment and personnel policy in the overseas setting*. New York: John Wiley.

4

Cultural Marginality: Identity Issues in Intercultural Training

Janet M. Bennett

...We are neither trapped nor free; we are always in interaction with our culture, our times, our realities, and we are always able to think about as well as within them (Minnich 1990, 165).

As educators struggle to come to terms with cultural pluralism in America, there is growing recognition of the identity challenges in the life of the bicultural or multicultural person.

Consider the story of Barack Obama, the first black ever to be elected president of the 102-year-old *Harvard Law Review*. Born to a Kenyan father and an American mother, Obama grew up in Hawaii. After his parents separated, he lived with his anthropologist mother in Indonesia. His teens were spent with his grandparents in Hawaii, his college years in Los Angeles and New York, followed by a short time in Chicago working for a church-based social action group. After a distinguished performance at Harvard Law School, he was elected president of the prestigious journal in February 1990.

Obama is described as "very unusual" by one of his professors, because he combines insight and diplomacy, self-confidence, and modesty. European-American students complain that too much attention is paid to his race; African-American students are angered that he failed to select more African Americans for positions at the *Review*. Some question his motives and find it puzzling that he is conciliatory toward conservatives; others say now that he has been elected, his feat is meaningless since he has become part of the Establishment. Still others point to his long record of social responsibility and apparent commitment to community work and political affairs.

In some ways, Obama presents us with an ideal case study of a man in the middle of many cultures. While various cultural groups may each seek his allegiance, he appears to claim for himself an identity that is beyond any single cultural perspective.

Looking around the United States in the 1990s, evidence of multicultural people like Obama is everywhere. Whether through immigration, sojourning, marriage, adoption, or birth, a wide range of people are actively carrying the frame of reference of two or more cultures.

One such group comprises the immigrants and refugees of the last three decades. They have developed and maintained a cultural presence in our society and have refused to melt away their cultures of origin. Unlike earlier immigrants, these "newcomers" are tending to stake out a bicultural way of life in the United States.

Global nomads (for example individuals such as Obama who have lived in several cultures as children) may be multicultural in their identities. Some nomads, called third-culture kids (TCKs), lived abroad while they were young with parents who were working for the government, the military, or for corporations. They returned to the U.S. as citizens of the world.

Individuals in bicultural marriages and their children also bridge two cultures. In cases where the couple is biracial, their children may develop a third cultural perspective within the family system by integrating the cultures of both parents. In cases where the culturally blended family has occurred through adoption, issues of cultural identity may present themselves in yet another way as parents and children explore each other's cultural identities.

Another group carrying two cultures may be long-term adult sojourners who have spent years living in another culture as missionaries, educators, anthropologists, students, international businesspersons, or volunteers. Never really detached from their past experiences, they continue to carry the perspectives gained through other cultural experiences.

Members of groups traditionally labeled "minority" (who no longer are "minority" in many places in the U.S.) frequently internalize two cultures, their own and the dominant culture, in order to function effectively in both. African Americans, Hispanic Americans, Asian Americans, and American Indians understand well the particular challenges that power and oppression bring to a dual cultural identity. The so-called "invisible minorities"— gays, lesbians, bisexuals, incest survivors, etc.—have similar challenges. Although their cultural differences may be hidden, they frequently consider themselves members of at least two cultures.

What these widely disparate individuals share is a sense of grappling with issues of self-concept and identity. As Goldberg suggests:

> ...When an individual shaped and molded by one culture is brought by migration, education, marriage, or other influences into permanent contact with a culture of a different content, or when an individual from birth is initiated into two or more historic traditions, languages, political loyalties, moral codes, or religions, then he is likely to find himself on the margin of each culture, but a member of neither (1941, 52).

In this same vein, Park comments:

> ...a cultural hybrid, a man living and sharing intimately in the cultural life and traditions of two distinct peoples; never quite willing to break, even if he were permitted to do so, with his past and his traditions, and not quite accepted...in the new society in which he now sought to find a place. He was a man on the margin of two cultures and two societies which never completely interpenetrated and fused (1928, 892).

Two potential responses to living on cultural margins are *constructive marginality* (M. Bennett 1986a, 1986b) and *encapsulated marginality*. Both will be explored here by examining some typical characteristics of each and how these characteristics relate to current intercultural and ethnic development models. Finally, suggestions will be made for possible strategies for intercultural educators and trainers to use in developing and implementing programs for culturally marginal people.

CULTURAL MARGINALITY

An individual who has internalized two or more cultural frames of reference frequently faces an *internal* culture shock. This intrapersonal response is not due so much to external interaction with a single different culture, but rather to the recognition of conflicts between two cultural voices competing for attention within oneself.

> All my life I had been looking for something, and everywhere I turned someone tried to tell me what it was. I accepted their answers, too, though they were often in contradiction and even self-contradictory....I was looking for myself, and asking everyone except myself questions which I, and only I, could answer" (Ellison 1972, 15).

Everett Stonequist, in his early work on marginality, describes this inner conflict with the "looking glass theory" of personality:

> The process of seeing one's self reflected in the attitudes of others toward one is so habitual with the ordinary individual that he is unaware of it...with the marginal person, it is as if he were placed simultaneously between two looking glasses, each representing a different image of himself. The clash in images cannot help but make the individual...conscious of the process —conscious of the two mirrors and...the two clashing images (1935, 7).

This description does not necessarily imply a personality disorder or serious maladjustment. Even healthy individuals experience stress when contradictory cultural values compete for ascendancy. Nevertheless, a number of writers have investigated some of the more exaggerated responses to marginality, which provide a glimpse of the inner conflicts the marginal person faces (Dean 1961; Goldberg 1941; Park 1928; Shibutani 1961; Sommers 1964; Stonequist 1935). They mention feelings of powerlessness, isolation, anxiety, insecurity, ambivalence, self-consciousness, malaise, and self-doubt. More recently, a wide range of writers have described the particular stresses of oppressed minorities living in a bicultural context (Cross 1978, 1991; Dyal and Dyal 1981; Levine and Evans 1991; Myers et al. 1991; Padilla 1980; Parham 1989; Phinney 1991; Poston 1990; Smith 1991). In addition to the feelings enumerated in the earlier literature, living within an oppressive culture may also foster low self-esteem, internalized prejudice, frustration, anger, a sense of inadequacy, guilt, hostility, and feelings of betrayal.

Figure 1: Characteristics of Cultural Marginality

ENCAPSULATED MARGINAL	CONSTRUCTIVE MARGINAL
Disintegration in shifting cultures	Self-differentiation
Loose boundary control	Well-developed boundary control
Difficulty in decision making	Self as choice maker
Alienation	Dynamic in-betweenness[2]
Self-absorption	Authenticity
No recognized reference group	Marginal reference group
Multiplistic[1]	Commitment within relativism[1]
Conscious of self	Conscious of choice
Troubled by ambiguity	Intrigued by complexity
Never "at home"	Never not "at home"

When a person responds to this internal dialogue with a compromised ability to establish boundaries and make judgments, we can say that the individual is "encapsulated" or trapped by marginality. The encapsulated marginal is a person who is buffeted by conflicting cultural loyalties and unable to construct a unified identity. In contrast, by maintaining control of choice and the construction of boundaries, a person may become a "constructive" marginal. A constructive marginal is a person who is able to construct context intentionally and consciously for the purpose of creating his or her own identity.

The use of the term "marginality" in this context carries no negative valence, but rather is intended to indicate a cultural lifestyle at the edges where two or more cultures meet, which can be either encapsulating or constructive. The thrust of this positive formulation of marginality compensates for previous views of this status as somehow negative. By construing marginality as a positive position, this formulation becomes a conceptual affirmative action against the imbalance of the past, in which such "deviance" was uniformly viewed as undesirable.

[1] Perry 1970.

[2] Yoshikawa 1987.

ENCAPSULATED MARGINALITY

The identity of the encapsulated marginal has experienced disjunction from constantly shifting cultural frames of reference. The intensity of this disintegration depends on a number of factors including: the situation, previous experience with cultural shifts, existing support systems, peer group identification, personality traits, and what can be termed "culture distance" (the degree of similarity between the internalized cultures). In addition, gender, sexual orientation, ethnicity, race, language, and power position seriously affect the internal culture shock and the self-identification of marginals.

Figure 2: Issues That Affect Self-identification of Marginals

1. Were you born in a country different from the one in which you now live?

2. If you identify with any group, does that group hold minority status in your place of residence?

3. Did you choose to migrate? Are you a refugee?

4. Are you a member of an indigenous group that was invaded by a colonial power?

5. Are you racially, ethnically, and/or culturally different from the dominant culture?

6. Do you speak the dominant language as a second or foreign language?

7. Are you female?

8. Are you gay, lesbian, or bisexual?

9. Do you feel that you don't share primary identification with any group?

10. Do you work/play/study at institutions staffed by people different from you?

Typically, the person described as an encapsulated marginal has grown to incorporate the worldviews of at least two cultures, but has difficulty controlling shifts between them. As Park suggests, the person "learns to look upon the world in which he was born and bred with something of the detachment of a stranger. He acquires, in short, an intellectual bias...not confined by...custom, piety or precedents" (Park 1928, 888). Conflicting loyalties and loose boundary control give decision making the character of a trial-and-error effort, as one attempts first to conform to the requirements of one perspective and then to the demands of the other.

Carl Jung reflects on this challenge:

> He will serve as his own group, consisting of a variety of opinions and tendencies—which need not necessarily be marching in the same direction. In fact, he will be at odds with himself and will find difficulty in uniting his own multiplicity for the purposes of common action....The disunion within himself may cause him to give up, to lapse into identity with his surroundings (1965, 342-43).

The encapsulated marginal is, therefore, vulnerable to a sense of alienation described variously as including powerlessness, meaninglessness, normlessness, cultural estrangement, self-estrangement, social isolation, anomie, or anxiety (Dean 1961, 754; Guthrie 1981, 105; McGuire and McDermott 1988, 101; Pearce and Kang 1988, 37).

The fact that persons with dual cultural membership may experience bouts of alienation can be related to the high degree of pressure placed on them by both of the cultures of which they are a part. Frequently, members of the original culture accuse the marginal of selling out to the new or dominant culture, of being corrupted by new friends, or of failing one's family. Meanwhile, the second culture may apply pressure to conform to unfamiliar roles in order to achieve acceptance or success. In the context of an oppressive second culture, integration or success may continually be thwarted. Establishing enduring goals, clear values, or strong personal attachments represents a major effort, given the conflicting pressures (Sommers 1964, 332).

Encapsulated marginals perceive themselves as so unique they may be incapable of envisioning a peer group with whom they can relate. This captive state can be called "terminal uniqueness," for it seems irresolvable to the encapsulated marginal. They may therefore appear self-conscious and self-absorbed. If power position is a factor, they may become engrossed with the process of assimilation (Parham 1989, 217). The encapsulated marginal may report feeling inauthentic all the time, as if any engagement in society is simply role-playing, and there is no way to ever feel "at home." A young female Vietnamese refugee reports:

> I began making progress in my career as a professional coordi-
> nating the Washington office of an association. Ironically, all of
> a sudden, the success I had striven for so arduously somehow
> became more of a mockery than an achievement. My self-
> confidence —critical in getting me through the first few years —
> quickly began to erode. The immense drive which I must have
> developed in order to survive the war and which I had put to use
> in rebuilding my life in America, lost its steam (*Oregonian*,
> 27 April 1985).

The sense of being alone with this cultural-identity struggle often
causes marginal people to feel detached from all reference groups and
forced to resolve these conflicts alone. If it is possible to seek support
among members of their own cultures, they are often unable to find peers
who have chosen a similar form of cultural adaptation. Many global
nomads, bicultural marriage partners, and adopted children have no
such peer-group option and are frequently unaware of the existence of a
global community of marginals with whom they might identify.

THE PERRY SCHEME

The difficulties of the encapsulated marginal as well as the necessary
tasks for becoming constructive can be illuminated by examining cultural marginality in light of Perry's (1970) scheme of intellectual and
ethical development. While the initial conceptualization of this model by
Perry had no relationship to cultural adaptation, the scheme lends itself
nicely to probing the issue of marginality.

Perry suggests that learners start from an initial position of ethical
dualism, where decisions are dictated by authority figures and have a
right/wrong quality to them. Randall Terry, founder of the controversial
pro-life group Operation Rescue, is quoted in an interview by Richard
Lacayo which illustrates this position:

> Why is theft always wrong? Because God says it's wrong. If you
> do not have the unchanging moral principles of higher law—
> and that's capital H and capital L—as the bedrock of your
> culture, then you are left with the ever-shifting sand of the
> newest fad, the latest whim (1991, 28).

Typically, individuals who have experienced deeply shifting frames of reference across cultures do not assume this kind of dualistic position.

When learners move beyond dualism, they arrive at a stage of *multiplicity* where the authorities are less clear, and choices are muddled by conflicting perspectives. The encapsulated marginal shares this multiplicity, being pulled in at least two directions for every thought, feeling, and behavior. The "terminal uniqueness" posture of the encapsulated marginal fosters multiplicity, where ambiguity seems overwhelming and strongly stated opinions seem prejudicial or biased.

In Perry's scheme, learners get beyond this confusing point through a recognition of the inevitability of ambiguity and of their own responsibility to think autonomously, based on an assessment of the context. In terms of the cultural marginal, this stage of *contextual relativism* allows random cultural-frame-of-reference shifting to become grounded in context. The individual assesses the cultural context before developing a position, taking care to be appropriate in the relevant cultural system. It also clarifies the inevitable responsibility for taking charge of one's own identity.

Once learners have achieved this recognition of context, they are prepared to move ahead to the final stages of the model: *commitment in relativism*. Here choice is an accepted responsibility. This stage is marked by respect for alternative opinions in the context of one's own commitments. The credibility attributed to authorities is based on qualitative judgments and critical thinking. The cultural marginal who can master this stage has become a constructive marginal, capable of constructing identity and making commitments in the face of ambiguity. The poignancy and strength of this position are best expressed by Wallace Stevens:

> The final belief is to believe in a fiction which we know to be a fiction, there being nothing else. The exquisite truth is to know that it is fiction and that you believe in it willingly (1957, 163).

CONSTRUCTIVE MARGINALITY

The constructive marginal also experiences disintegration as a function of cultural shifts, but in that process has become fully conscious of self-differentiation and the need to assume personal responsibility for choosing and constructing value sets. The concept of personal choice, while not necessarily a part of the person's previous cultural worldview, may be essential to forming clear boundaries in the face of multiple cultural perspectives. It is not so much a case of becoming individualistic as it is of becoming self-reflective.

Consciousness of one's own cultural marginality, of one's role in creating a unique cultural identity, has been called a state of "dynamic in-betweenness" by Muneo Yoshikawa. The suggestion here is of continual and comfortable movement between cultural identities such that an integrated, multicultural existence is maintained, and where conscious, deliberate choice making and management of alternative frames prevail. Yoshikawa depicts the final stage of cross-cultural adaptation as a Möbius strip or mathematical infinity symbol, reflecting twofold movement, paradoxical relationships, and "identity-in-unity," with realities that are complementary and constantly in interaction (1988, 143).

This awareness of living on the margins of at least two cultures eliminates being overly dependent upon a single culture for identity. Rather, individuals who are constructive in their marginality tend to "...experience wholeness and integration...recognize and value all of their ethnic identities...[and] develop a secure, integrated identity" (Poston 1990, 154). Frequently, this marginal identity is recognized as a resource to be harnessed for professional or social advantage. As Stonequist noted, "the stimulus of the [marginal] situation may create a superior personality or mind...dual contacts may give him an advantage, making him a leader...." (1935, 11). Several authors have noted the additive element in biculturality or multiculturality, suggesting that the acculturation process need not substitute new cultural values for old. Rather, acculturation may add new behaviors and constructs that allow for cultural-frame-of-reference shifting (Dyal and Dyal, 1981). Saltzman's 150 percent person represents just such a culturally expanded individual (1986).

Unlike the encapsulated marginal, the constructive marginal feels authentic and recognizes that one is never *not* at home in the world. This comfort may be partially due to the acknowledgment that indeed one does have a peer group. It is not fellow members of one's own culture, but rather a group of fellow marginals with whom one has more in common than with anyone else.

Most importantly, the constructive marginal is no longer at a multiplistic stage of cognitive and ethical development. In terms of Perry's scheme, the individual has moved into relativism and perceives that knowledge is constructed from context, not from "truth" as given by authorities. This stage depends on the person's ability to tolerate ambiguity, respect other perspectives, and define his or her own frame of reference. Ultimately, it requires the person to make a commitment to a value system honed from many contexts and an identity actively affirmed and based solidly on self as choice maker. It requires an ability to empathize with others, balanced by skill at withdrawing from empathy, and flexibility of boundaries, balanced by skill at defining them. This stage of commitment within relativism is exemplary of constructive marginality.

DEVELOPMENTAL MODELS

Designing educational programming for marginals is particularly challenging to the trainer or educator, who may well ask: What represents development for these individuals? How can they be inspired to greater cognitive, affective, and behavioral development? In the past two decades, many writers have addressed this question by creating models of development from various intercultural and ethnic perspectives. Many of these models focus on psychosocial-identity development for different cultural groups.

For instance, recent research has focused on African-American identity (Cross 1978; Parham 1989), sexual identity (Cass 1979; Levine and Evans 1991), ethnic identity in general (Banks 1988; Smith 1991; Sue and Sue 1990; Phinney 1991), oppressed peoples' identity (Myers et al., 1991), minority identity (Atkinson, Morten, and Sue 1983), biracial identity (Poston 1990), and white identity (Helms 1984, 1990; Sabnani, Ponterotto, and Borodovsky, 1991). Each of these models attempts to describe the development of identity from the perspective of self and group, indicating the degree of identification the person has with the cultural group at various stages and the relationship patterns that typically develop with other cultures. Nearly all of these models suggest a final stage of development which closely resembles the image of the constructive marginal described above; many of them also include a stage which resembles encapsulated marginality.

Another model relevant to the discussion of marginality is the developmental model of intercultural sensitivity (M. Bennett 1986a, 1986b). Not an identity model as such, this model examines the individual's response to cultural difference and suggests a series of stages through which a person from any culture might expect to move when experiencing other cultures. The final stage of this model describes the nature of constructive marginality and its relationship to intercultural-sensitivity development.

Suggesting some similarities among developmental models is not intended to obscure the very definite differences that exist in identity-development issues among various groups. Self-directed sojourners who have chosen to live overseas for ten years may become bicultural and face many of the issues of the cultural marginal. Members of minority ethnic groups living in a dominant culture may face some similar issues, but they also frequently grapple with different issues of power and status as they relate to the majority culture. (The words "minority" and "majority" are used here reluctantly to reflect a political status that continues, at least temporarily, despite rapidly changing demographics.) Responsible trainers will want to familiarize themselves with the specific concerns of the individuals and groups with whom they work.

A review of these models is useful to the educator for a number of reasons. First, it familiarizes us with the essential developmental tasks which are being pursued by learners in our programs. Second, it provides us with tools for "audience analysis" of our learners. Finally, it can inform our approach to designing and sequencing learning opportunities for members of different cultures.

What these models share is an approach to development which frequently construes the final stage in terms that resemble constructive marginality. While this comparison should not be made without caution, nevertheless many authors of different cultures have clearly experienced and researched the developmental processes of persons living on the edge of two or more cultures and come to similar conclusions. They tend to describe this stage as integrated, synergetic, aware, ethnorelative, multicultural, secure, appreciative of self and others, and committed.

The characteristic most often emphasized in these final stages is integration of identity. Smith points out that members of ethnic groups face conflict between "ethnic identity fragmentation" and "ethnic identity integration" (1991). This conflict is one which mirrors the struggle of the encapsulated marginal in making sense of multiple frames of reference. In discussing biracial identity development, Poston also labels his final stage "integration," noting that individuals at this stage "recognize and value all their ethnic identities" (1990). Similarly, in analyzing sexual identity, Cass (1979) describes stages of confusion, comparison, tolerance, acceptance, and pride with a final state she calls identity synthesis. Banks's model of ethnicity concludes with a stage he calls "globalism," which engenders "a delicate balance of ethnic, national, and global identifications, commitments, literacy, and behaviors" (1988). Milton Bennett's model of intercultural sensitivity also ends in a stage labeled integration, "where difference is integral to identity" (1986a,1986b).

Another trait widely emphasized in cultural-identity models is the trait of personal commitment. Like learners who represent the later stages in the Perry scheme (commitment in relativism), constructive marginals need to be able to take action and achieve commitment with a great deal of tolerance of ambiguity: "Complexity, especially the conflict between value systems, demands a capacity to tolerate paradox in the midst of responsible action" (1970, 166). This need for commitment is central to many of the models' final stages. In particular, Cross outlines a stage of black identity development which he describes as reflecting "ideological flexibility, psychological openness and self-confidence." He expands on this in a final stage of "internalization/commitment," in which "to achieve a lasting political significance, the 'self'...must become or continue to be involved in the resolution of problems shared by the 'group'..." (1978, 18). Other models (Banks 1988; Parham 1989; Phinney 1991) also reinforce the need for personal commitment to values (in Perry's terms) as well as a commitment to justice, or world consciousness (in the terms of the cultural models). Simply stated, the resolution of multicultural identity requires an integration of both the psychological and social aspects of self and society.

There are both limits and strengths in applying such models to training and education. While most of these models have not been empirically validated, they have a great deal of heuristic value for the practitioner who is responsible about understanding learners. While some models may be too simplistic to reflect accurately the needs or experiences of any given group, they do provide a place to begin and some goals to be achieved, goals which seem to be shared by a wide range of culturally diverse scholars over time. As with all issues of cultural difference and, in particular, issues of cultural marginality, the educator needs to proceed with caution in recognition of the profound complexity of the process.

TRAINING

For the intercultural trainer, the rewards and challenges of teaching and learning with a group of marginals are immense. It is not sufficient to run a simple orientation for learners who are generally quite sophisticated about moving from culture to culture. It is too simplistic to train multicultural members of a diverse work force with a skills set for improved functioning in the workplace. Rather, trainers are increasingly faced with marginals who want to know more than who, what, when, where, and how; they want to know why. The need for this deeper understanding requires that trainers assume a frankly developmental perspective on their programming. They must begin to educate their learners on why as well as train them how or orient them to who, what, when, and where.

To meet this challenge, trainers and educators are well advised to familiarize themselves not only with the cultural-identity models discussed above, but also with a range of developmental models exploring epistemology and ethics, two subjects which continually trouble the marginal person (Belenky et al., 1986; Fowler 1981; Gilligan 1982; Knefelkamp, Widick, and Parker 1978; Kohlberg and Mayer 1972; Perry 1970). By approaching programs with a conscious organized intent to foster the perspective transformation, trainers can become developmental educators.

In order to consider the development needs of both the encapsulated and the constructive marginal, trainers can borrow a framework from educator Nevitt Sanford's influential text *Self and Society* (1966) in which he discusses the ideas of challenge and support. For each learner, depending on his/her developmental stage, educators need to examine what aspects of the learning context can provide needed supports and what aspects present challenges. If the learner is overly supported, no learning takes place. If the learner is overly challenged, the learner flees the learning context. The educator needs to assess the needs of the participants and carefully balance challenge and support to maximize learning.

Further, this idea of challenge and support relates both to the content and process of the program. Depending on their developmental stage, learners may find certain content, such as culture shock, very challenging or very affirming of their experience. Depending on their learning style, they may find certain processes, such as role plays, very rewarding or very demanding.

Figure 3:   Content and Process: Balancing Challenge

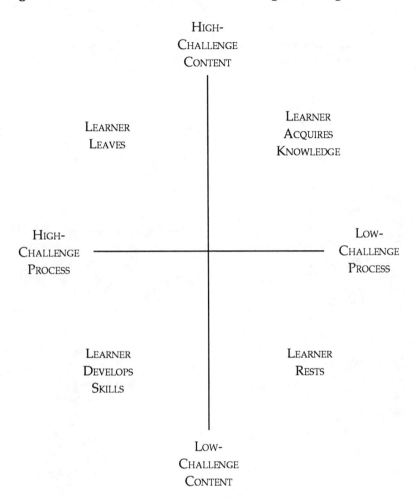

TRAINING THE ENCAPSULATED MARGINAL

By fully understanding the developmental supports and challenges for the encapsulated marginal, the trainer can better facilitate movement to greater constructiveness.

Figure 4:   Issues in Training Marginals

ENCAPSULATED MARGINALS	CONSTRUCTIVE MARGINALS
Support	*Support*
Identify a peer group	Share with peers the exploration of cultural values and commitments
Reinforce connections between experience and knowledge	Reinforce commitments based on experience and knowledge
Model appreciation for diversity of perspective	Model constructive marginality
Challenge	*Challenge*
Primary task: learning how to think critically	Primary task: learning how to think in context
Develop distinctions between "connected knowing" and "separate knowing"	Synthesize "connected knowing" and "separate knowing"
Encourage individual responsibility	Encourage individual choice
Explore cultural decision-making methods	Explore cultural mediation methods
Examine cultural issues that require synthetic thinking	Examine cultural issues that require reflective judgment
Question view of self-as-object	Promote view of self-as-process
Present models of cultural-identity development	Present models of ethical development
Encourage exploration of boundary expansion and contraction	Encourage commitments and boundary setting

Encapsulated Marginals: Supports

In order to support these participants, the trainer should model for them a consistent appreciation for diversity of perspectives. Encapsulated marginals frequently bring multiple frames of reference to the training context, and this ability to demonstrate such shifts needs to be rewarded. In addition, as deeply experienced multicultural persons, these learners can benefit from an educational context that respects that experience and reinforces the connections between their own "real life" events and academic knowledge. "Experience rich, but theory poor" in the intercultural context often stimulates superb learning opportunities. Finally, the encapsulated marginal's sense of "terminal uniqueness" often denies the marginal any recognition of a peer group. One of the most supportive contributions a trainer can make to cultural marginals is to help them identify their true peer group, which is other cultural marginals.

Encapsulated Marginals: Challenges

The primary challenge for these individuals is learning how to think critically about the contradictory perspectives their cultural knowledge and experience have provided. If they are indeed encapsulated by the whirlwind of equally valid (to them) cultural frames of reference, they need to develop standards for assessing those frames.

Valuable insights into this process are provided by Belenky et al., in *Women's Ways of Knowing*. Based on a distinction made earlier by Gilligan (1982), women's development is discussed in terms of "two contrasting epistemological orientations: a separate epistemology, based on impersonal procedures for establishing truth, and a connected epistemology, in which truth emerges through care" (Belenky et al. 1986, 102). Central to separate knowing are objectivity, critical thinking, detachment, debate, argumentation, logic, and impersonality. Central to connected knowing are empathy, subjectivity, experience, nonjudgmentalness, patience, feelings, and intuition. Connected knowing may be related to Peter Elbow's concept of the "believing game," in which the learner's first response to new information is to believe and to look for ways to empathize. In contrast, his notion of the "doubting game" fits with separate knowing, in which the learner first doubts, initially trying to find something wrong with the new information (Elbow 1973).

Professionals who have had frequent contact with cultural marginals might be inclined to suggest that the believing game is somewhat more representative of this group than is the doubting game. Based on wide and complex experiences, marginals have learned to avoid cultural judgments, to use intuition in intercultural situations, and to appreciate the subjectivity of their experience—all attributes of the believing game. Trainers thus may find that they need to spend more time teaching the doubting game than they do the believing game.

If training for encapsulated marginals is to be developmental, the learners must understand the distinctions between these two modes of thinking and set about learning to construe their intercultural experiences in both ways. For example, Barack Obama, mentioned in the case study at the beginning of this chapter, would need to explore the frustrations of the African-American students both by doubting and believing. In doubting, he might analyze their stages of ethnic development and see their anger as symptomatic of identity issues. In believing, he would empathize with them, attempting to see their point of view from their perspective, and take full account of the affective dimension.

The doubting game and separate knowing build an effective foundation for the encapsulated marginal who needs to master contextual decision making. In teaching critical thinking to these learners, the trainer should encourage them to take responsibility for their own learning through goal-setting and self-assessment methods. Marginals can be relied upon to provide critical incidents, case studies, and the content of role plays. Their rich experiences provide complex examples, and by connecting the application of the concepts to their own experience, the trainer will enhance the "real life" value of learning, powerfully connecting theory to practice.

In addition to critical thinking, the encapsulated marginal must also master models of decision making. Having been buffeted by multiplistic values, the marginal can benefit from training in a variety of decision-making approaches ranging from values clarification to creative problem solving. In each case, the emphasis should be on closure: "How can we come to the best resolution on this matter?"

Cultural issues that require synthetic thinking are ideal examples for these problem-solving exercises. By requiring that learners synthesize their many perspectives to achieve resolution and closure, the trainer is capitalizing on the creative strength of marginals and limiting their tendency to indecisiveness.

While critical thinking and decision making are essential skills, intrapsychic processes cannot be ignored. Self-absorption may be a preoccupation of those who have internalized several cultures, and much time may be spent on the "who am I?" question. Psychologist Don Hamachek provides a perspective useful to the trainer working with marginals:

> As the *self* has evolved in psychological literature, it has come to have two distinct meanings. From one view it is defined as a person's attitudes and feelings about himself, and from another it is regarded as a group of psychological processes which influence behavior and adjustment. The first meaning can be looked at as a *self-as-object* definition, as it conveys a person's attitudes, feelings, and perceptions of himself as an object. That is, it is as if one could stand outside of himself and evaluate what he sees from a more or less detached point of view. In this sense, the self is what a person thinks of himself. The second meaning may be called the *self-as-process* definition. In other words, the self is a doer, in the sense that it includes an active group of processes such as thinking, remembering, and perceiving (1971, 8).

Watching the self and becoming a collectivity of intrapersonal impressions of one's own fluid identity are hazards of marginality. While certainly not recommending the unexamined life, a trainer can assist marginals in recognizing the limits of self-as-object, moving toward a more constructivist perspective of self-as-process.

In order to facilitate this movement, it is often helpful if the trainer familiarizes the participants with various models of cultural-identity development, as suggested above. The final stages of all these models clearly identify the attitudes and characteristics of individuals who have achieved comfort with their multicultural position. In these late stages, the majority of these models describe individuals who view themselves not as objects, but as process creators.

Finally, when the learners are familiar with cultural-identity development, they can begin to practice skills of boundary expansion and contraction. So often, persons who excel at empathy will complain of being unable to control the extent and duration of their empathic response. Encapsulated marginals sometimes struggle with a similar issue: how to control the extent and duration of their frame-of-reference shifting? Just as the overly empathic counselor experiences burnout, so does the unbounded marginal. This ability to open boundaries and let many cultural frames of reference come to bear needs to be tempered with the ability to arrive at a conclusion, to end the input, and, once again, achieve closure.

TRAINING THE CONSTRUCTIVE MARGINAL

By fully understanding the supports and challenges for the constructive marginal, the trainer can better facilitate movement toward increasing the potential, both personal and professional, of these individuals.

Constructive Marginals: Supports

In order to support constructive marginals, the trainer needs to model the attitudes, behaviors, and commitments of this stage of development. Many multicultural individuals are eager to experience role models who have succeeded in maintaining their multicultural identities while functioning effectively. Either through personal actions and expressions of the trainer or through the use of reading or media, learners should have the opportunity to experience a variety of approaches to life as a comfortable multicultural person.

Constructive marginals find great support in learning from each other. Rather than encouraging individual introspection and responsibility as indicated in training encapsulated marginals, the trainer should structure learning opportunities that fully capitalize on the resources of the group. One highly effective process is cooperative learning, an educational method orginally developed in primary and secondary schools. Cooperative learning strategies designed for older learners reinforce both personal and group responsibility and take advantage of all available expertise (Cooper et al. 1990; Johnson, Johnson, and Smith 1991). Effort at group work with marginals also cements their recognition of the marginal peer group and counteracts a sense of alienation.

Finally, the trainer can support this group by validating commitments learners make based on both their experience and their knowledge, on both doubting and believing. Affirmation of self-as-process and of constructivist thinking is an important part of development.

Constructive Marginals: Challenges

The primary challenge for these individuals is learning how to think in a context defined and assessed by their construction of reality. In a sense, they are coming to terms with the reality that all knowledge is constructed, and what they will ultimately value and believe is what they choose, based on the context and frame of reference they construct.

During the encapsulated phase, they learned to practice both believing and doubting, connected and separate knowledge. As constructive marginals, their task now is to synthesize this thinking and, through establishing their own value commitments, arrive at personal choices. The warring frames of reference must be resolved by the only persons in authority: the marginals themselves. A rich example is provided by Eva Hoffman, in her book *Lost in Translation* (1989, 199):

"Should I marry him?" I asked myself in English. "Yes."
"Should I marry him?" I asked myself in Polish. "No."

Obviously, this sort of question cannot remain a multiplistic riddle forever, and only she herself can make the choice. While she may be "dynamically in-between" two cultures, only one frame of reference can provide the context for the choice—the one she constructs. It may be that she chooses to conform to a Polish identity. It may be that she chooses to abandon that life and maintain an American identity. More likely, she will make a commitment to some values from each perspective, or other cultural perspectives as well, and create an identity uniquely her own.

The trainer working with learners at this stage of development should be cautious not to interpret this as an individualistic process, based on a Western concept of how life is best lived. It is rather a self-reflective process, which may involve either a more Western field-independent approach or a more field-sensitive approach. Persons who have a major component of group interdependence in their cultural makeup can maintain their field-sensitivity orientation by identifying with their peer group of cultural marginals. This can provide a great deal of support to marginals who no longer feel they can conform to the original cultural group but who wish to retain the field-sensitive rather than the field-independent identity.

This form of synthetic thinking, what Belenky et al. (1986) call constructed knowledge, should be applied to cultural issues that call for reflective judgment. The trainer is now calling for evaluation and is facilitating the learners in making value commitments. In support of this process, the trainer may wish to familiarize the learners with cultural-mediation models, in recognition that multicultural specialists are superb candidates for training as mediators. The combination of multiple frames of reference, connected and separate knowing, and commitment in the context of relativism makes an ideal background for a rational, empathic go-between.

Once again, the intrapsychic processes cannot be ignored, as the constructive marginal comes to full terms with the responsibilities of self-as-process, in Hamachek's phraseology. Being one's own authority figure and one's own choice maker may be viewed by some cultures or individuals as an unrealistic challenge. Having relied for part of a lifetime on the culture around them for their identity, they may struggle long and hard with this issue.

They can be assisted by an understanding of models of ethical development and a realization of the place they are trying to achieve in a developmental context. William Perry's model of intellectual and ethical development is particularly useful in this training. In addition, understanding their own place on Milton Bennett's model of intercultural sensitivity can reinforce their accomplishment.

While encapsulated marginals practice boundary expansion and contraction, constructive marginals are mastering commitments and boundary setting. Constructive marginals tend to avoid getting lost in every new cultural frame of reference that presents itself. While being able to understand the other frame, constructives do not reinvent their identities on a weekly basis. At this stage of development, the trainer must provide learning opportunities to set boundaries, make value commitments, and put these constructions into practice.

REFERENCES

Amir, Yehuda (1969). "Contact hypothesis in ethnic relations." *Psychological Bulletin* 71, no. 5: 319-42.

Atkinson, Donald R., George Morten, and Derald Wing Sue (1983). *Counseling American minorities: A cross-cultural perspective* (2d ed.). Dubuque, IA: William C. Brown.

Banks, James A. (1988). *Multiethnic education: Theory and practice* (2d ed). Newton, MA: Allyn and Bacon.

Belenky, M., B. Clinchy, N. Goldberger, and J. Tarule (1986). *Women's ways of knowing: The development of self, voice, and mind.* New York: Basic Books.

Bennett, Milton J. (1986a). "A developmental approach to training for intercultural sensitivity." *International Journal of Intercultural Relations* 10: 179-96.

———— (1986b). "Towards ethnorelativism: A developmental model of intercultural sensitivity." In R. Michael Paige (Ed.), *Cross-cultural orientation: New conceptualizations and applications.* Lanham, MD: University Press of America.

Bochner, Stephen, Anli Lin, and Beverly M. McLeod (1979). "Cross-cultural contact and the development of an international perspective." *Journal of Social Psychology* 107: 29-41.

Cass, V. C. (1979). "Homosexual identity formation: A theoretical model." *Journal of Homosexuality* 4: 219-35.

Cooper, James, Susan Prescott, Lenora Cook, Lyle Smith, Randall Mueck, and Joseph Cuseo (1990). *Cooperative learning and college instruction: Effective use of student learning teams.* Long Beach: California State University Foundation.

Cross, William E., Jr. (1978). "The Thomas and Cross models of psychological nigrescence: A review." *Journal of Black Psychology* 5, no. 1: 13-31.

———— (1991). *Shades of black: Diversity in African-American identity.* Philadelphia: Temple University Press.

Dean, Dwight G. (1961). "Alienation: Its meaning and measurement." *American Sociological Review* 26: 753-58.

Drummond, Tam Merlin (1 April 1990). "The Barack Obama story." *San Francisco Chronicle.*

Dyal, James A., and Ruth Y. Dyal (1981). "Acculturation, stress and coping: Some implications for research and education." *International Journal of Intercultural Relations* 5: 301-28.

Elbow, Peter (1973). *Writing without teachers*. London: Oxford University Press.

Ellison, Ralph (1972). *Invisible man*. New York: Random-Vintage.

Fowler, J. W. (1981). *Stages of faith: The psychology of human development and the quest for meaning*. San Francisco: Harper and Row.

Furnham, Adrian (1988). "The adjustment of sojourners." In Young Yun Kim and William B. Gudykunst (Eds.), Cross-cultural adaptation: Current approaches. *International and Intercultural Communication Annual* 11. Newbury Park, CA: Sage.

Furnham, Adrian, and Stephen Bochner (1986). *Culture shock: Psychological reactions to unfamiliar environments*. New York: Methuen.

Gilligan, Carol (1982). *In a different voice: Psychological theory and women's development*. Cambridge, MA: Harvard University Press.

Goldberg, Milton M. (1941). "A qualification of the marginal man theory." *American Sociological Review* 6: 52-58.

Grove, Cornelius Lee, and Ingemar Torbiörn (1985). "A new conceptualization of intercultural adjustment and the goals of training." *International Journal of Intercultural Relations* 9: 205-33.

Gudykunst, William B., and Mitchell R. Hammer (1988). "Strangers and hosts: An uncertainty-reduction-based theory of intercultural adaptation." In Young Yun Kim and William B. Gudykunst (Eds.), Cross-cultural adaptation: Current approaches. *International and Intercultural Communication Annual* 11. Newbury Park, CA: Sage.

Guthrie, George M. (1981). "What you need is continuity." In Stephen Bochner (Ed.), *The mediating person*. Cambridge, MA: Schenkman.

Hamachek, Don E. (1971). *Encounters with the self*. New York: Holt.

Harari, Herbert, Catherine A. Jones, and Helena Sek (1988). "Stress syndromes and stress predictors in American and Polish college students." *Journal of Cross-Cultural Psychology* 19, no. 2: 243-55.

Helms, Janet E. (1984). "Toward a theoretical explanation of the effects of race on counseling: A black and white model." *Counseling Psychologist* 12: 153-65.

_____ (1990). *Black and white racial identity theory, research, and practice.* New York: Greenwood Press.

Hoffman, Eva (1989). *Lost in Ttranslation.* New York: Dutton.

Johnson, David W., Roger T. Johnson, and Karl A. Smith (1991). *Active learning: Cooperation in the college classroom.* Edina, MN: Interaction.

Jung, Carl G. (1965). *Memories, dreams and reflections.* New York: Vintage.

Knefelkamp, L. Lee, Carol Widick, and Clyde A. Parker (Eds.) (1978). *Applying new developmental findings.* New Directions for Student Services 4. San Francisco: Jossey-Bass.

Kohlberg, Lawrence, and Rochelle Mayer (1972). "Development as the aim of education." *Harvard Educational Review* 42: 449-96.

Lacayo, Richard (1991). "Interview with Randall Terry: Crusading against the pro-choice movement." *Time* 21 (October): 26-28.

Levine, Heidi, and Nancy J. Evans (1991). "The development of gay, lesbian, and bisexual identities." In Nancy J. Evans and Vernon A. Wall (Eds.), *Beyond tolerance: Gays, lesbians and bisexuals on campus.* Alexandria, VA: American College Personnel Association.

McGuire, Michael, and Steven McDermott (1988). "Communication in assimilation, deviance, and alienation states." In Young Yun Kim and William B. Gudykunst (Eds.), Cross-cultural adaptation: Current approaches. *International and Intercultural Communication Annual* 11. Newbury Park, CA: Sage.

Minnich, Elizabeth K. (1990). *Transforming knowledge.* Philadelphia: Temple University Press.

Myers, Linda J., et al. (1991). "Identity development and worldview: Toward an optimal conceptualization." *Journal of Counseling and Development* 70, no. 1: 54-63.

Oregonian, 27 April 1985.

Padilla, Amado M. (1980). *Acculturation: Theories, models and some new findings.* Boulder, CO: Westview.

Parham, Thomas A. (1989). "Cycles of psychological nigrescence." *Counseling Psychologist* 17, no. 2: 187-226.

Park, Robert E. (1928). "Human migration and the marginal man." *American Journal of Sociology* 3, no. 6: 881-93.

Pearce, W. Barnett, and Kyung-Wha Kang (1988). "Conceptual migrations: Understanding 'travelers tales' for cross-cultural adaptation." In Young Yun Kim and William B. Gudykunst (Eds.), Cross-cultural adaptation: Current approaches. *International and Intercultural Communication Annual* 11. Newbury Park, CA: Sage.

Perry, William G. (1970). *Forms of intellectual and ethical development in the college years: A scheme.* New York: Holt.

Phinney, Jean S. (1991). "Ethnic identity and self-esteem: A review and integration." *Hispanic Journal of Behavioral Sciences* 13, no. 2: 193-208.

Poston, W. S. Carlos (1990). "The biracial identity development model: A needed addition." *Journal of Counseling and Development* 69: 152-55.

Sabnani, Haresh B., Joseph G. Ponterotto, and Lisa G. Borodovsky (1991). "White racial identity development and cross-cultural counselor training: A stage model." *Counseling Psychologist* 19, no. 1: 76-102.

Saltzman, Carol E. (1986). "One hundred and fifty percent persons: Models for orienting international students." In R. Michael Paige (Ed.), *Cross-cultural orientation: New conceptualizations and applications.* Lanham, MD: University Press of America. 247-68.

Sanford, Nevitt (1966). *Self and society: Social change and individual development.* New York: Atherton Press.

Schlossberg, Nancy K., Ann Q. Lynch, and Arthur W. Chickering (1989). *Improving higher education environments for adults.* San Francisco: Jossey-Bass.

Schuetz, Alfred (1945). "The homecomer." *American Journal of Sociology* 50: 369-76.

Shibutani, Tomatsu (1961). "Social change and personal growth." *Society and Personality.* Englewood Cliffs, NJ: Prentice-Hall. 567-96.

Smith, Elsie J. (1991). "Ethnic identity development: Toward the development of a theory within the context of majority/minority status." *Journal of Counseling and Development* 70, no. 1: 181-88.

Sommers, Vita S. (1964). "The impact of dual-cultural membership on identity." *Psychiatry: Journal for the Study of Interpersonal Processes* 27: 332-44.

Stevens, Wallace (1957). *Opus posthumous.* New York: A. Knopf.

Stonequist, Everett V. (1935). "The problem of the marginal man." *American Journal of Sociology:* 1-12.

Sue, Derald Wing, and David Sue (1990). *Counseling the culturally different* (2d ed.). New York: Wiley.

Taylor, Kathe Elizabeth (1990). *The dilemma of difference: The relationship of the intellectual development, racial identity, and self-esteem of black and white students to their tolerance for diversity.* Doctoral dissertation, University of Maryland, College Park, 1990.

Taylor, Kathe Elizabeth, and William S. Moore (1991). "Education as transformation: Thinking about general education and the college classroom environment from a Perry perspective." Association for General and Liberal Studies, National Conference, Washington, DC. October 17.

Useem, John, John D. Donoghue, and Ruth Hill Useem (1963). "Men in the middle of the third culture." *Human Organization* 22: 169-79.

Widick, Carole, L. Lee Knefelkamp, and Clyde A. Parker (1975). "The counselor as a developmental instructor." *Counselor Education and Supervision* 14: 286-96.

Yoshikawa, Muneo J. (1987). "The double-swing model of intercultural communication between the east and the west." In D. Lawrence Kincaid (Ed.), *Communication theory: Eastern and Western perspectives.* San Diego: Academic Press.

_____ (1988). "Cross-cultural adaptation and perceptual development." In Young Yun Kim and William B. Gudykunst (Eds.), Cross-cultural adaptation: Current approaches. *International and Intercultural Communication Annual* 11. Newbury Park, CA: Sage.

Yum, June O. (1988). "Locus of control and communication patterns of immigrants." In Young Yun Kim and William B. Gudykunst (Eds.), Cross-cultural adaptation: Current approaches. *International and Intercultural Communication Annual* 11. Beverly Hills, CA: Sage.

5

Understanding and Coping with Cross-Cultural Adjustment Stress

Gary R. Weaver

WHAT IS "CULTURE SHOCK"?

The phrase "culture shock," coined by Cora DuBois in 1951, was first used in the cross-cultural literature by anthropologist Kalvero Oberg (1960) to describe problems of acculturation and adjustment among Americans who were working in a health project in Brazil. He viewed it as "an occupational disease of people who have suddenly been transported abroad [which] is precipitated by the anxiety that results from losing all our familiar signs and symbols of social intercourse." Oberg viewed culture shock as a specific ailment with its own symptoms and cures. However, in the past thirty years the phrase has become a basic part of the international sojourner's jargon and is now commonly used to describe almost any physical or emotional discomfort experienced by those adjusting to a new environment. "Homesickness," "adjustment difficulties," "uprooting" (Zwingmann and Gunn 1983), and numerous other terms are often used to describe the same phenomenon as culture shock. While that term may be a bit too strong, the other labels fail to focus on cultural factors and are overly euphemistic. Most cross-cultural trainers use the term culture shock because of historical tradition and the attention-getting value of the words.

Symptoms may range from mild emotional disorders and stress-related physiological ailments to psychosis. The types and intensity of reactions to a new cultural environment depend upon the nature and duration of the stressful situation and, more importantly, the psychological makeup of an individual. Some people quickly develop useful coping strategies which allow them to adjust easily while, at the other extreme, some resort to the use of progressively more inappropriate and maladaptive neurotic defense mechanisms which may eventually develop into such severe psychological disorders as psychosis, alcoholism, and even suicide.

Most studies suggest that such severe reactions account for less than 10 percent of all sojourners, and it may well be that they were predisposed to an inability to cope with sudden traumatic stress before they traveled overseas. The vast majority of sojourners experience moderate reactions and successfully overcome culture shock. In fact, some may actually come through culture shock more psychologically sound than before they left their own culture.

In the past decade severe culture shock has also been measured in terms of a so-called "dropout rate." It has been informally estimated, for example, that the Peace Corps has a dropout rate of between 30 and 40 percent. These are volunteers who return home before completing their term of service overseas. The implication is that these volunteers terminated their stays because of the stress of cross-cultural adjustment or an inability to adapt overseas. Of course, there may be many other factors to account for such termination including family difficulties, health problems unrelated to stress, or differences with management overseas.

The severity of culture shock is generally much greater when the adjustment involves a completely different culture, because there is a greater loss of Oberg's "familiar signs and symbols of social intercourse" in an entirely new environment. On the other hand, anticipation of a stressful event also affects the severity of the reaction. It seems that if we do not anticipate a stressful event we are much less capable of coping with it. This would explain why we still experience culture shock when entering a slightly different cultural environment or when returning home to our native culture. Most Americans do not anticipate stress when adapting to London and few anticipate the stress of reentering their home culture.

Ultimately the psychological makeup of the individual may be the most important factor. Some people can tolerate a great deal of stress caused by change, ambiguity, and unpredictability while others demand an unchanging, unambiguous, predictable environment to feel psychologically secure. Psychological traits, rather than cross-cultural adjustment skills or cultural awareness, may be of primary importance (Brislin 1981, 40-71) in determining the success with which one adapts to another culture.

While Oberg considered culture shock to be a separate "ailment," thereby suggesting a medical disease model to explain the phenomenon, some have come to consider it a normal and natural growth or transition process as we adapt to another culture (N. Adler 1985; P. Adler 1974). As with growth or adaptation there is disorientation, ambiguity, and pain, but we often come through this state more stable and centered than ever before. The object is not to eliminate or avoid culture shock but rather to make it a less stressful and more positive experience. Culture shock is most probably the result of a normal process of adaptation and may be no more harmful than the psychological reactions we experience when adapting to such new environmental situations as entering college or moving to another city in our own culture. Those who claim they have never experienced any form of culture shock overseas are either fairly unaware of their own feelings or have never really cross-culturally adjusted. Tourists and those who remain enmeshed within conational groups generally do not experience culture shock.

WHY DOES CULTURE SHOCK OCCUR?

In the literature on culture shock there are three basic causal explanations: (1) the loss of familiar cues, (2) the breakdown of interpersonal communication, and (3) an identity crisis. All three disorienting states occur in adjustment to any new social environment. However, in a cross-cultural situation they are greatly exaggerated and exacerbated by cultural differences. While each of these explanations takes a slightly different approach, they are not mutually exclusive nor is any single one adequate to fully understand the phenomenon. Indeed, they overlap and complement each other.

Loss of Cues or Reinforcers

This explanation is the most behavioral in that it primarily focuses on that which is tangible and observable. Everyone is surrounded by thousands of physical and social cues which have been present since childhood and therefore are taken for granted until they are absent. Behavioral or social cues, which Oberg refers to as signs and signals, provide order in interpersonal relations. Physical cues include objects which we have become accustomed to in our home culture which are changed or missing in a new culture. These familiar cues make us feel comfortable and make life predictable. When they are absent we begin to feel like a fish out of water.

Cues are signposts which guide us through our daily activities in an acceptable fashion which is consistent with the total social environment. They may be words, gestures, facial expressions, postures, or customs which help us make sense out of the social world that surrounds us. They tell us when and how to give gifts or tips, when to be serious or to be humorous, how to speak to leaders and subordinates, who has status, what to say when we meet people, when and how to shake hands, how to eat, and so on. They make us feel comfortable because they seem so automatic and natural.

Cues serve as reinforcers of behavior because they signal if things are being done inappropriately. In a new social environment, behavior is no longer clearly right or wrong, but instead becomes very ambiguous. This ambiguity is especially painful for many Euro-Americans because they are accustomed to clear verbal messages and feedback, explicit rules of behavior, and the ability to predict the behavior of others. In many other cultures, people may say yes when they mean maybe because they seek to please. Or they may say maybe when they mean no because they don't want to give negative feedback to another person.

The low-context, loosely integrated, and heterogeneous nature of Euro-American societies (Hall 1976) is built upon clear, explicit, overt rules of behavior which ensure predictability. In high-context, non-Western cultures, rules of behavior are often vague, implicit, and tacitly learned simply by growing up in that culture. They are buried or embedded deeply within the context of the culture. The society is usually more tightly integrated and homogeneous. Thus, one can infer from his or her own behavior what is appropriate for everyone else. For Euro-Americans, on the other hand, there are fewer rules of behavior and they are less easily identified. Consequently, there is less predictability. When familiar cues or reinforcers are no longer elicited by their behavior, they experience pain and frustration. In fact, the loss of a reinforcer or cue is actually a form of punishment (Azrin 1970) in terms of their psychological reactions. Thousands of times Euro-Americans deposit coins into a soft drink machine which results in the drop of a can or cup. If one day no can or cup drops down after depositing their money, they may react to this lack of an expected reinforcer by irrationally kicking the machine. It usually does not cause the can or cup to drop down nor does the machine return the money. But they may feel better because they have vented their anger over the loss of the reinforcer.

In a new culture, our messages of "good morning," "thank you," "how are you," no longer bring the response we are accustomed to in our native culture. It is not even clear when one should smile or laugh. These simple behaviors that we have used to interact with others no longer elicit the reinforcers we have received throughout our lives. And the reaction is often frustration and anger which is irrationally displaced onto others whom we perceive to be lower in our social hierarchy, such as taxi drivers, waiters, porters, and secretaries.

Cues also involve how we use time and space (Hall 1959, 1966, 1976). They include the very rhythm or synchrony of speech and movement which we acquire during the first few weeks of life (Hall 1983) and the social distance we maintain between ourselves and others. How late we can arrive without making an apology; the rhythm of conversation including pauses between words and phrases; and the appropriate pace, amount, and kind of body movement are learned implicitly or tacitly from the social or cultural environment during the first few years of life.

When we enter another culture we feel out of sync and, yet, we often do not realize the cause of our awkwardness because we learned our own kinesic, proxemic, and chronemic cues simply by growing up in our own culture. This silent language, or nonverbal communication, is especially important for the communication of feelings (Mehrabian 1968) and yet is almost totally beyond the conscious awareness of the average person.

The very act of changing physical environments causes stress. It is true that we are adaptable, but within limits. Moreover, adaptation always produces some stress, whether it is to a better or a worse condition. As both Alvin Toffler (1970) and Philip Slater (1974) point out, there is a direct correlation between the number of major changes experienced in a given period and the likelihood of the person falling ill. Selye's (1956, 1974) and Barna's (1983) research on stress as it relates to change clearly suggests that change of physical environments in and of itself produces much of the stress that may be attributed to culture shock.

There probably is a form of "object loss" when we experience loss of cues and reinforcers, and one may actually go through various stages of acute grief (Lindemann 1944). Disorientation can lead to a form of "learned helplessness" (Siligman 1975) which often results in depression. While everyone going through culture shock feels disoriented, some people panic psychologically and become extremely self-destructive.

Fortunately, most of us adapt to new environments and, in the process, acquire new skills and ways of looking at the world. Through the process of adaptation we often gain insights into our own personality and the great impact our culture has had in shaping it. But this awareness and personal growth necessarily involves some pain.

The Breakdown of Communication

Identifying a breakdown of communication as a cause of culture shock emphasizes the process of interpersonal interaction and is much less behavioral than the other possible causes. In fact, it approaches humanistic psychology with its emphasis on the psychodynamics of human interaction. A basic assumption in this explanation is that a breakdown of communication, on both the conscious and unconscious levels, causes frustration and anxiety and is a source of alienation from others.

Proponents of this explanation may emphasize any part or link in a communication system. Some might concentrate on the inefficiency and misunderstandings brought about by different meanings given to messages. Others might carry this approach into the areas of transactional analysis or even existential psychology, stressing the inability to communicate on an "authentic level" with others as the source of stress (Laing 1967, 1970). These latter theorists dovetail into the third explanation of cause—an identity crisis—with their emphasis on self and human interaction.

From a cross-cultural or orientation-training standpoint, the communication-breakdown explanation allows for an understanding of the process of cross-cultural adjustment and provides a paradigm for identifying the various components of any cross-cultural interaction. One may begin with a simple cybernetics model of communication to illustrate how the breakdown of communication inevitably takes place as one interacts with people in a new culture. The simple model on the following page may serve as an illustration.

Basic Cybernetics Model of Communication

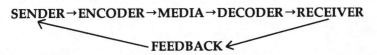

SENDER → ENCODER → MEDIA → DECODER → RECEIVER

FEEDBACK

As this cybernetics model suggests, the breakdown of any part or link between parts in the system causes the entire system to break down, somewhat like a tube blowing on an old radio. For example, focusing on the *sender* and *receiver*, it is clear that we send messages, not meanings. If the sender and receiver come from different cultures, the same messages may elicit completely different meanings in their respective minds.

At the *encoder* and *decoder* stages, the obvious source of breakdown involves different languages. However, nonverbal codes are probably even more significant in cross-cultural communication because these codes are learned implicitly and thus are generally unconscious. They are mostly culture-specific and are used primarily for communicating messages regarding feelings (Mehrabian 1968). One can easily identify the breakdown of verbal messages, whereas the breakdown of nonverbal messages is less obvious but more significant in that we feel emotionally confused and cut off from others.

Feedback involves both verbal and nonverbal messages and certainly varies with each culture. In many non-Western cultures, feedback is circuitous and subtle, whereas Americans prefer direct and unambiguous feedback. Americans want a clear yes or no, not "it is the will of God," "it is difficult," or "maybe."

When communication breaks down or becomes ineffective, we experience pain. Passive-aggressive individuals are especially effective at cutting off communication with others to induce frustration and pain. Victims of this aggression often have no conscious awareness of why and how the passive-aggressive causes them so much distress. Because most humans communicate quite effectively before the age of three or four, we take the ability to communicate for granted and seldom are consciously aware that the source of much of our pain in human interaction is the breakdown of communication.

When any animal experiences pain, it reacts by fleeing the source of pain (escape or avoidance behavior), displacing aggression (fight behavior), or distorting, simplifying, and denying the complexity and reality of the painful situation. Note that, in human beings, all of these reactions, when carried to extremes, are both unconscious and highly neurotic.

People going through culture shock are not aware of what is causing them pain nor why they often behave in such irrational ways. They have a sense of hopelessness and helplessness. The situation is controlling them, and, unless they understand the process of communication breakdown, they fail to develop coping strategies, lose their sense of control, and cannot find alternative ways of behaving. Instead of acting, they end up reacting.

By considering culture shock as a result of the breakdown of communication, one can apply many psychological constructs to explain the behavior of those going through the stress of cross-cultural adjustment. These include learned helplessness, autistic hostility, psychosomatic reactions, displacement of aggression, projection, the conflict cycle, image theory, and attribution theory.

This explanation is especially useful for helping sojourners understand the underlying dynamics of culture shock. Furthermore, it suggests that culture shock is an inevitable but natural process of cross-cultural adjustment which can be overcome with conscious awareness of one's own reactions. While this explanation offers no specific answers for overcoming culture shock, it does help sojourners replace neurotic reactions with coping strategies.

An Identity Crisis

This explanation of culture shock draws together behavioral, psychoanalytical, and existential approaches with an overlay of cognitive theory. This is by far the most complicated yet the most fascinating explanation of culture shock, because it implies that there is genuine psychological growth that occurs when one successfully overcomes culture shock.

The loss of cues or reinforcers is disorienting, but the disorientation frees people from habitual ways of doing and perceiving things and allows them to perceive and adopt new cues. It also brings to conscious awareness the grip that our culture has on our behavior and personality.

We might consider culture as analogous to a computer program, that is, our culture determines what information gets into our heads and how we use that information to solve problems. To this extent, culture is indeed synonymous with mind (Hall 1976). This culture "program" in turn determines our behavior. To understand someone's behavior (output) it is necessary to understand how the person experiences or perceives the world (input) and how that person has learned to organize and utilize that information (program).

Computer Analogy of Culture

INPUT ⟶ **PROGRAM** ⟶ **OUTPUT**

selective perception   thought pattern   behavior

information   values   actions and reactions

When we enter another culture, the program which has worked so well since childhood no longer is adequate. The system of selective perception and interpretation (N. Adler 1985) no longer wards off the bombardment of millions of new stimuli or cues, and it is no longer clear what one should pay attention to or what the stimuli mean.

The ways in which we have been programmed by our culture to solve problems or to think no longer work effectively. The environment makes new demands upon us. Finally, we are overwhelmed by the bombardment of stimuli and demands and must temporarily experience the sense of confusion of not knowing what to pay attention to or how to solve problems. This period may be similar to the transitional stages we experience during other life crises such as adolescence. The ways in which we select out that which is relevant or abstract from our social and physical environment, that which is significant, are obsolete. We are overwhelmed and can no longer cope.

The transitional period is very associative or relational (Weaver 1975) in that everything seems to flow together somewhat chaotically. But this is how we begin to see new relationships and new ways of ordering our perceptual and intellectual world. We are gradually expanding our cultural program, image system, and subjective knowledge structure.

As with any other identity crisis, culture shock allows us to give up an inadequate perceptual and problem-solving system to allow another more expanded and adequate system to be born. It is somewhat of a death-rebirth cycle.

In her book *Passages*, Gail Sheehy suggests that we human beings are similar to hardy crustaceans. "The lobster grows by developing and shedding a series of protective shells. Each time it expands from within, the confining shell must be sloughed off. It is left exposed and vulnerable until, in time, a new covering grows to replace the old." As with the passages from one stage of human growth to the next, when we go through culture shock, "we must shed a protective structure and are left exposed and vulnerable—but also yeasty and embryonic again, capable of stretching in ways we hadn't known before" (Sheehy 1977, 29). Fundamentally the lobster is still the same except more mature. And when we come through culture shock, we are fundamentally still the same except that we may now see the world in different ways and have a host of new alternatives for solving problems and considering reality.

The breakdown of communication may be more of a breakthrough to new ways of interacting with others, and it might give us insight into our own need for human interaction on an authentic level. Ways of accomplishing tasks, solving problems, and thinking which may have worked effectively all our lives may be ineffective in a new culture. When we go through culture shock, we become aware of how our culture has shaped our thinking and perception, and we may become more conscious of our "hidden culture" (Hall 1976) and, in turn, transcend it.

As with the psychoanalytic cathartic event and the existential crisis, there is pain and risk involved in the culture-shock experience (Blanchard 1970). Some do not want to be freed from the cultural prison they have been born into, and not all make it to the other side when they take an existential leap. A certain percentage of people will be unable to tolerate the stress of giving up an inadequate problem-solving system or an identity which gave them a sense of security and predictability for so long. Every soldier who goes into battle does not experience the kind of acute psychosis associated with shell shock. And everyone who goes through culture shock does not experience the reactive or acute psychosis associated with severe adjustment difficulties. A great deal depends upon the predisposition of the individual and his or her psychological makeup.

The overseas experience, like that of an encounter or sensitivity group, offers a new social milieu in which to examine one's behavior, perceptions, values, and thought patterns. An experience close to psychosis may be required to take one outside the collective pressures and assumptions of our culture. We may discover things about ourselves that allow for great personal growth. Yet it may be an ego-shattering experience. Great personal insight can occur for many, while others may find it very destructive (Blanchard 1970). Whether the experience will eventually become positive or negative, a source of personal growth or destruction, depends upon one's expectations, adaptability, tolerance for ambiguity and stress, and an understanding that there inevitably will be pain which can be handled and overcome.

The analogy between the overseas experience and the encounter group is even more apropos when we consider that both involve emotional and somewhat irrational situations. Moreover, both demand full participation and emotional involvement. Frustration is only heightened when one attempts to cope with the situation as an aloof, rational, objective observer. It is a total experience of mind and body, the intellectual and sensual, and the objective and subjective person.

It is not so much that the individual is a fish out of water as it is that he or she is a youngster being thrown into the water who must learn how to swim. People cannot intellectualize the experience nor simply observe others swimming. They must try to swim by moving their arms and legs in the water, by participating kinesthetically in the aquatic environment. This is not a simple theoretical or intellectual exercise. Eventually most will experience the ecstasy of being able to swim. Some, however, rush to the shore, never to set foot in the water again. Some even drown.

CULTURE SHOCK IS NOT A DISEASE

For over a hundred years psychologists have been trying to overcome the medical model of emotional disorders which originated with Sigmund Freud. The problem with the model is that it suggests that an emotional disorder is actually an illness or disease which you can catch like a cold or tuberculosis. It implies that it has a distinct set of symptoms which can be cured. This relieves the person and others in his or her life of any responsibility for the disorder, it ignores the reality that most disorders are directly related to complex interpersonal relationships, and it suggests that we may find a magic-bullet cure of some sort. Worst of all, it causes both the observer and the participant to focus on the pathological aspects of emotional disorder rather than the growth process and positive benefits.

The medical model also leads us to label emotional disorders and identify specific pathological symptoms. Once the label is applied to an individual, it is very difficult for that person to convince others that he or she is not schizophrenic, psychotic, or neurotic (Rosenhan 1973). That is, people tend to perceive selectively that behavior which fits the label while ignoring behavior which contradicts the label. Even worse, the individual often adjusts his or her behavior to fit the label, thereby creating a self-fulfilling prophecy.

As noted earlier, Oberg described culture shock as an ailment with distinct symptoms and cures, thereby establishing a medical model to explain cross-cultural adjustment stress. Orientation trainers often uncritically accept this model and seek to give trainees a clear diagnosis, set of symptoms, prognosis, and cure. They may resort to using flip charts listing distinct symptoms ranging from diarrhea to insomnia. Sometimes they produce U- and W-curve charts to illustrate a clear pattern of progression or phases of the disease. Some even suggest a list of cures or specific ways of overcoming culture shock.

When someone in our own family has an emotional disorder, we really like to believe that it struck the person arbitrarily, like some mysterious germ. When we discuss the disorder with a therapist, most of us are not interested in hearing all the theoretical explanations of cause or responsibility. We would like a clear diagnosis, a label for the disease with a list of specific symptoms which can be cured by following concrete procedures. Ideally, we would like to hear that it is biochemically caused and thus can be biochemically cured. That is, give us a simple explanation of cause, a clear description of symptoms, and some prescription to cure the illness.

The medical, or illness, model of culture shock is counterproductive and misleading, yet is an unfortunate result of the desire of many sojourners to have a simple formula for dealing with it. Of course, when they get overseas they find they may not have all the symptoms, and stress may manifest itself in complex psychological disorders such as depression, confusion, irrational behavior and thoughts, and a sense of lacking control. These are all internal, not external, symptoms. The distress does not follow any particular pattern and the sojourners are not sure where they are on the so-called U- or W-curve of adjustment. The resultant confusion adds to their stress and gives them a lack of confidence in their predeparture training.

Most people going overseas are not really interested in understanding the causes of culture shock or the process of cross-cultural adjustment. They want specific information, not analysis and interpretation. They want cookbooks and a list of do's and don't's for dealing with the new culture and cross-cultural adjustment stress. And some cross-cultural trainers will sell them their favorite cookbook with catchy labels and simple, concrete examples of symptoms and cures.

New situations often come up that were not covered in the training, and their vague psychological malaise fits into none of the distinct categories on the trainers' charts. The sojourners mentally thumb through the index of their cookbook but to no avail. At this point, panic often sets in. It would have been much more useful to have a broad framework within which they could analyze and interpret their reactions. Knowing the causes of culture shock and the process of cross-cultural adjustment would have helped them understand that it is a normal reaction which does, in fact, end—sooner or later.

No cure will work for everyone because there are so many variables involved. What might work for one person in a specific environment may not work for others in different environments. Wives may react differently from husbands, and children differently from adults. Rather than traveling overseas with a false sense of confidence in cure-alls, it would have been much more helpful to develop coping strategies which allow each individual to find his or her own way of dealing with and overcoming the stress of cross-cultural adaptation.

The most common symptom of culture shock is a lack of control or helplessness. Unconscious reactions to the situation control us unless we understand what is going on. Thus, simply understanding the process of cross-cultural adjustment or adaptation is probably the best way of overcoming culture shock. Then we have a sense of control and can act instead of reacting.

Culture shock is primarily an unconscious phenomenon. Most people have no idea why they are behaving as they are or feeling as they do. By understanding the process of adaptation, one sees that it is a normal reaction to a new cultural or social environment which everyone goes through to some extent. Furthermore, it can be a very positive experience which allows for personal insight and growth.

COPING WITH CROSS-CULTURAL ADJUSTMENT STRESS

The various reactions to the stress of cross-cultural adjustment are much akin to what Sigmund Freud (1936, 1955) and his daughter Anna (1970) described as defense mechanisms—unconscious steps we take to protect our ego or self from a painful reality. Most neurotics have a sense of hopelessness, helplessness, and lack of control. They are victims of a situation that they cannot realistically change, and they are controlled by their unconscious reactions.

Of course, many neurotics fully understand the cause and process of their neurosis but they are still highly neurotic. Understanding is the beginning step in overcoming a neurosis, but ultimately each individual must develop a sense of control over his or her reactions and must cope with a painful reality which cannot be changed.

A conscious understanding of the process of adaptation and the expectation that culture shock will occur eliminates a great deal of the pain caused by uncertainty and lack of predictability. It helps if we know that our reactions are part of the process of adjustment to the reality of another culture which we cannot change. However, this knowledge is not enough. There are conscious steps we can take which allow us to control our reactions and minimize the length and severity of the stress. These coping mechanisms or strategies (Allport 1961; Maslow 1970) permit sojourners to *act* instead of simply *reacting* to the new culture, to face reality and decide what to do about it, and to find various alternative ways of dealing with the adjustment problems.

It is important to distinguish between *coping* and *defense* mechanisms. Defense mechanisms are unconscious reactions to a stressful or painful reality. The situation controls the individual by causing the reactions. These defenses help one avoid the painful reality through such unconscious processes as denial, distortion, withdrawal, and repression. They are normal and explicable, but ineffective, ways of dealing with the situation and the resultant stress.

Coping mechanisms are actions, not reactions, which one consciously takes to give one a sense of self-control and to respond effectively to a situation. They provide strategies, methods, or steps for dealing with the stressors and the stress, and they increase effectiveness. One cannot change another culture, and the goal of cross-cultural adaptation is not to avoid the source of stress (people in the host culture) but to increase interaction with the local people. Thus, one of the primary ways to minimize defensive reactions, to provide greater self-control, and to maximize effective interaction in another culture is to develop coping strategies.

While each person must develop his or her own ways of coping, the following brief list of broad strategies may be applied by most sojourners. They are a logical extension of the discussion of the process of cross-cultural adjustment.

Understand the Process of Adjustment

By understanding the process of adjustment, we can anticipate stress and this, in and of itself, helps minimize the severity of our reactions. Furthermore, this understanding gives sojourners a way to make sense out of the confusion, ambiguity, and disorientation which are symptomatic of culture shock. It suggests that there are strategies one may take to cope with the stress and more effectively overcome the causes of culture shock. And, most importantly, it makes the pattern of cross-cultural adjustment predictable and clearly shows most people that they will overcome the stress and may even be better for having gone through it.

Loss of control, helplessness, and hopelessness are some of the more obvious symptoms of culture shock, and they result from a lack of understanding of what is happening. These symptoms cannot be controlled unless there is an understanding that culture shock is not some mysterious disease. Moreover, most sojourners will realize that they have gone through this process before, such as their first day of school, summer camp, or military training. These parallel experiences were overcome and some of the same reactions and coping strategies will work again. We can build upon this reservoir of experience much as reverse culture shock or reentry/transition stress can be overcome by building upon the experience of having gone through culture shock (Weaver and Uncapher 1981).

If you understand the process of cross-cultural adjustment, it is fairly easy to recognize the symptoms of culture shock. Withdrawal, displacement of anger, building little American communities, going native, and various psychosomatic illnesses are all obvious symptoms which can be controlled. Simply knowing that these are symptoms and not causes eases a great deal of the stress.

Control the Symptoms or Reactions to Cross-Cultural Adjustment Stress

Before you can treat the root causes of culture shock, it is necessary to control the symptoms. If one is paralyzed with frustration and anxiety and feels overwhelmed by the stress, it is difficult to perceive alternative ways of behaving or coping. Thus, the first step is to develop first-aid techniques which will allow for greater control of reaction to stress.

From our understanding of culture shock, it is obvious that some behavior is counterproductive and will only inhibit adjustment. For example, if culture shock results from a breakdown of communication, withdrawing from host nationals may alleviate the pain temporarily but ultimately will not help one adjust. The withdrawal behavior is defensive, and extreme withdrawal and paranoia are danger signs that culture shock may be getting worse (Silverman 1970).

Some sojourners decide to leave behind all reminders of home and start off anew in another culture. However, from our understanding of what happens in the loss of familiar cultural cues, this will actually increase the stress of adjustment. Transferring potent reminders from one's home culture, such as favorite CDs or photographs, may be an effective coping strategy to temporarily ease the pain of loss of cues until new potent ones are adopted (David 1976). Modifying things in the host environment so that they are somewhat similar to those in the home culture is another coping strategy that may ease the stress. One can make a hamburger of sorts out of almost any meat.

According to research on reactive or acute schizophrenia, interfering with the normal death/rebirth or growth process can make the situation worse (Silverman 1970; Maher 1968). If culture shock is understood as an identity crisis, then abruptly interfering with the process, such as returning home during the crisis period, is not a wise course of action. Rather, intensifying the sharing of feelings with others who understand the process of adaptation helps one through the transition. Temporarily cutting down stimuli by withdrawing somewhat from host nationals may be a wise conscious strategy in light of this paradigm. But that is not an unconscious retreat from a painful reality—it is a strategic withdrawal. There is a clear difference.

Often, people intuitively adopt coping strategies which help control the symptoms of culture shock. For example, during the first few weeks or months of an overseas experience, sojourners write numerous long letters to their loved ones at home. Certainly people back home are not all that interested in every meal or experience the sojourner has had. However, for the sojourner it provides a way of communicating authentically with those who share the same meaning system. That is, it may be an unconscious form of compensation for the breakdown of communication overseas. And, as one gradually adjusts to the new culture and begins communicating effectively with host nationals, the letter writing usually decreases. Loved ones back home may be concerned that something has happened when letters stop coming with such frequency and detail, but, in fact, the sojourner is probably happier than when the copious letter writing was taking place.

As with any stressful situation, relaxation, desensitization, and counterconditioning techniques are very useful for minimizing reactions (Barna 1983; Walton 1990). Knowing that too much stress and overstimulation can be traumatic allows one to develop stress-control techniques such as decreasing stimuli, relaxing, minimizing the number of changes in a short period of time, and withdrawing temporarily.

These first-aid strategies ultimately do not treat the root causes of culture shock or help one adjust to another culture. However, they do give sojourners a greater sense of control and prevent the symptoms from overwhelming them.

Developing Coping Strategies That Facilitate Adjustment

Just as understanding the process of cross-cultural adjustment leads to logical methods for controlling the symptoms of culture shock, it also leads to ways in which we can more quickly and effectively adjust to another culture. Cross-cultural adjustment is the final goal.

If withdrawing from others is ultimately maladaptive, increased communication with host nationals is ultimately adaptive. Temporarily this may actually increase stress because host nationals are the stressors (Barna 1983). But in the long run it will speed up the process of adjustment. Learning the verbal and nonverbal language in the context of the culture and consciously placing oneself in situations where there is greater likelihood of interacting with host nationals are coping strategies which lead toward greater cross-cultural understanding. Furthermore, they will allow for the development of cross-cultural communication skills.

In researching the process of cross-cultural adjustment with over a thousand Nigerian students who studied in the U.S. (Weaver and Uncapher 1981) and with hundreds of international students at The American University, it was found that most identified a fairly clear U-curve pattern with an initial high or honeymoon period (Oberg 1960) followed by a sharp emotional downturn. Almost all came out of the slump with an emotional upswing as they adjusted to American culture. When asked what single event seemed to be most responsible for the upturn, the vast majority responded that they had developed a friend-ship with a host national. Interpersonal communication with host-national friends seemed to turn the tide.

When we go through culture shock, there is often a sense that there is some personal weakness or inadequacy on our part which inhibits our adjustment. Sometimes irrational behavior such as displacement of anger causes feelings of guilt. The apparent lack of concern by host nationals for our misery may be interpreted as enjoyment of our discomfort.

To overcome this sense of personal inadequacy and paranoia, it is helpful also to associate with those who have gone through culture shock. Host nationals may have never experienced culture shock and are actually quite unaware of what is happening to us. Experienced sojourn-ers have gone through this before and can provide assurance that it is both normal and transitional. They also may model strategies to over-.

come the stress and successfully adapt. Caution must be taken that this association with other sojourners not be exclusively conational or reactionary in nature (i.e., gripe sessions). Otherwise, it may lead to avoidance of host nationals and inhibit successful adjustment.

Learn Something about the New Culture before Leaving Home

Just as it helps to anticipate reactions to stress, it helps to have some knowledge of the new culture before departure. It is fairly easy to acquire information on history, geography, food, customs, dress, language, and religion before leaving. This information, if understood as incomplete and simply a descriptive set of broad generalizations, may help diminish negative stereotypes and give some confidence that you will know what is going on. Having realistic expectations of the new culture obviously helps decrease stress.

This culture-specific knowledge also provides conversational currency. It helps sojourners coming to the U.S. if they already know something of American sports, politics, history, and music. They then have the basis for a conversation with almost any American. This predeparture, culture-specific knowledge also communicates to host nationals that you care enough about them to gather the information.

While no "cookbook" for another culture can be written, we can acquire a list of basic do's and don't's which at least get us started on the right foot, helping us avoid grossly offensive behavior and giving us the confidence that we can at least greet people correctly, know when and how to tip, avoid gestures that will be interpreted as obscene, and eat in a manner that does not upset everyone else present. As long as this knowledge does not become a security blanket or crutch which inhibits our ability to accept its incompleteness and even inaccuracy, it is useful during the transition period.

The tendency to judge others in terms of one's own cultural experiences and expectations (ethnocentrism) is diminished if we have some predeparture, culture-specific knowledge. We are more likely to understand the behavior of our hosts in terms of their cultural experiences. While complete empathy is almost impossible unless we actually grew up in that culture, we can at least become less ethnocentric and rein in our prejudices. In a lecture some years ago, if my memory hasn't betrayed me, Edmund Glenn defined prejudice as "being down on that which you are not up on." It is more difficult to be down on people in the new culture if you have more culture-specific information about them which explains their behavior.

This knowledge also helps to lessen the tendency sojourners have of making trait attributions of host-national behavior instead of situational attributions (Brislin 1981, 72-108; Martin 1983). When we behave negatively, we usually explain the behavior in terms of the particular situation—normally, we don't behave badly. But, when *they* behave negatively it is because of innate personality traits. For example, "*I* cheated because it was a surprise exam and the professor didn't give me a chance to study for it. *They* cheat because they are basically dishonest people." If we understand their culture we can see that their behavior is simply a matter of cultural background, and they behave in ways we consider negative in many cases because of particular situations.

Caution must be taken when gathering culture-specific, predeparture information. It can never be complete or accurate in every situation. Even worse, it may predispose you to have expectations which are not met. The consequence is that some people, after they arrive in-country, may take perverse pleasure in selecting out that which contradicts what they learned before coming. This distortion and selective attention may inhibit successful adjustment and true understanding of the culture.

Develop Skills Which Will Facilitate Cross-Cultural Understanding, Communication, and Adaptation

Personality may be the most important determinant of successful cross-cultural adaptation. There are skills, however, which can be developed through cross-cultural training or orientation which will allow one to cope more effectively with culture shock and understand the new culture without memorizing lists of do's and don't's.

These skills can best be developed experientially. One need not go overseas to experience the disorientation, confusion, and ambiguity of entering another culture. There are enough subcultural communities in the U.S. to experience the same feelings without going overseas. This kind of experience can serve as an inoculation against culture shock. The various ethnic communities of metropolitan areas provide excellent opportunities for this type of experience, and the coping strategies developed during these brief encounters can be transferred overseas.

These domestic experiences also allow for the development of analytical, interpretive, and communicative skills. What causes the behavior of people within the ethnic community? Why do they take offense at particular expressions? What do particular nonverbal and verbal messages mean in the context of their community? And what causes the conflict between members of this community and outsiders? We could go on and on considering questions which aid in the development of cross-cultural understanding and cross-cultural adaptation and communication skills.

Of course, language ability is a basic skill which can be developed before departure. However, it is especially important to remember that nonverbal messages cannot be learned effectively outside the context of the culture. In fact, most people in the culture are unaware of how they give meaning to particular messages. Sometimes sojourners are overconfident that they can communicate effectively when they have studied the host culture's language before departure. Because they do not anticipate any stress in communicating, their culture shock is sometimes even more severe than those with little prior knowledge of the language.

SOME IMPLICATIONS FOR CROSS-CULTURAL ORIENTATION OR TRAINING

Cross-cultural trainers are often expected to give advice on how best to adjust quickly and painlessly to another culture. Furthermore, they are to describe the other culture in a colorful manner without ambiguity or complexity. Many sojourners do not want theoretical or abstract culture-general presentations which emphasize process. Rather, they want their training short, concrete, painless, entertaining, and simple.

It is very tempting to give these sojourners what they want—cookbooks, do's-and-don't's lists, fancy charts and graphs, and a multitude of clever anecdotes. Some might even prefer to watch slick, fast-paced films which they feel can eliminate the trainer altogether (Duncan 1985). The films are often simplistic and humorous, thereby suggesting that there is little pain involved in cross-cultural adjustment. They usually offer clear-cut advice on how to minimize the stress of culture shock and quickly adjust overseas.

Like the self-help psychology books and the various forms of sensitivity training of a couple of decades ago, it is doubtful that these quickie, cure-all, painless approaches are productive. In fact, they may be quite counterproductive (Blanchard 1970) in giving sojourners a false sense of confidence in their abilities, false expectations about the ease of cross-cultural adjustment, misleading and inaccurate stereotypes about other cultures, and a lack of true understanding of the dynamics of culture shock.

Of course, trainers must be entertaining simply to get and hold the attention and interest of clients who may not be accustomed to didactic presentations or complex conceptual frameworks. Stage presence, anecdotes which make a point or concretely illustrate a concept, and sometimes even graphs, charts, and films are necessary. Even stereotypes are useful so long as they are accurate and lead to conceptual understanding. But all of these should have the clear purpose of (1) helping the client anticipate the stress of cross-cultural adaptation and his or her reactions to the stress, (2) facilitating the development of coping strategies, (3) giving the sojourner confidence that he or she can adjust to another culture and interact effectively with host nationals, and (4) helping the client understand the process of cross-cultural adaptation.

While there is no one formula which is best for orienting sojourners, a solid training program should include many of the following guidelines, approaches, and goals which flow logically from our discussion of cross-cultural adaptation.

Understand the Concept of Culture

Culture is an abstraction which must be understood before we can begin discussing our own culture, the cultures of others, or the process of cross-cultural adaptation and interaction. Just as we cannot discuss individual human behavior without understanding the concept of personality, it is almost impossible to discuss intelligently the behavior of people in particular societies without understanding the concept of culture.

Many, if not most, people think of culture as what is often called "high culture"—art, literature, music, and the like. This culture is set in the framework of history and of social, political, and economic structures. Sojourners often think that if they have learned about these aspects of a culture they are prepared to enter it.

Actually, the most important part of culture for a sojourner is that which is internal and hidden (Hall 1976), but which governs the behavior they encounter. This dimension of culture can be seen as an iceberg with the tip sticking above the water level of conscious awareness. By far the most significant part, however, is unconscious or below the water level of awareness and includes values and thought patterns.

Knowledge of internal culture gives a framework for analyzing and interpreting behavior and customs both of others and of ourselves. For

example, individualism, the achievement motive, and the linear time
orientation of Americans causes them to be competitive and concerned
about actions and earned status rather than with harmony and ascribed
status. These values also explain the American concern with punctuality,
time scheduling, and the future. Unless there is some understanding of
these basic values, it is almost impossible to explain why Americans
behave as they do.

Another example is patterns of thinking. There is a particular way of
solving problems or thinking which is logical to people in each culture.
Americans tend to be low-context (Hall 1976), abstractive (Glenn 1981;
Weaver 1975), analytical (Cohen 1969) thinkers, typical of complex,
loosely integrated, urban or Gesellschaft societies (Tonnies 1940). At the
other end of the continuum are high-context, associative, relational
thinkers, typical of traditional, homogeneous, rural communities or
Gemeinschaft societies.

This kind of cross-cultural analysis offers analytical and interpretive
tools which can give sojourners confidence in their ability to explain their
own behavior and that of others in cross-cultural situations.

All of this is to suggest that cross-cultural training ought to help
sojourners move from the overt and descriptive level to the analytical
and interpretive. This requires didactic presentations to provide a framework or system for understanding the interrelationship of the various
facets of cultures and the process of cross-cultural interaction. These
concepts provide keys to understanding and even to predicting individual behavior within the context of particular cultures.

Understand the Dynamics of Cross-Cultural Communication and Adaptation

If the breakdown of communication is one of the primary causes of
culture shock, sojourners must understand the dynamics of interpersonal communication. The cybernetics model already mentioned helps
them conceptualize the process of communication and identify the basic
parts and links in a face-to-face communication system. Furthermore, it
helps participants identify why, where, and how communication breaks
down and anticipate reactions to it.

Basic to any discussion of cross-cultural communication is nonverbal communication. If the vast majority of messages which communicate
feelings are sent nonverbally (Mehrabian 1968) and the meanings we
give to nonverbal messages are culture-specific and unconsciously ac-

quired, then it is vital that considerable attention be paid to nonverbal communication.

There are many tangential concepts which add breadth and depth to the discussion of cross-cultural interaction. For example, synchrony, the rhythm of body movement and speech (Hall 1983), helps explain how each culture has its own rhythm which members learn within the first few hours or days of birth. When we enter another culture, much of the discomfort we feel may be because we are out of sync with movement in the culture.

Action chains (Hall 1976) are culture-specific sequences of behavior which we unconsciously follow to reach goals. They include courting behavior, the way conflict escalates or is resolved, and even how friendships develop. Perhaps one reason multicultural meetings seem to get out of hand is that each participant carries unconscious assumptions about the pertinent action chain, how a leader is selected, how discussion ought to progress, or how an agenda should be developed (Althen 1983). As with synchrony, action chains are unconscious and acquired simply by growing up in a particular culture.

The "Iceberg Analogy" of Culture

Understanding the dynamics of cross-cultural adaptation or culture shock, including the three explanations of cause, is essential to realizing that one's reactions are normal and that there are steps one can take to cope with both the stress and stressors. Again, it is important to focus on internal or subjective culture (Triandis 1972). When one enters another culture, it is somewhat like two icebergs colliding—the real clash occurs beneath the water where values and thought patterns conflict. This model serves as a device for explaining a fairly complex concept and causes participants to focus on culture as a system, rather than trying to memorize lists of culture-specific behaviors.

The terms "internal" and "external" culture are used by Edward T. Hall in his book *Beyond Culture* (1976). He suggests that what we normally refer to as "mind" is actually internal culture, which we have embodied here in the iceberg analogy of culture. This is similar to Freud's concept of personality which he also compares to an iceberg, with conscious mind represented by the tip and unconscious or subconscious mind represented by the part below the water level. Hall argues that the only way to really learn the internal culture of others is on a gut level by actively participating in their culture. In the process, one becomes more aware or conscious of his or her own internal culture. That is, the collision of culture causes one to raise to the conscious level that part of culture which is internal or unconscious.

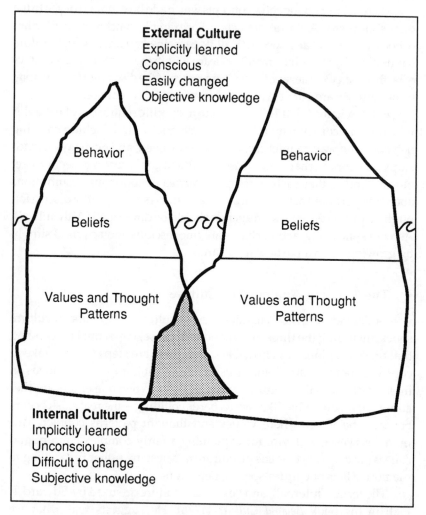

External Culture
Explicitly learned
Conscious
Easily changed
Objective knowledge

Behavior

Behavior

Beliefs

Beliefs

Values and Thought
Patterns

Values and Thought
Patterns

Internal Culture
Implicitly learned
Unconscious
Difficult to change
Subjective knowledge

The Sequence of Topics Is Very Important

Training programs which begin with culture-specific information alone suggest that the focus is on "those people," and participants naturally expect to be given a cookbook, which starts them off on the wrong foot.

Training programs which move from the culture-general to the culture-specific finesse this desire for cookbooks. In turn, sojourners are more likely to develop coping strategies and gain understanding rather than simply amassing questionable information. Culture-specific knowledge is important and should be available with as much depth and breadth as possible. But the mind-set which aids cross-cultural adaptation best is one oriented toward interaction and process and focused on "us" rather than simply "them."

Training which begins with the study of "those people" also implies we need not examine or understand our own culture. How can sojourners understand the impact of culture on the behavior, perceptions, values, and thought patterns of "those people" if they do not understand the impact of their own culture on their personality? An admonition that might be taken to heart by all trainers is "know thy own culture first."

For Americans, this is a special problem because most people are culturally unaware. They may have studied American literature and history; few have systematically studied their own culture. Because of geographic isolation during the formative period of the United States, the unique background of early immigrants, the frontier experience, the continually expanding economy, the seemingly unlimited natural resources, and the economic and political success of the United States, Americans are fairly parochial and take their own culture for granted.

Surely any training program designed for Americans would raise consciousness of their own culture. That in turn would tend to decrease ethnocentrism and make it clear that American behaviors, values, thought patterns, and ways of viewing the world are a result of their historical experiences and not necessarily appropriate or normal for the rest of the world.

The contrast-culture approach of Kluckhohn and Strodtbeck (1961) and Stewart (1969), deals by necessity with oversimplifications and even stereotypes. Nevertheless, it provides a solid conceptual framework which focuses on values and thought patterns as the determinants of behavior. Once the interrelatedness of American values and behaviors is understood, they can be contrasted quite easily with non-Western cultures such as those of the traditional Middle East, Africa, and Asia. The model can then be expanded to suggest a continuum moving from high to low context, associative to abstractive, and analytical to relational cultures, and sojourners can place themselves and others along such a continuum. Consequently, they move beyond the simple contrasts to understand that there are also similarities among various cultures around the globe and that differences along the continuum are a matter of degree.

Use Participatory or Experiential Exercises

While many of the basic concepts require some didactic presentation and every trainer must have a sound command of theoretical frameworks and concepts, a good training program ought to allow each participant an opportunity to experience some of the ambiguity, confusion, uncertainty, and frustration involved in cross-cultural adaptation and intercultural communication. If culture can only be learned at a gut level (as Hall argues; see above), then participatory exercises, such as role playing, are extremely useful in facilitating learning.

These exercises also provide a laboratory experience in applying the various concepts and approaches discussed here and in the development of coping, interpretive, analytical, and communicative skills. In fact, unless they have these clear purposes they may be perceived as childish (Weaver and Uncapher 1981) and meaningless.

A trainer should be able to model analytical and interpretive skills which may be adopted by participants as they develop their own techniques. In no way should the trainer cause a dependency relationship to develop where sojourners expect advice which they feel must be followed if they are to succeed overseas. Rather, the ultimate goal of training is that each sojourner assume the responsibility of developing his or her own strategies for cross-cultural adjustment and communication.

A trainer is then a facilitator who provides the conceptual frameworks for understanding as well as the opportunities to apply them in a participatory manner. Experiential exercises can include contrast-culture games such as *Bafá Bafá* or other contrast-culture simulation exercises. Because of their ambiguity, they produce stress and force participants to apply conceptual frameworks which help them interpret and analyze their own reactions and the behavior of others. Furthermore, they encourage the development of communication and coping skills.

Again, it is important that these exercises be culture-general and that only afterward does the trainer move to a culture-specific focus. Seldom do culture-specific role plays and exercises actually replicate situations or persons in the actual overseas culture, and they encourage cookbook thinking, provide false and misleading stereotypes, and promote unrealistic expectations. The major goal of the exercises is not to enable the participants to fully understand another specific culture but rather to help them develop strategies for understanding any other culture they might encounter and to examine their reactions to the stresses of cross-cultural communication and interaction.

Contrast-culture models are especially useful because they are ambiguous and culture-general. For example, the famous Khan contrast-culture simulation (Stewart, Danielian, and Foster 1969) involves rather open-ended scenarios in which Khan plays the role of a person who comes from a culture and behaves in a way that is generally non-Western, associative, high-context, and relational. "Mr. Khan" (not his real name) is a man of non-European background specifically trained by Stewart and his colleagues to play this role—commonly referred to as "contrast American"—in interactions with American participants. The role-play scenarios were originally created for American advisors going abroad on technical assistance projects but are now used for a variety of cross-cultural training purposes. If Khan were to represent a member of a particular culture with which participants were familiar, they would probably resort to their stereotypes of that culture to explain his behavior. Rather than applying the conceptual models, developing coping skills, or examining their reactions, they would mentally leaf through the cookbook for that country. When Khan is culture-general and simply a contrast to the mainstream American culture, he acts as a cultural Rorschach inkblot upon which Americans project their unconscious assumptions regarding people from other cultures. This in turn brings out revealing thoughts and behavior from the Americans.

Inoculate Sojourners

Just as one inoculates people against physical disease by giving them a little dose of the disease to build up their resistance, training should inoculate sojourners to the stress of cross-cultural adaptation and the difficulties of cross-cultural communication. This may be done with participatory exercises which allow participants to experience the discomfort, uncertainty, and ambiguity of dealing with someone who behaves and thinks differently.

Barna (1983) refers to this as "stress inoculation training" and finds that "an underlying premise of this approach is that the effective management of stress and anxiety is the goal, not stress avoidance" (35). Consequently, various coping strategies can be used such as modeling desired behaviors, imagery rehearsal, relaxation training, desensitization, and counterconditioning. But, first of all, the client must understand the nature of stress and reactions to stress and have an opportunity to experience a stressful situation to practice coping skills. These skills give the sojourner a sense of greater control over his or her behavior in a stressful situation.

Inoculation also involves helping sojourners anticipate the stress of cross-cultural adaptation and communication and their reactions to it. Thus, they begin to worry somewhat as they proceed through the training program. The training normally raises the anxiety levels of sojourners because they have become more aware of communication and adaptation difficulties.

They also have been helped in developing the skills to cope with these difficulties and the confidence to overcome them. The anxiety produced through inoculation should be balanced by the assurance and confidence that sojourners have within themselves adequate knowledge and skills to cope with these stresses.

CONCLUSION

If there is a medical or illness analogy for culture shock, the common cold is probably it. Like the common cold, there is no way to prevent culture shock and one can catch it over and over again. Each time we adjust to another culture or readjust to our own culture, we go through culture shock.

The symptoms of a cold are relatively harmless unless we fail to take minimal precautions to prevent the cold from weakening our immune system. The body can only take so much physical stress at any one time. A certain percentage of people who get colds experience severe reactions. The same is true of culture shock—the symptoms are relatively harmless unless we have experienced too many life changes in too short a time period (Selye 1974), and a certain percentage of people going abroad may be unable to tolerate the additional stress of cross-cultural adaptation.

A cold follows a somewhat regular pattern; it will eventually come to an end, and you will eventually be as healthy as ever. Knowing the "cold process" prevents you from thinking that every cough, sniffle, or pain is symptomatic of some more severe, or perhaps even terminal, disease. And you can control the symptoms by getting rest, drinking plenty of liquids, eating chicken soup, etc. However, there is no one cure for a cold, and each person probably has a personal remedy that seems to work.

In the end, each of us will develop our own set of coping strategies. We can manage culture shock. Like the cold, there is no real cure or prevention, but understanding the process gives us a sense of control and predictability and allows us to cope better with the symptoms and achieve some new level of cross-cultural skill.

REFERENCES

Adler, Nancy J. (1985). *International dimensions of organizational behavior.* Cambridge, MA: Kent.

Adler, Peter S. (August 1974). "Beyond cultural identity: Reflections on cultural and multicultural man." *Topics in Culture Learning* 2: 23-41.

_____ (1975). "The transitional experience: An alternative view of culture shock." *Journal of Humanistic Psychology* 15: 13-23.

Adorno, Theodor, E. L. Frenkel-Brunswick, D. Levinson, and R. Stanford (1950). *The authoritarian personality.* New York: Harper.

Allport, Gordon W. (1961). *Pattern and growth in personality.* New York: Holt, Rinehart & Winston.

Althen, Gary L. (1983). "The intercultural meeting." In *The handbook of foreign student advising.* Yarmouth, ME: Intercultural Press.

Azrin, Nathan (1970). "Pain and aggression." In N. T. Adler (Ed.), *Readings in experimental psychology today.* Del Mar, CA: CRM Books.

Barna, LaRay M. (1983). "The stress factor in intercultural relations." In Dan Landis and Richard W. Brislin (Eds.), *Handbook of intercultural training* 2, Elmsford, NY: Pergamon.

Blanchard, William H. (1970). "Ecstasy without agony is baloney." *Psychology Today* 3, no. 8: 8, 10, 64.

Brislin, Richard W. (1981). *Cross-cultural encounters: Face-to-face interaction.* Elmsford, NY: Pergamon.

Cohen, R. A. (1969). "Conceptual styles, culture conflict and nonverbal tests of intelligence." *American Anthropologist* 71: 828-56.

David, Kenneth H. (1976). "The use of social-learning theory in preventing intercultural adjustment problems." In Paul Pedersen, W. J. Lonner, and J. G. Draguns (Eds.), *Counseling across cultures.* Honolulu: University of Hawaii Press.

Duncan, Michael (1985). "American corporations learn a lesson in cross-cultural business." *OAG Frequent Flyer* (Part 2, OAG Pocket Flight Guide). (March): 59-62.

Freud, Anna (1970). *The ego and the mechanisms of defense* (rev. ed.). New York: International Universities Press.

Freud, Sigmund (1936). *The problem of anxiety.* New York: W. W. Norton.

_____ (1955). *Little Hans.* London: Hogarth Press.

Glenn, Edmund S. (1969). "The university and revolution: New left or new right?" In G. R. Weaver and J. H. Weaver, *The university and revolution.* Englewood Cliffs, NJ: Prentice-Hall.

_____ (1981). *Man and mankind: Conflict and communication between cultures.* Norwood, NJ: ABLEX.

Hall, Edward T. (1959). *The silent language.* New York: Doubleday.

_____ (1966). *The hidden dimension.* New York: Doubleday.

_____ (1976). *Beyond culture.* Garden City, NY: Anchor Press/Doubleday.

_____ (1983). *The dance of life.* New York: Doubleday.

Kluckhohn, Florence R., and Frederick L. Strodtbeck (1961). *Variation in value orientations.* New York: Row, Peterson.

Laing, Roland D. (1967). *The divided self.* New York: Pantheon (originally published, 1959.)

_____ (1970). *The self and others.* New York: Pantheon.

Lindemann, E. (1944). "Symptomatology and management of acute grief." *American Journal of Psychiatry* 101: 141-48

Maher, B. (1968). "The shattered language of schizophrenia." *Psychology Today* 2, no. 6: 30-33, 60.

Martin, R. P. (1983). "Consultant, consultee, and client expectations of each other's behavior in consultation." *School of Psychology Review* 12, no. 1: 35-41.

Maslow, Abraham (1970). *Motivation and personality* (2d ed.), New York: Harper and Row.

Mehrabian, Albert (1968). "Communication without words." *Psychology Today* 2, no. 4: 53-55.

Oberg, Kalvero (1960). "Cultural shock: Adjustment to new cultural environments." *Practical Anthropology* 7: 177-82.

Rosenhan, D. L. (1973). "On being sane in insane places." *Science* 179: 250-58.

Selye, Hans (1956). *The stress of life.* New York: McGraw-Hill.

_____ (1974). *Stress without distress.* Philadelphia, PA: Lippincott.

Sheehy, Gail (1977). *Passages: Predictable crises of adult life.* New York: Bantam.

Siligman, Martin E. P. (1975). *Helplessness*. San Francisco: Freeman.

Silverman, J. (1970). "When schizophrenia helps." *Psychology Today* 4, no. 4: 63-66, 68, 70.

Slater, Philip (1974). *Earthwalk*. Garden City, NY: Doubleday.

Stewart, Edward C., and Milton J. Bennett (1991). *American cultural patterns: A cross-cultural perspective*. Yarmouth, ME: Intercultural Press.

Stewart, Edward C., Jack Danielian, and R. J. Foster (May 1969). *Simulating intercultural communication through role-playing*. Washington, DC: George Washington University Human Resources Research Office (HumRRO Division No. 7, Technical Report 69-77).

Toffler, Alvin (1970). *Future shock*. New York: Bantam.

Tonnies, Ferdinand (1940). *Gemeinschaft and gesellschaft*. Tubingen, Germany: Mohr 1937. C. P. Loomis (trans.), *Fundamental concepts of sociology*. New York: John Wiley.

Triandis, Harry C. (1972). *The analysis of subjective culture*. New York: Wiley.

Walton, S. (1990). "Stress management training for overseas effectiveness." *International Journal of Intercultural Relations* 14, no. 4: 507-27.

Weaver, Gary (1975). "American identity movements: A cross-cultural confrontation." *Intellect* (March): 377-80.

Weaver, Gary, and Philip Uncapher (1981). "The Nigerian experience: Overseas living and value change." Paper and workshop presented at Seventh Annual SIETAR Conference, Vancouver, BC, Canada. March 11.

Zwingmann, Charles A., and A. D. C. Gunn (1983). *Uprooting and health: Psycho-social problems of students from abroad*. Geneva, Switzerland: Geneva World Health Organization, Division of Mental Health (WHO/MNH/83.8).

6

Trainer Competencies for International and Intercultural Programs

R. Michael Paige

> The complexities and demands of culture learning require exceptional competencies of the trainer. These include a high degree of self-awareness and a recognition of one's skills limitations, sensitivity to the needs of the learners, the ability to respond to the problems that culture learners encounter, an awareness of the ethical issues involved in cross-cultural training, conceptual/theoretical understanding, program-design skills, and research/evaluation skills (Paige and Martin 1983, 57).

During the past twenty-five years, there has been enormous growth in the field of intercultural training coterminous with developments in international educational exchange and, more recently, multicultural education. Today, intercultural training programs are being conducted for a wide variety of audiences including international students, business personnel, government officials, teachers, and others. Associated with this growth has been the emergence of a sizable intercultural training literature; the development of a professional association for intercultural specialists, the International Society for Intercultural Education, Training and Research (SIETAR International); and of a journal,

169

the *International Journal of Intercultural Relations,* which, since 1982, has included a specifically designated training section. In many respects, the field of intercultural training is in the very healthy process of coming of age. It is somewhat surprising, in light of these other advances, that little has been written about intercultural trainers and the competencies they must have to be effective in their work. In my view, the literature should more systematically examine (1) trainer skills, (2) appropriate settings—time, place, and audience—for specific learning activities, (3) potential difficulties learners will have with these activities and appropriate trainer responses, and (4) ethical issues associated with training programs and trainer behavior. This missing element, trainer competencies, represents a deficiency in the training literature.

The purpose here is to address this shortcoming by conceptualizing specific cognitive understandings, behavioral skills, and personal qualities that would characterize the competent intercultural trainer. First, I will briefly review two relevant literatures (intercultural effectiveness and intercultural training) and extract from them the major implications for trainers. A discussion of the central ethical issues will also be presented so that the challenges facing trainers will be seen in their moral as well as pragmatic contexts. The chapter will then conclude with a more elaborate detailed discussion of the trainer competencies.

INTERCULTURAL EFFECTIVENESS

Virtually millions of persons...have by now successfully interacted with persons from other cultures in obtaining academic degrees, concluding business deals, negotiating treaties, and collaborating to bring about advances in the sciences and arts. Yet it is only within the last few decades that there has been any systematic attempt to understand either the persons or the situations in which these successes occurred (Dinges 1983, 176).

For training programs to have meaningful goals and objectives, it is necessary for trainers to understand what constitutes effectiveness in the target culture and what the factors are that influence success. The study of effectiveness has long been a major issue in intercultural communication, and there have been noteworthy advances in both the theoretical and the research literatures (Dinges 1983; Kim and Gudykunst 1988, Kim 1988; Hannigan 1990; Grove and Torbiörn, this volume; and M. Bennett, this volume). In 1989, the *International Journal of Intercultural Relations* devoted an entire issue to intercultural competence (Martin 1989).

The conceptual model that emerges from these studies is a complex one. Intercultural effectiveness is positively influenced by (1) knowledge about the target culture, (2) personal qualities such as openness, flexibility, tolerance of ambiguity, and sense of humor, (3) behavioral skills such as communicative competency, culturally appropriate role behavior and ability to relate well to others, (4) self-awareness, especially with respect to one's own values and beliefs, (5) technical skills, including the ability to accomplish the task within the new cultural setting, and (6) situational factors such as relative similarity of the target culture to one's home culture, receptivity to foreigners, political/economic/social conditions in the second culture, clarity of expectations regarding the role and the position of the foreigner, and the psychological pressures associated with the experience (Paige, this volume, chapter 1).

The complexity of the intercultural experience has important implications for trainers. They must know which factors can or cannot be influenced by the program, which types of learning activities can affect different types of learning outcomes, and how to prepare the learner to continue the learning process. The more clearly trainers can accurately conceptualize intercultural effectiveness, the more likely they are to design and implement a sound training program. Ignorance of these concepts can result in poorly designed and poorly delivered programs, unrealistic expectations among the learners, and harmful misperceptions.

INTERCULTURAL TRAINING AND ORIENTATION

> ...the purpose of a cross-cultural training program is to provide a *functional awareness* of the cultural dynamic present in intercultural relations and assist trainees in becoming more *effective* in cross-cultural situations (Pusch et al. 1981, 73).

Trainers now have an extensive literature to draw upon regarding such key topics as: training activities (Batchelder and Warner 1977; Weeks, Pedersen, and Brislin 1977; Casse 1979; Hoopes and Ventura 1979; Pusch 1979; M. Bennett 1986b); training design issues (Gudykunst and Hammer 1983; Landis and Brislin 1983); and evaluation of intercultural training (Renwick 1979; Blake and Heslin 1983). In this section we will examine some of the major issues associated with training that emerge from the literature.

Content and Pedagogy

In their work on intercultural training, Gudykunst and Hammer (1983) introduce two issues they consider central to training: didactic versus experiential approaches to instruction and culture-general versus culture-specific content. The first issue concerns the method of instruction to be employed. Many of the early training programs relied on the didactic approach (alternately referred to as the intellectual, cognitive, or university models), which emphasized the lecture-discussion format to transmit information about the target culture. The many deficiencies of the university model were articulated in a seminal article by Harrison and Hopkins (1967), and experiential learning activities started to be utilized with increasing frequency. However, many experiential approaches were seriously flawed because the trainers lacked the conceptual framework to assist the learner in reflecting upon and making some sense out of the experience. In their extreme forms, neither the didactic nor the experiential approach alone proved suitable for intercultural training (J. Bennett, 1986).

The intriguing culture-general versus culture-specific issue concerns the content of training. Early programs relied almost entirely on culture-specific content, i.e., information about the target culture, society, political system, economic structure, history, etc. Although at the time this seemed like a logical approach, it eventually became clear that: (1) individual cultures are diverse, fluid, and difficult to comprehend and (2) self-awareness and an understanding of the dynamics and influence of culture, in general terms, are equally, if not more, important than information about cultural specifics. An overemphasis on culture-specific training can deceive the learners into thinking that they are much better prepared for the experience than they actually are. Paradoxically, the learners themselves are generally more positive toward culture-specific than culture-general learning because the former is more concrete and less threatening. Trainers thus face the dilemma of (1) having to include learning activities that may be resisted, but, according to training-design theory, will be more relevant to overseas effectiveness or (2) eliminating these activities and risk failing to prepare the learner adequately. An integrated training design is the solution suggested by Gudykunst and Hammer (1983) and Janet Bennett (1986).

Three Challenges of Intercultural Training Programs

Intercultural training programs have some unique features that pose challenges for trainers. *The first is the challenge of helping learners wrestle with the issue of assimilation.* The pressures of assimilation are particularly strong upon long-term sojourners (e.g, foreign students) who will be completely immersed in a new culture. As the learners begin to recognize that pressure will be placed on them to acquire new ways of thinking and behaving, they will begin to pose difficult questions about cultural identity, personal integrity with respect to belief and behàvior systems, and other issues that penetrate below the surface of the training process. While there are no correct answers to these questions that will apply equally to all learners, trainers must avoid giving simplistic or misleading responses. Rather, they should emphasize that the intercultural experience will require learners to make some difficult behavioral and attitudinal choices. Trainers can point out that attaining mastery of another language and culture will be a source of great personal accomplishment. But during the adjustment phase, sojourners face the dilemma of wanting to become fully functioning members of the new culture, on the one hand, without having to sacrifice their own identity on the other. It takes a skilled trainer to assist learners in working through these questions and maintaining their enthusiasm for the forthcoming intercultural experience.

The second challenge for trainers is that of helping learners conceptualize and deal with the experience of becoming multicultural, which is the capacity to integrate alternate cultural frames of reference into one's life and function effectively in two or more cultures. As Mestenhauser (1983) and Milton Bennett (this volume) point out, acquiring that capacity requires a "paradigm shift," which can be defined as a cognitive, behavioral, and affective shift away from one's monocultural, ethnocentric frame of reference. Such a shift is often accompanied by a sense of loss and confusion as the learner begins to systematically confront deeply held value orientations, assumptions about human behavior, and perspectives about the world. Unquestionably, the processes of culture learning and becoming multicultural subject the learner to certain psychological stresses and tensions (P. Adler 1974; Brislin et al. 1986).

The trainer must be able to assist the learner in sorting out these feelings and in developing new strategies for coping with stresses (Barna 1983; Walton 1990; Weaver, this volume). Some trainers may be sufficiently uncomfortable themselves with the learning issues surrounding the paradigm shift that they do not incorporate any activities into their program that would induce these more substantive, and difficult, dimensions of culture learning. In Milton Bennett's conceptual model of intercultural sensitivity (1986a; 1986b; and this volume), such training would end at the minimization stage rather than encourage movement to the ethnorelative stages of acceptance, adaptation, and integration. Avoidance of these issues, however, is not the answer. It is my opinion that the effective intercultural trainer will be able to provide learners both with opportunities to experience the paradigm shift and with conceptual frameworks to help them understand this profoundly important aspect of culture learning. The experienced trainer, above all else, will have the ability to provide personal support to the learner by means of effective listening, advising, and counseling.

The third challenge is for trainers to be able to handle learner resistance, defensiveness, and frustration. These are the normal responses of individuals undergoing a challenging, self-confrontational learning experience. Learners will take their frustrations out on the trainers. They will rationalize inadequate performances and resist certain learning activities. They may reject the program in its entirety. Experienced trainers will be familiar with these negative reactions and will know how important it is to be patient, sensitive, and nondefensive with the learners. Such trainers will recognize that, as the program progresses toward its more provocative segments, the trainer may become less, rather than more, popular with the learners and should be able to accept that being liked is not always synonymous with being effective as a trainer.

In summary, intercultural trainers must understand and be able to act upon a great deal of information, including the basic assumptions underlying their programs, content and process issues, and the interpersonal dynamics of the learner-trainer relationship. They must also be aware of the central ethical issues involved, which are presented in the following section.

THE ETHICS OF INTERCULTURAL TRAINING AND ORIENTATION

The neglect of ethical concerns and ethical implications of cross-cultural training programs stands in sharp contrast to the extensive discussions on research ethics and professional conduct in the traditional social sciences disciplines (Brislin, Landis, and Brandt 1983, 27).

There are many ethical questions that confront individual trainers and the profession as a whole, but only recently have these issues become the focus of any systematic attention. This relatively new concern with ethics is the result of several factors: the sizable increase in the number of intercultural practitioners, the absence of certification and licensure mechanisms to govern trainer activities, various instances of abuse (e.g., exaggerated claims made for training programs and trainers, poorly implemented programs), and the desire of many to strengthen the profession. Significant contributions in conceptualizing ethical issues and developing ethical standards have been made by Barnlund (1982), Howards et al. (1982), Howell (1982), and Paige and Martin (1983). The purpose of this section is to further elaborate the emerging definition of the "ethical trainer."

Key Ethical Questions in Intercultural Training and Orientation

The central ethical questions that have been presented in the literature and discussed among trainers are:

1. What goals and objectives are appropriate for intercultural training and orientation? For example, is it ethical to attempt to change the individual's behavior, attitudes, or values? To promote multiculturalism?

2. What constitutes an ethical training environment? For example, should intercultural training be conducted in an extremely competitive social-psychological context? What kind of fit should be established between the learning environment and the personal characteristics of the learners?

3. What characterizes an ethical pedagogy? For example, are there certain types of learning activities (e.g., experiential simulations) that would be inappropriate under certain circumstances?

4. What characterizes an "ethical client" and under what circumstances might a training program contract be rejected? Are there ethical standards that can and should be applied to the long-term purposes of clients for acquiring intercultural skills?

5. What constitutes ethical marketing of trainers and their programs? Under what circumstances should we be making claims regarding our own skills and the outcomes attributed to our programs?

6. What characterizes an ethical trainer-learner relationship? For example, is the "expert" posture an appropriate one for the trainer to take? (See McCaffery, this volume.)

7. What risks are associated with training for the learners and how would the ethical trainer respond to them? What skills should the trainer have in order to effectively and sensitively use learning activities which call upon the learner to risk failure and self-disclosure and/or might threaten the learner's self-esteem and personal identity?

8. What qualities characterize ethical trainers? Are there behavioral patterns, values, and levels of understanding that distinguish ethical trainers?

9. What steps can our profession take to promote an ethics of intercultural training? Are there practical steps our professional associations can take to encourage further development of ethical guidelines and standards?

These are extremely difficult questions to answer, but they are central to the development of our profession, how it will be perceived in the public mind in the years ahead, and how we as individual trainers will be received and judged. If we ignore these questions and fail to provide ethical guidelines for our work, ill-informed practices will likely increase, and our collective professional reputation will be compromised.

The Emerging Ethics of Intercultural Training and Orientation

Although an absolute consensus does not yet exist with respect to all of the questions posed above, healthy discussion and debate are occurring. Paige and Martin (1983), for example, have offered useful responses to a number of these issues. Regarding the goals and objectives of training, they suggest that intercultural training is inherently "transformative," i.e., intended to change learner cognition, behavior, and affect. But they add that the ethical trainer is both fully aware of this "person-transformation imperative" and able to help move learners through the challenges and difficulties of culture learning. The unethical trainer may induce change without being aware of it or lack the skills to assist learners who are going through significant personal development. Regarding the training environment, the authors suggest that an ethical trainer will seek to establish a climate of trust and will strive to fit the learning environment to the learning styles of the clients.

On the matter of training pedagogy, Paige and Martin (1983, 54-56) discuss the sequencing of learning activities and the importance of debriefing skills for trainers. They also address the question of ethical clients, urging trainers to inquire into the long-range purposes of the client and to reject contracts if they determine that the acquired intercultural skills would be used for unethical purposes (e.g., exploitation of others). An ethical marketing approach would base claims about trainers and programs on solid evaluation research. The trainer's prior experience and skills would be accurately represented, not exaggerated. The trainer-learner relationship is discussed later in this chapter, emphasizing the need to avoid creating dependency relationships and the importance of helping the learners to become independently resourceful in learning about the target culture. Paige and Martin (1983) and Paige (this volume, chapter 1) also identify certain risks (e.g., self-disclosure and failure) related to training. Paige and Martin suggest that ethical trainers—through awareness of these risks, proper sequencing of activities, and debriefing skills—can reduce the element of risk for learners. A recent and very important development has been SIETAR International's effort to formulate ethical guidelines for interculturalists. SIETAR members around the world have been involved in the process of generating and refining the SIETAR position on ethics.

We can anticipate that these answers will be considerably refined in the future as more is written about ethics, as more conference programs on ethics are presented, and as our reflections on ethics become more sophisticated. Fortunately, a solid start has been made.

The Ethical Trainer

In light of the above considerations, suggestions for behavioral qualities that would characterize the ethical trainer can be made. Specifically, ethical trainers will:

1. Strive to acquire relevant conceptual/theoretical foundations for intercultural training from the fields of intercultural communication, psychology (in particular, cross-cultural psychology, counseling psychology, social psychology), education (curriculum, pedagogy, learning theory), anthropology, etc.

2. Keep abreast of ethical issues via the literature, conference programs, and dialogues with professional colleagues.

3. Keep informed about training issues through the literature, professional association meetings, workshops, etc.

4. Seek constantly to develop their professional skills.

5. Use only those training methods and learning activities that are congruent with their own skills as trainers.

6. Be openly self-reflective and critical regarding their own skills, levels of self-awareness, training biases, etc.

7. Seek to establish ethical training environments, training pedagogies, and trainer-learner relationships.

8. Market themselves and their programs honestly and accurately.

9. Recognize the change imperative of training and the risks associated with certain learning activities and acquire the skills to conduct training in general, and these activities in particular, with sensitivity to the needs and concerns of the learners.

10. Strive to help the profession identify ethical issues and forge a consensus regarding ethical behavior.

TRAINER COMPETENCIES

Training design, duration, intensity, and size vary. Participants vary. Countries of destination vary....And from that builds my conviction that this most challenging of challenges...deserves extraordinary, inventive modes of teaching (Ackermann 1976, 304).

In this section, trainer competencies will be categorized in terms of cognitive knowledge, behavioral skills, and personal attributes. Some of these cognitive and behavioral competencies and many of the personal attributes have been mentioned in the general training and intercultural effectiveness literatures. Thus, I am indebted to my colleagues for their prior work in this field. The intent here is to pull these ideas together and present a detailed description of trainer competencies.

No given trainer, of course, will possess all of these skills and attributes, but the best and most ethical trainers will be striving constantly to improve their knowledge base, behavioral performance, and personal qualities. They will recognize their own strengths and weaknesses as trainers and will seek to function in those areas where they can be most effective.

Trainer Competencies in the Cognitive Domain

Competent trainers must have a sound conceptual foundation for their work. Knowledge serves as the basis for action and must be regularly expanded in the light of new research findings, conceptual models, and theories. Figure 1 classifies cognitive competency into eight knowledge areas and thirty-two knowledge specifics that are subsumed under each of these broader areas. Together, these knowledge areas and specifics represent the cognitive competencies of the exemplary trainer.

Figure 1: Trainer Competencies: Cognitive Domain

Knowledge Area	Knowledge Specifics
Intercultural Phenomena	1. intercultural effectiveness, competence
	2. intercultural adjustment, culture shock
	3. reentry adjustment
	4. culture learning
	5. the psychological and social dynamics of the intercultural experience
Intercultural Training	6. training-program assumptions: program philosophy, conceptual foundations of training, perspectives on learner needs, etc.
	7. program-planning principles: client-needs assessment, audience analysis, staff training, logistics, timing, length, setting
	8. key training variables: audience diversity, trainer skills, length of program, predicted intensity of the intercultural experience, amount of affective and behavioral training
	9. realistic understanding of what training can and cannot accomplish
	10. realistic understanding of the relationship of training to performance in the target culture

11. training design: goals and objectives, appropriate use of experiential and didactic methods, culture-specific and culture-general content, cognitive/affective/behavioral learning, and integrated training designs which incorporate these elements

12. training pedagogy: appropriate selection and sequencing of learning activities, alternative training techniques, purposes of different activities, techniques for preparing culture learners (learning how to learn)

13. program evaluation principles and methods

Trainer-Learner Issues

14. debriefing principles and strategies

15. the social-psychological dynamics of the trainer-learner relationship: power, role modeling, risk of learner dependence on trainer

16. the nature and sources of learner resistance to training and potential learner reactions to intense training experiences (stress, anxiety, frustration, anger)

17. major learner concerns: threat to cultural identity, pressures to assimilate, challenge of becoming multicultural, becoming immobilized in a state of cultural relativism

Ethical Issues

18. ethical issues in training: appropriate management of risks faced by learners (failure, self-disclosure), proper handling of the transformation imperative of training, creating a supportive rather than destructive learning environment

19. the intercultural trainer's code of ethics

Culture-Specific Content	20.	the target culture: political, economic, social, cultural, demographic, religious, historical, and other factors
	21.	situational factors in the target culture: host-counterpart expectations, job clarity, openness to outsiders, host-culture/country relationship to own culture/country, host-culture country aspirations
	22.	predominant values, attitudes, and behaviors in the host culture
	23.	the nature of the occupational position: job roles and requirements
Trainer Issues	24.	the role of the trainer in the learning process
	25.	the pressures that face trainers and methods for coping with them
	26.	one's own strengths and limitations as a trainer
International Issues	27.	theories of development, social change, transfer of technology
	28.	the issues of international relations: dependence versus interdependence, neocolonialism, parity versus dominance
Multicultural Issues	29.	cultural pluralism and diversity: diversity and intercultural interactions in the workplace and in society
	30.	the nature and impact of racism, sexism, and other forms of prejudice and discrimination; institutionalized forms of prejudice and discrimination
	31.	history of oppression and discrimination of groups being trained; history of intergroup relations among groups being trained
	32.	the psychology of cultural marginality and multiculturalism

Intercultural Phenomena

This area is at the core of the trainer's knowledge. It includes understanding what it means to make the transition to another culture and to live and work effectively in it. The dynamics of cultural adjustment and the challenges of culture learning are well understood, as is the process of reentry adjustment, which has emerged in the literature as a major intercultural issue (Martin, this volume). The trainer who understands the excitement as well as the frustration of the intercultural experience will be better able to empathize with and assist the learner on the verge of having that experience.

Intercultural Training

There is a great deal to understand in this second area, as the eight knowledge specifics suggest. From basic programmatic assumptions to follow-up evaluation, the competent trainer must have a command of all aspects of training. A sophisticated program design requires an in-depth awareness of key issues. The development of a pedagogy relevant to learner needs and program goals requires a detailed understanding of content and process alternatives. The skilled trainer will know what factors influence the process of training as well as how intercultural training impacts on the sojourner's subsequent effectiveness.

Trainer/Learner Issues

It is critical for the trainer to understand the dynamics of the trainer-learner relationship. Above all else, the competent trainer will understand the principles of "debriefing," i.e., processing (discussing and interpreting) a learning experience in a way which enables the learners to better understand the meaning of what they have experienced and to integrate it into the structure of knowledge and skills they currently possess. Debriefing skills are especially important when learners are experiencing stress, confusion, anxiety, or frustration. The trainer should also have a conceptual grasp of alternative learner reactions to program activities, in particular the ways in which resistance might be expressed.

Ethical Issues

The competent trainer must be aware of the major ethical issues in the field of intercultural training, such as those mentioned earlier in this chapter. There will be an understanding of the code of ethics that is emerging and a realization that this code will be refined in the years ahead.

Culture-Specific Content

This knowledge area complements the trainer's general understanding of intercultural phenomena by including specific items of information about the sojourner's target culture and assignment. Obviously, trainers cannot be experts regarding the many target cultures they are preparing sojourners to enter, but they can and should (1) learn as much as possible about the host culture and the participants' assignments therein prior to the program and (2) know how to bring together the appropriate human and material resources to convey relevant information to them.

Trainer Issues

Competent trainers will have a clear understanding of their role in the learning process. Rather than serve as experts and risk creating dependency relationships with learners, they will understand the principles of culture learning and thus encourage learners to discover for themselves the realities of the target culture (see McCaffery, this volume). Trainers will also understand the pressures on learners and will know the methods for coping with them. They will also know their own strengths and weaknesses.

International Issues

Many training programs today are preparing sojourners to live, work, and study in the so-called developing nations. Trainers preparing persons for these assignments have a special obligation to understand and convey to the learners information about: (1) alternative theories and perspectives of social change or development, (2) the concerns and aspirations of Third-World peoples, and (3) the importance of establishing relationships based on parity rather than dominance.

Multicultural Issues

Numerous programs focus on domestic issues associated with cultural pluralism and diversity (e.g., workplace diversity, multicultural education in the schools, racism, and prejudice). Trainers working in this arena must have a great deal of knowledge about the history, cultures, and political and economic realities of the individuals they are serving. Multicultural training is extremely challenging because trainers are working on fundamental societal questions regarding oppression and inequality; such training is often highly controversial, politicized, and stressful. Trainers must also understand the psychology of marginality and multiculturalism (J. Bennett, this volume).

Trainer Competencies in the Behavioral Domain

Figure 2 presents the behavioral competencies. These are organized into the same eight areas as listed in the cognitive domain and are further described in terms of thirty-two specific behavioral skills or capacities. In many instances, the behavioral specific is the performance equivalent of cognitive competency.

Figure 2:   Trainer Competencies: Behavioral Domain

Behavioral Area	Specific Behavioral Capacities
Intercultural Phenomena	1. capacity to promote learner acquisition of skills, knowledge, and personal qualities relevant to intercultural effectiveness
	2. capacity to induce a cultural-adjustment experience and to provide a culture-general conceptual framework to assist learners in coping with adjustment stresses
	3. capacity to conceptualize reentry issues and provide concrete ways for learners to maintain their connectedness with their home culture
	4. capacity to conceptualize the culture-learning phenomenon as a framework for thinking about intercultural experiences

5. capacity to present theories and concepts regarding the psychological and social dynamics of the intercultural experience: culture shock, intercultural communication and interaction, intercultural competence, etc.

Intercultural Training

6. ability to articulate a clear, theory- and research-based training philosophy and a statement of central training-program assumptions
7. ability to conduct planning activities including staff training and development, needs analysis, audience assessment
8. ability to effectively consider key training variables in program planning, design, and pedagogy
9. ability to make appropriate claims for what training can and cannot accomplish
10. ability to make appropriate claims regarding the relationship of training to performance in the target culture
11. ability to design integrated training programs having the appropriate mix of experiential and didactic methods, culture-specific and culture-general content, cognitive/affective/behavioral-learning activities
12. ability to implement training pedagogy which effectively selects and sequences learning activities; utilizes alternative training techniques; clearly realizes the cognitive, affective, and behavioral purposes of different learning activities; and incorporates appropriate techniques for preparing culture learners (learning how to learn)

13. ability to conduct formative and summative program evaluations

Trainer-Learner Issues

14. ability to debrief learning activities with individuals and groups
15. capacity to establish effective relationships with learners which reduce risk of learner dependence, minimize power and status differentials, build trust in the learning community
16. capacity to help learners deal with stress, anxiety, frustration, etc.; ability to respond effectively and with sensitivity to learner resistance
17. capacity to effectively treat difficult issues—cultural identity, assimilation, multiculturalism, cultural relativism— in training design and pedagogy

Ethical Issues

18. capacity to incorporate ethical standards into all aspects of training
19. capacity to adhere firmly to the intercultural trainer's code of ethics, the ethical guidelines of the profession; this includes the willingness to improve one's own professional skills

Culture-Specific Content

20. capacity to secure appropriate information about and resources on the target culture: values, attitudes, politics, history, geography, etc.
21. capacity to assess situational factors in the field that will affect the work of the sojourner
22. ability to assess and describe specific job roles, duties, and host-counterpart expectations
23. ability to provide instruction regarding target culture

Trainer Issues	24. capacity to articulate, model, and orient learners to a clear philosophy of the trainer's role and to serve as a resource
	25. ability to handle the stress and pressures of training
	26. ability to conduct training activities in one's areas of strength; using skilled trainers for other activities where one has more limited skills
International Issues	27. ability to present theories of development, social change, transfer of technology
	28. ability to engage learners in thinking about the central issues of international relations, especially as these will affect them personally: dependence versus interdependence, impact of the colonial legacy, parity versus dominance or superiority
Multicultural Issues	29. capacity to provide instruction about cultural pluralism and diversity and on intercultural interactions in the workplace and in society
	30. capacity to provide consciousness-raising education about the nature and impact of racism, sexism, and other forms of prejudice and discrimination
	31. capacity to design training programs which are sensitive to the history of oppression, discrimination, and intergroup relations of the groups being trained
	32. capacity to conceptualize and provide supportive social and psychological mechanisms for dealing with cultural marginality and multiculturalism

Intercultural Phenomena

These behavioral specifics are related to the trainer's ability to prepare learners for their encounters with intercultural processes and phenomena such as cultural adjustment (including culture shock), culture learning, intercultural communication, intercultural relations, and reentry adjustment. The competent trainer must be able to construct activities that will enable learners to think about, feel, and behaviorally react to these phenomena. The acquisition of new ways of thinking, behaving, and feeling (i.e., the paradigm shift) must begin during training, irrespective of the target culture, because it can be anticipated that all sojourners will experience these phenomena to some degree.

Intercultural Training

Many behavioral skills are required of the trainer in this area. The capacity to assess the needs of prospective learners is basic. The planning process includes conducting a client-needs analysis and audience assessment, making the necessary logistical arrangements, and conducting staff training. The specifics of program design include: identifying goals and objectives and relating training activities to them, integrating a variety of content areas and instructional methods into the program, and doing all of this by systematically considering the critical variables associated with training as they apply to this program. In the specific realm of pedagogy, the trainer must be able to design appropriate learning activities and properly sequence them, making certain that they are reasonably congruent with the learning styles of the trainers and/or that alternative activities are available. They will promote learner independence in cultural training, emphasizing "learning how to learn" skills (Hughes-Weiner 1986). Trainers must also develop formative (ongoing) and summative (cumulative) evaluation procedures.

Trainer/Learner Issues

Competent trainers will not only have a keen awareness of learner concerns and dynamics, they will also be able to respond effectively to them. By providing conceptual frameworks and establishing an atmosphere of trust, trainers will be able to promote culture learning and the skills of intercultural effectiveness. They will be able to debrief difficult learning issues with program participants, especially when certain activities have produced strong reactions. They must resist being placed in the expert role to avoid dependency relationships with learners. At all times, they will demonstrate sensitivity to what the learner is experiencing.

Ethical Issues

Ethical trainers will conduct themselves in ways that will advance the profession. They will promise only what they can deliver. They will be prepared to design and implement a sophisticated program. They will refuse contracts if the client's purposes are themselves unethical. They will promote public trust and confidence in intercultural training by adhering to the professional code of ethics.

Culture-Specific Content

This behavioral area is comprised of two distinct competencies: the ability to secure information about the setting within which the sojourner will be working (using interviews and other assessment strategies) and the ability to provide instruction about the specific features of the target culture. The competent trainer also takes care that the learners do not overemphasize culture-specific information and use it as a crutch.

Trainer Issues

The behaviorally competent trainer must possess some unusual abilities: the capacity to serve as a resource, but not an expert; the capacity to create learning activities that are stressful combined with the ability to help learners deal with the stresses of culture leaning; the capacity to be a strong individual, but also serve as part of a team. Competent trainers derive their professional identity from functioning effectively in the many roles of the trainer: programmer, educator, advisor, etc. Unlike many inexperienced trainers, their professional self-concept is not dependent on having lived and worked in a specific culture, nor on praise from the learners. They have moved beyond these initial, but ultimately limiting, sources of identity.

International Issues

Intercultural trainers, most certainly those preparing sojourners for Third-World assignments, should have the capacity to build theoretical content into the program related to social change and development. They' must be able to instruct learners about the pressing concerns of peoples in developing nations, some perspectives of which may be significantly different from the learners' own perceptions of global reality. In particular, they must familiarize learners with host-counterpart concerns about dependence, cultural dominance/arrogance/superiority, and other factors often associated with a past history of colonization.

Multicultural Issues

Trainers in multicultural programs must be able to handle the controversies and tensions associated with training about extremely sensitive issues such as racism. Program participants often experience feelings of anger, frustration, or guilt when the discussion turns to the oppression of certain groups by others in society. Some learners will reject such propositions and resist the content and process of training. Multicultural trainers must be able to manage conflict among group members. Perhaps the most important behavioral skill of the multicultural trainer is the capacity to promote a positive vision of diversity, one which helps equip the learners to view differences as a resource rather than a problem.

PERSONAL ATTRIBUTES OF THE INTERCULTURAL TRAINER

Figure 3 lists twelve personal characteristics the literature suggests are positive attributes of the effective and competent intercultural trainer (see Kealey and Ruben 1983 for a useful discussion of intercultural effectiveness and personal qualities).

Figure 3:   Trainer Competencies: Personal Attributes

1. Tolerance of ambiguity
2. Cognitive and behavioral flexibility
3. Personal self-awareness, strong personal identity
4. Cultural self-awareness
5. Patience

6. Enthusiasm and commitment

7. Interpersonal sensitivity

8. Tolerance of differences

9. Openness to new experiences and to people who are different

10. Empathy

11. Sense of humility

12. Sense of humor

Tolerance of Ambiguity

Virtually every training program is unique and to some degree unpredictable. The configuration of elements—staff composition, learner characteristics, design features, learning dynamics—changes from program to program. Thus, there is some inherent ambiguity built into programs that trainers must be able to tolerate.

Cognitive and Behavioral Flexibility

Given the complex and somewhat unpredictable nature of training as a learning enterprise, programs demand cognitive and behavioral flexibility on the part of the trainer. Trainers must be able to adjust their expectations and learning activities to the diverse needs, learning styles, and varying responses of the participants to the training processes and content. The pace of learning may differ from the trainers' expectations. Certain activities may be effective, while others are not. As a function of the learners' experiences, new conceptual explanations may be required. The competent trainer will be flexible enough to respond effectively to these dynamics of training.

Personal Self-Awareness, Strong Personal Identity

In light of the fact that trainers are often going to be challenged by learners, it is important for them to be confident in their own identity and to possess a high level of self-awareness. Then they can serve as models for learners, be more open and honest in their relationships with them, and more effectively help them deal with the issues of culture learning.

Cultural Self-Awareness

Cultural self-awareness means understanding the role of culture in the formation of one's own values, beliefs, patterns of behavior, problem-solving orientation, and the like. It also means awareness of one's uniqueness as well as the degree to which one shares the prevailing cultural norms. The competent trainer will be able to teach this concept to others.

Patience

Patience is extremely important because in every program there will be logistical problems, delays, and other disruptions to test the mettle of the trainer. Most importantly, trainers must be patient with learners. They should also encourage learners to be patient in their effort to become proficient in a second language and culture, so discouragement does not result when progress seems slow.

Enthusiasm and Commitment

Many of the most competent trainers inspire learners by communicating a sense of enthusiasm for the subject matter and a spirit of commitment to the pursuit of intercultural knowledge and skills. Such trainers never lose sight of the exciting aspect of intercultural learning in spite of the many challenges. Their great gift is the ability to motivate learners by means of their own demonstrable enthusiasm and commitment to the culture-learning experience.

Interpersonal Sensitivity

Intercultural trainers must be very adept at interpersonal relations and especially sensitive to the needs and concerns of learners. They must be able to relate well to the wide variety of individuals who comprise the learning community. They must also be skilled at working with other trainers, resource people, community volunteers, and administrators who are involved with the program.

Tolerance of Differences

The ability to tolerate differences (e.g., in values, beliefs, behavior) is one of the hallmarks of the effective trainer, who is often working in extremely heterogeneous learning communities. This trait will frequently be tested by learners who do not fit the norm and by colleagues with different perspectives on training.

Openness to New Experiences and to People Who Are Different

An authentic openness to new experiences and different peoples is a quality which leads many into the intercultural field in the first place and it is a most important attribute for culture learning. The competent trainer will be motivated in this way and will communicate that openness to learners in patterns of thought, feeling, and action.

Empathy

Empathy here means the ability to project oneself into the mind, feelings, and role of another. The empathic trainer will have the capacity to sense how the learner is doing and to respond appropriately. Such a trainer will appreciate the learner's anxieties and difficulties as well as his or her sense of accomplishment.

Sense of Humility

This does not mean a false sense of modesty, but an honest respect for the complexities, challenges, and uncertainties of intercultural learning. The competent trainer will first acknowledge that there is much to learn about intercultural phenomena. This trainer will also appreciate that training is not a perfect science, that creativity in design and technique is still possible and desirable, and that future research and evaluation will have much to reveal about the intercultural experience. Fundamentally, this sense of humility stems from the competent trainer's deep respect for the intricate and varied nature of cultures.

Sense of Humor

This particular attribute can help trainers and learners cope more effectively with the pressures of training and help learners cope with the subsequent stresses of adjustment to a new culture. By being able to laugh at themselves and at the peculiarities of intercultural relationships, competent trainers can help break the tension and maintain the learners' enthusiasm.

This section has dealt in detail with the ideal cognitive and behavioral competencies and personal attributes one would look for in a trainer. Unquestionably, other qualities could be mentioned and some exceptions could be taken to those listed here. No ideal typology can do complete justice to the variation in style and approach that exists among competent trainers. Assuming, however, that the attributes I've discussed above are reasonably accurate, there is then the question as to how prospective trainers can acquire those competencies.

THE TRAINING OF TRAINERS

If preparing sojourners in an intercultural training program is a complex educational enterprise requiring many trainer competencies, the training of trainers is even more complex and challenging. Such training requires learners to make a quantum leap from a basic understanding of intercultural experience and grasp of intercultural skills to a point where they can apply that foundation of knowledge and skills as intercultural educators. That basic foundation, however, does not automatically make persons with intercultural skills trainers, although it is sometimes assumed that such is the case. I have worked in training programs for the Peace Corps with many newly returned sojourners serving as trainers. It generally takes several programs' worth of experience for them to begin to understand and effectively deal with the learning dynamics, design questions, and pedagogical issues of training. With time and the support of experienced trainers, they can become increasingly more competent trainers themselves.

The point to be made is that one does not quickly or easily become a competent, professional trainer. The problem for the aspiring trainer is that there are few established experiential or academic pathways into the profession. Thus, it is incumbent on the profession and its experienced practitioners to:

1. Identify relevant academic programs at the undergraduate and graduate levels

2. Continue to articulate and refine the body of knowledge trainers must acquire

3. Provide more opportunities for prospective trainers to gain experience under the guidance of seasoned professionals

4. Refine and offer more programs for the training of trainers.

Programs intended to train trainers will have to be sophisticated in combining experiential opportunities to acquire training skills with sound conceptual content regarding the critical training variables and dynamics. These programs should include learning exercises focused on overall program design and the construction of specific learning activities. Logistical planning and program evaluation should be reviewed. Program objectives and assessment measures should be examined. The challenging dynamics of the trainer-learner relationship should be thoroughly explored. These are just a few of the elements that would comprise a training-of-trainers program.

Fortunately, there are several training workshops offered annually under the sponsorship of professional associations and organizations such as SIETAR International, NAFSA: Association of International Educators, and the Intercultural Communication Institute. They are intensive in nature, but also limited in time (one or two weeks). Thus, they cannot substitute for the long-term effort the prospective trainer must make to acquire experience and knowledge. Indeed, trainers should seek professional-development opportunities throughout their careers.

CONCLUSION

Many thousands of programs have been conducted in the past thirty years, and the field has become increasingly sophisticated. Intercultural training demands of its practitioners the command of a large body of knowledge, a wide range of behavioral competencies, and a number of special personal qualities. This author would submit that it takes extensive exposure to another culture, relevant academic training, years of experience, and exposure to skilled professionals to become an authentically competent trainer. This requires considerable commitment to this field and an ability, indeed a sense of delight, in discovering ways to achieve one's own intercultural effectiveness and competency as a trainer.

REFERENCES

Ackermann, Jean Marie (1976). "Skill training for foreign assignment: The reluctant U.S. case." In Larry A. Samovar and Richard E. Porter (Eds.), *Intercultural communication: A reader*. Belmont, CA: Wadsworth.

Adler, Peter S. (1974). "Beyond cultural identity: Reflections upon cultural and multicultural man." *Topics in Culture Learning* 2: 23-41.

Barna, LaRay M. (1983). "The stress factor in intercultural relations." In Dan Landis and Richard W. Brislin (Eds.), *Handbook of intercultural training* 2. Elmsford, NY: Pergamon.

Barnlund, Dean C. (1982). "The cross-cultural arena: An ethical void." In Larry A. Samovar and Richard E. Porter (Eds.), *Intercultural communication: A reader*. Belmont, CA: Wadsworth. 378-83.

Batchelder, Don, and Elizabeth C. Warner (Eds.) (1977). *Beyond experience*. Brattleboro, VT: Experiment in International Living.

Bennett, Janet M. (1986). "Modes of cross-cultural training: Conceptualizing cross-cultural training as education." *International Journal of Intercultural Relations* 10, no. 2: 117-34.

Bennett, Milton J. (1986a). "A developmental approach to training for intercultural sensitivity." *International Journal of Intercultural Relations* 10, no. 2: 179-96.

_____ (1986b). "Towards ethnorelativism: A developmental model of intercultural sensitivity." In R. Michael Paige (Ed.), *Cross-cultural orientation: New conceptualizations and applications*. Lanham, MD: University Press of America.

Blake, Brian F., and Richard Heslin (1983). "Evaluating cross-cultural training." In Dan Landis and Richard W. Brislin (Eds.), *Handbook of Intercultural training* 1. Elmsford, NY: Pergamon.

Brislin, Richard, Dan Landis, and Mary Ellen Brandt (1983). "Conceptualizations of intercultural behavior and training." In Dan Landis and Richard W. Brislin (Eds.), *Handbook of intercultural training* 1. Elmsford, NY: Pergamon.

Brislin, Richard, Kenneth Cushner, Craig Cherrie, and Mahealani Yong (1986). *Intercultural interactions: A practical guide*. Beverly Hills, CA: Sage.

Casse, Pierre (1979). *Training for the cross-cultural mind*. Washington, DC: Society for Intercultural Education, Training, and Research.

Dinges, Norman (1983). "Intercultural competence." In Dan Landis and Richard W. Brislin (Eds.), *Handbook of Intercultural training* 1. Elmsford, NY: Pergamon.

Gudykunst, William B., and Mitchell R. Hammer (1983). "Basic training design: Approaches to intercultural training." In Dan Landis and Richard W. Brislin (Eds.), *Handbook of intercultural training* 1. Elmsford, NY: Pergamon.

Hannigan, Terence P. (1990). "Traits, attitudes, and skills that are related to intercultural effectiveness and their implication for cross-cultural training: A review of the literature." *International Journal of Intercultural Relations* 14, no. 1: 89-111.

Harrison, Roger, and Robbins Hopkins (1967). "The design of cross-cultural training: An alternative to the university model." *Journal of Applied Behavioral Science* 3: 341-60.

Hoopes, David S., and Paul Ventura (Eds.) (1979). *Intercultural sourcebook.* Washington, DC: Society for Intercultural Education, Training, and Research.

Howards, Susan, et al. (1982). Guest editorial. *International Journal of Intercultural Relations* 6, no. 3: 225-26.

Howell, William S. (1982). *The empathic communicator.* Belmont, CA: Wadsworth.

Hughes-Weiner, Gail (1986). "The 'learning-how-to-learn' approach to cross-cultural orientation." *International Journal of Intercultural Relations* 10, no. 4: 485-505.

Kealey, Dan J., and Brent D. Ruben (1983). "Cross-cultural personnel selection criteria, issues, and methods." In Dan Landis and Richard W. Brislin (Eds.), *Handbook of intercultural training* 1. Elmsford, NY: Pergamon.

Kim, Young Y. (1988). *Communication and cross-cultural adaptation.* Clevedon, England: Multilingual Matters.

Kim, Young Y., and William B. Gudykunst (Eds.) (1988). *Cross-cultural adaptation: Current approaches.* Newbury Park, CA: Sage.

Landis, Dan, and Richard W. Brislin (Eds.) (1983). *Handbook of intercultural training* (3 vols.). Elmsford, NY: Pergamon.

Martin, Judith N. (Ed.) (1989). Intercultural Communication Competence. *International Journal of Intercultural Relations* 13, no. 3.

Mestenhauser, Josef A. (1983). "Learning from sojourners." In Dan Landis and Richard W. Brislin (Eds.), *Handbook of intercultural training* 2. Elmsford, NY: Pergamon.

Paige, R. Michael, and Judith N. Martin (1983). "Ethical issues and ethics in cross-cultural training." In Dan Landis and Richard W. Brislin (Eds.), *Handbook of intercultural training* 1. Elmsford, NY: Pergamon.

Pusch, Margaret D. (Ed.) (1979). *Multicultural education: A cross-cultural training approach*. Yarmouth, ME: Intercultural Press.

Pusch, Margaret D., Alexander Patico, George W. Renwick, and Carol Saltzman (1981). "Cross-cultural training." In G. Althen (Ed.), *Learning across cultures*, Washington, DC: National Association for Foreign Student Affairs.

Renwick, George W. (1979). *Evaluation handbook*. Yarmouth, ME: Intercultural Press.

Ruben, Brent (1989). "The study of cross-cultural effectiveness: Traditions and contemporary issues." *International Journal of Intercultural Relations* 13, no. 3: 229-40.

Walton, Sally (1990). "Stress management training for overseas effectiveness." *International Journal of Intercultural Relations* 14, no. 4: 507-28.

Weeks, William, Paul B. Pedersen, and Richard W. Brislin (1977). *A manual of structured experiences for cross-cultural learning*. Yarmouth, ME: Intercultural Press.

7

The First Step in Cross-Cultural Orientation: Defining the Problem

Kristin A. Juffer

Situation: You have just received a contract to provide orientation training for a new group of cross-cultural sojourners.[1] As usual, the time you will have with them will be limited. Which one of the following approaches to orientation training would you most likely choose:

Provide a basic knowledge of the differences sojourners will encounter in the new environment or situation so they will know what to expect in the new host culture, e.g., transportation, communication, clothing, climate, foods, restaurant behavior, etc.

Provide training to improve sojourners' cross-cultural and interpersonal communication skills in the host culture such as nonverbal communication training, survival language training, knowledge of the host culture's value system, etc.

Provide training concentrating on developing the sojourner's self-awareness including values exploration, discussion of characteristics that promote cross-cultural success, review of the adjustment curve, and symptoms of culture shock. Stress how to overcome culture shock, etc.

Provide training that demonstrates to the sojourner that familiar patterns of behaving and interpreting others' behavior will not produce the expected positive results in the new culture and then train them to behave in new ways that will be positively reinforced in the new environment, etc.

Provide training that will assist them in learning *how* to learn about a new culture, teaching strategies to enable sojourners to become independent, cross-cultural learners; emphasize that the purpose of travel is to develop "world-mindedness" and that the travel experience will be a positive growth experience for self-development, etc.

After choosing the *one* method you would most likely use, explain your reasons for selecting that particular approach over the others. Was it chosen because it is similar to previous sessions you have organized or similar to previous orientations you have attended or observed? Are there other reasons that you used in making your decision to choose that particular approach? What are they?

The object of this exercise is to dramatize and focus on the kind of value judgments trainers make (consciously or otherwise) when designing orientation programming. Often trainers choose an approach or technique because the trainer feels comfortable with it for a variety of reasons, such as (1) they themselves were trained using that approach, (2) they have observed it working for other trainers with other groups and they would like to duplicate that success, or (3) they feel they have mastered it and need to spend little time in additional preparation in order to make it work.

But a question must be asked of professional trainers who are intent on upgrading both their own effectiveness and the cross-cultural field: "Are the *trainer's* comfort, chance exposure to a particular method, sense of having mastered a particular kind of training to the point that it is easy, or even personal belief system adequate criteria on which to base design decisions for truly effective cross-cultural orientation programming for clients?"

For the professional trainer, the answer must be no. *Effective training must be client-centered* and *results-oriented*. The result clients most expect when contracting for cross-cultural training is improved cross-cultural adjustment by the trainees when they are overseas.

How, then, can training be improved to better meet these expectations? It is, in fact, deceptively simple, for the answer lies within the problem. *How the problem of cross-cultural adjustment is conceptualized should prescribe the design of any training program.* In other words, before trainers will be consistently able to design more effective and successful orientation programs, they will have to analyze more carefully the cross-cultural adjustment phenomenon and its components, for it is there that they will find answers to program-design questions.

To assist trainers in improving training, this chapter will provide an overview of the different approaches to conceptualizing the adjustment process, particularly focusing on the culture-shock aspect as described by over thirty-five cross-cultural writers and researchers. It will then relate these conceptualizations or theories of cross-cultural adjustment to existing training techniques and provide an approach to help trainers better design training as an integrated whole.

NATURE OF THE PROBLEM—ADAPTATION

Generally, cross-cultural trainers have considered the desired result of training to be assisting the sojourner to adapt (or adjust)[2] to the new culture. However, as Ruben, Askling, and Kealey (1977) noted, there are at least three different ways of defining or understanding the term "adaptation" currently accepted in the cross-cultural field. They include:

- ameliorating the sojourner's culture-shock experience;
- improving the sojourner's psychological adjustment (comfort, satisfaction with the stay); and
- increasing the sojourner's effectiveness[3] in the new culture.

Since these definitions also closely parallel the goals of cross-cultural training, it is important that trainers make it clear, both to themselves and to their clients, which of these distinct goals is the intended purpose of a particular program. This not only brings clarity to cross-cultural training, it enhances the trainer's credibility. (Trainers should also make it clear during orientation which of these definitions is being implied whenever they use the terms "adjust" or "adapt.")

Although each of these three definitions/orientation goals is distinct from the others, they are also highly interrelated. The first question to be examined is how they are interrelated.

1. It seems apparent that these three adaptational goals may or may not all be present in any given cross-cultural adaptation experience.

    For instance, a tourist's goal may be to increase psychological adjustment, comfort, and self-satisfaction while abroad, with mild culture shock being the primary problem to overcome. On the other hand, Peace Corps volunteers must first overcome culture shock before they can achieve the fairly high degree of psychological satisfaction necessary for successfully achieving cross-cultural effectiveness with host nationals, before they can accomplish Peace Corps goals.

2. It also seems apparent that these adaptational goals may interact on one another in a number of ways to compound the adjustment problem.

    For instance, in the previous example of the Peace Corps volunteers, the volunteers' feeling of psychological satisfaction would probably be associated with their degree of cross-cultural effectiveness.

3. It is further hypothesized that the accomplishment of each of the adjustment goals is generally hierarchical in nature.

    Until most culture-shock symptoms are alleviated, psychological satisfaction in the new culture is unlikely to be achieved; and until the sojourner's psychological self-satisfaction is largely achieved, a high degree of cross-cultural effectiveness is unlikely to be realized.

4. Further, the sequencing is such that each goal is increasingly complex and difficult to achieve.

    For example, if a sojourner is suffering strong culture-shock symptoms of loneliness, homesickness, anxiety, and anger toward the host nationals, it is improbable that she or he is experiencing much psychological satisfaction with the stay. On the other hand, if culture-shock symptoms abate and psychological satisfaction with the stay increases, it is still entirely possible that the sojourner's effectiveness in the new culture could be low. For example, some foreign students who successfully network and become immersed with other foreign students similar to themselves may find themselves no longer lonely, anxious, or homesick. They may have successfully navigated the host country's educational system and consequently are able to achieve acceptable marks in their studies, but they have yet to learn how to interact effectively on a day-in, day-out basis with host-culture members even though immersed in the host culture. They have not learned to interact with host-culture members using their "deep culture"[4] as a basis for understanding. Finally, as they become more effective in the new culture, their satisfaction will become even greater. In this sense, the relationship among the three goals as well as their achievement has a hierarchical character.

5. It is also hypothesized that when culture shock does occur, it becomes the first adjustment goal of the sojourner.

Although culture shock may not occur in every cross-cultural encounter, it is theorized by Ruben, Askling, and Kealey (1977) that culture shock is a phenomenon that always accompanies authentic culture learning and is a prerequisite to true cross-cultural effectiveness. If this is true and the achievement of the three adjustment goals is hierarchical, then understanding more about the culture-shock experience and how to prepare sojourners to cope with and eventually overcome culture shock may be prerequisite to achieving the other adjustment goals.

NATURE OF THE PROBLEM—CULTURE SHOCK

In spite of the fact that people have been migrating to new cultures for unnumbered centuries, it was not until 1953 that the phenomenon known as culture shock began to receive serious attention when anthropologist Kalvero Oberg used the term in an address to the American Women's Club in Rio de Janeiro, Brazil, while working with foreign service officers there (see Oberg 1958).

Since Oberg's description of the culture-shock experience, varying conceptual approaches have been proposed. Nagler (1977), after examining the research literature, found that "there is general agreement on the broad definition of culture shock as a reactive phenomenon occurring as a result of culture change and including both cognitive and affective components combining to produce extraordinary stress on the individual migrant. The locus of this stress is variously identified. It is alternately regarded as the *source* and the *result* of alienation in the new culture" (35).

Juffer (1983a; 1983b; 1984), scrutinizing more than thirty-five definitions of culture shock found in research literature, categorized the prevailing definitions of culture shock using the following causal schema:

1. Culture shock is caused by confronting a new *environment* or *situation*.

   Example definition: "Culture shock...refers to an overall reaction that individuals from one cultural milieu experience in confronting a different, less familiar one" (Baker 1976, 442).

2. Culture shock is caused by ineffectiveness of *intercultural* or *interpersonal communication*.

   Example definition: "Culture shock happens as a result of a disjunction or mismatch between the cognitive meaning structures of the interactors and their cultures" (Noesjirwan and Freestone 1979, 189).

3. Culture shock is caused by a threat to the *emotional* or *intrapsychic well-being* of the sojourner.

   Example definitions: "Culture shock is the effect that immersion in a strange culture has on the unprepared visitor....The culture-shock phenomenon accounts for much of the bewilderment, frustration, and disorientation that plagues Americans in their dealings with other societies. It causes a breakdown in communication, a misreading of reality, and inability to cope" (Toffler 1970, 6-7).

   "Culture shock profoundly tests the over-all adequacy of personality functioning, is accompanied by mourning for the abandoned culture, and severely threatens the newcomer's identity" (Garza-Guerrero 1974, 409).

4. Culture shock is caused by the need to *modify behavior* to regain *positive reinforcement* from the new environment.

   Example definitions: "Culture shock is defined as the sudden inability to anticipate events correctly, and the discontinuity between one's behavior and expected consequences. Social interaction no longer appears to follow one's internalized rules; the social text is characterized by ambiguity, shifting role demands, and status loss. In short, familiar reference points of personal identity appear lost, a condition which for many individuals is a source of anxiety and stress" (Higginbotham 1979, 53).

   "Culture shock is primarily a set of emotional reactions to the loss of perceptual reinforcement from one's own culture, to new culture stimuli which have little or no meaning, and to the misunderstanding of new and diverse experiences" (P. Adler 1975, 13).

5. Culture shock is caused by *growth experience*.

Example definition: "Although culture shock is most often associated with negative consequences, it can be an important aspect of cultural learning, self-development, and personal growth.... [T]he problems and frustration encountered in the culture-shock process are important to an understanding of...transitional experience which can be the source of higher levels of personality development. Implicit in the conflict and tension posed by the transitional experience lies the potential for authentic growth and development; 'the transcendence from environmental to self-support'" (F. Perls, as quoted in P. Adler 1975, 14).

The above schema categorizing prevailing definitions of culture shock is of interest to the cross-cultural trainer because it clearly demonstrates the major trends in how culture shock is conceptualized. The schema assists trainers in understanding the problems being addressed in greater depth and sophistication by the training. Extensive consideration of this schema is outside the scope of this discussion, but briefly, it provides the practitioner an overview of the hypothesized components of culture shock and its causes and effects. Understanding these elements is critical for effective training; these are the elements that trainers should address through effective training design. Suggestions on how to use this schema in designing comprehensive, integrated orientation training is the subject of the remainder of this chapter.

EMPLOYING THE CULTURE-SHOCK SCHEMA TO CLASSIFY TYPES OF ORIENTATION TRAINING

In developing and evaluating comprehensive and integrated training, it is important for trainers to understand the characteristics of and differences between each of the five categories or definitions described above. This schema will be used in analyzing different types of training in order to assist trainers in identifying the techniques that are appropriately applied in each case. The categories will be considered in the same order as they appeared above.

1. Culture shock is caused by confronting a new *environment* or *situation*.

This category of culture-shock definitions theorizes that culture-shock problems are largely situational or environmental and will affect, to some degree, all persons in a foreign environment. As Harris and Moran (1979) observed, "Culture shock describes the impact of a new and different environment on the individual" (164). Hall (1959) expands this view by observing that culture shock can result from not only perceiving a new environment, but also from missing or misinterpreting old familiar things. "Culture shock is a removal or distortion of many of the familiar cues one encounters at home and substitution for them of other cues which are strange" (156).

If culture-shock problems are largely situational or environmental and will affect, to some degree, all persons in a foreign environment or situation, then training should prepare sojourners for the new environment by informing them of what to expect. Informing sojourners what to expect should take the newness and the unexpected out of the situation, thereby minimizing the shock of the experience.

Types of training that address the culture-shock problem as it is conceptualized in this set of definitions include:

a. Providing orientation to the physical environment (city, campus, transportation system, Laundromats, geography, climate, traditions, holidays, foods, etc.)

b. Providing sojourners with survival skills and a list of do's and don't's to guide them in the new environment

c. Providing sojourners with fact sheets about the customs and traditions; history of the country; political, religious, and cultural background; dominant social trends, etc.

d. Using a *National Geographic* approach to orientation, including interesting pictures of the country, vignettes of the people and their customs, a brief history, with an emphasis on highlighting the differences between home and host countries. This technique is often called a travelogue approach.

The purpose of this type of orientation is to familiarize the sojourners with what they can expect to experience while in the new country. It is primarily concerned with the differences sojourners will experience in their physical environment (including the concepts of time and space) and is considered to be, by many people, elementary and somewhat controversial, since it often leaves the client with a stereotype of the new culture. Elements of this kind of training have to be incorporated into almost any training design since sojourners usually have physical survival concerns that have to be addressed initially to clear their personal agendas. But as a sole technique it is best suited to orientation for short-term sojourners. This approach corresponds with the first one listed in the exercise at the beginning of the chapter.

2. Culture shock is caused by ineffectiveness of *intercultural* or *interpersonal communication*.

   This theory states that intercultural and interpersonal communication problems are the causes of culture shock. In other words, culture shock occurs when interpersonal communication between interactors from different cultures breaks down (Brein and David 1971, 222-23). This breakdown occurs when people cannot understand and predict others' behavior, when their categories of experience no longer seem to be relevant, and when their accustomed behavior elicits apparently weird responses (Torbiörn 1982, 94-95).

   This concept of culture shock as an interpersonal communication problem is addressed in training which:

   a. focuses on person-to-person interactions and how to improve interpersonal cross-cultural communication,
   b. focuses on the culturally determined cognitive meaning structures of the people interacting and how they are matched or mismatched,
   c. focuses on understanding the new culture's social motivators, mores, values, and expectations,
   d. explores the new culture's social structure and sociology,
   e. addresses the concept of role ambiguity,

f. uses controlled goal-oriented cross-cultural communication tasks in which the sojourners explore communication and culture in the new community and report back to the group regarding outcomes and perceptions,

g. uses *Bafá Bafá* or other simulations to demonstrate different communication and value systems,

h. uses culture assimilators to demonstrate how actions in the host culture are often misinterpreted and to sharpen trainee communication skills in the new culture on several levels.

These types of orientation training activities particularly address the interpersonal and intercultural communication problems and, as such, represent a more sophisticated approach to training (and correspond to the second approach listed at the beginning of the chapter).

3. Culture shock is caused by a threat to the *emotional* or *intrapsychic well-being* of the sojourner.

A number of writers refer to the culture-shock experience as a mental illness or disease (Foster 1962; Oberg 1958). These definitions range in seriousness from "temporary personality disorientation" (Lundstedt 1963; Marsh 1975; Gama and Pedersen 1977) to a "massive psychic reaction" (Anderson 1971). The problem is seen to be an internal one within the sojourner: "Culture shock designates the massive psychic reaction which takes place within the individual plunged into a culture vastly different from his or her own. The 'shock' imagery suggests some resultant failure in appropriate response mechanisms, a derangement of control related to psychic injury or incapacitation—a neurotic condition" (Anderson 1971, 121). In referring to students, Gosnell (1979) speaks about culture shock as being an internal condition: "All too often new international students become casualties of culture shock, a condition of disorientation, anxiety, and confusion caused by an inability (or reluctance) to adjust to the new culture" (viii).

Training that specifically addresses this concept of culture shock is not often included in predeparture training, although it should be provided to sojourners to prepare them for the emotional experience of cultural adjustment. It is found more frequently in postarrival, host-country counseling settings. When it is found in predeparture training, it usually takes the following forms:

a. Providing information to sojourners about the cross-cultural adjustment process, focusing on culture shock, especially symptoms of culture shock including psychological reactions, psychosomatic illnesses, etc., so that sojourners will be able to identify them for what they are and not overreact.

b. Openly discussing the adjustment process, including the U-curve of adjustment, to inform sojourners that feeling confused, disoriented, anxious, uncertain, homesick, frustrated, or angry is normal to anyone coping in a cross-cultural situation. This approach attempts to prepare sojourners for culture shock in order to diffuse its intensity and the accompanying fear and resistance and to create more opportunity for openness to the new culture.

c. Discussing personality characteristics that promote cross-cultural adjustment: flexibility, openness, tolerance for ambiguity, etc.

d. Providing sojourners with the knowledge of several coping strategies which can be implemented while in the new culture to help them get through the culture-shock experience. Examples of such coping techniques are provided in letter f below.

For the most part, this type of training or orientation takes place after the arrival of the sojourner in the new culture, often after the individual realizes she or he is not adjusting as well as expected. Although a wide variety of counseling techniques are used by cross-cultural counselors in one-on-one counseling sessions, there are several that can also be used by trainers with groups of sojourners aimed at furthering their intrapsychic and emotional well-being. They would include the methods listed above plus the following:

a. Providing stress-reduction exercises such as transcendental meditation, imaging, deep breathing, etc.

b. Emphasizing the importance of a "wellness" orientation:

eating regularly and well, getting plenty of exercise, pursuing healthy recreational activities.

c. Establishing and promoting use of peer support groups and networking.

d. Examining the culture-shock experience from the perspective of grieving or mourning theory.

e. Presenting the General Adaptation Syndrome (GAS), which emphasizes the intrapsychic aspects of the cross-cultural encounter to explain culture-shock phenomena.

f. Presenting diagrams and information that deal with culture shock as stress including
   • sources of stress in the cross-cultural experience; and
   • individual variables that either diffuse or intensify stress (personality factors, the nature of one's situation, the support or lack of support one gets).

Available coping strategies:
   • self-management: vigorous exercise, nutrition;
   • letting-go exercises: centering and focusing techniques, finishing unfinished business, relaxation, meditation, prayer;
   • self-awareness: needs, desires, idiosyncrasies, congruence, assertiveness; and
   • personal planning: time management, life and career planning, life choices.

These are examples of training that can be provided to groups of sojourners who are having ongoing emotional and intrapsychic problems with culture shock.

4. Culture shock is caused by the need to *modify behavior* to regain *positive reinforcement* from the new environment.

This theory of culture shock is more instrumental in nature. In this theory, a behaviorist perspective (complete with behaviorist terminology) is clearly evident: individuals grope for appropriate responses in reaction to needs, and it is the lack of fit between one's behavior and anticipated consequences that causes the anxious reaction. For example, Peter Adler (1975) defined culture shock as "primarily a set of emotional reactions to the loss of perceptual reinforcement from one's own culture, to new cultural stimuli which have little or no meaning, and to the misunderstanding of new and diverse experiences" (13).

This type of training is often particularly difficult to achieve effectively in predeparture situations. The reality of the cultural differences to be encountered in the future and the need to adjust are removed, so motivation to change behavior is superficial and not highly internalized. However limited the immediate results of this type of training may be, it does provide a future sojourner an opportunity to practice new desired behaviors.

Based on behaviorist theory of stimulus and response and patterning of behavior theory, training of this type would involve the following methodologies:

a. The introduction, reintroduction, and consistent positive reinforcement of favorable attitudes toward new cultural forms such as foods, music, art, modes of dress, etc., in order to accustom the sojourners' senses to the new cultural environment and to condition the sojourners to accept different cultural forms more easily.

b. The practicing of certain behaviors until they become automatic, using the concept of "spaced repetition" (similar to the audiolingual approach in language training).

c. The use of culture assimilators to show sojourners experientially that there will be a need to adjust behavior abroad.

d. The programming of role playing and simulation games to simulate certain conditions and to practice certain behaviors, especially *Bafá Bafá* which demonstrates to sojourners how they learn via trial and error and gives them an opportunity to practice and internalize cross-cultural learning behaviors.

e. The identification of favorable role models whose behavior sojourners can emulate.

f. The explanation and application of attribution theory and how it molds people's perception through stimulus/response and positive/negative reinforcement.

Although there are many other training techniques that fall into this category, these will provide an example of those that take a behaviorist approach to cross-cultural training. These methods are similar to the fourth group at the beginning of the chapter.

5. Culture shock is caused by *growth experience.*

Culture shock is viewed by other researchers as a natural transition state that has potential for positive learning and growth. For instance, Crisler (1977) describes culture shock as being "a transition state...[which] may lead to either maladaptive, self-destructive behavior or to a stronger sense of personal growth and personal identity." Brislin (1981) frames the culture-shock experience in this same positive sense: "The constant demand of coping with differences in climate, housing, transportation, food, and social norms leads to frustration and sometimes a sense of worthlessness. It is important to view this condition as a normal part of cross-cultural contact, not as an anomaly which signifies failure. Culture shock has positive aspects, including a motivation component which encourages people to learn about their feelings so that frustration is reduced" (138). Some of the techniques and approaches which would be used here include:

a. Training sojourners to analyze the new culture and their experiences in it using "meta-structures" and/or anthropological "tools of perception."

b. Focusing orientation programming on the positive aspects of the personal-growth experience (for self-development and learning).

c. Presenting culture adjustment as being a natural part of personal change, evolution, and transition toward higher levels of personality development.

d. Emphasizing that growth overseas will begin with an encounter of a new culture and will evolve into an encounter with the self.

e. Using role plays and simulations that actually foster changes in the sojourners which are internalized and personalized (not just experienced on a superficial level).

CONCLUSION

The major premise of this chapter has been that alternative conceptualizations of the cross-cultural adjustment phenomenon prescribe alternative cross-cultural orientation techniques and methods. By focusing first on the five theories regarding the causes of culture shock, the trainer will then be able to design an integrated, well-defined training program which will effectively meet clients' needs. In the final analysis, if all the critical variables discussed in this chapter are factored into the selection of adaptation frameworks, an appropriate training design should emerge which will produce the expected results.

ENDNOTES

1. For the purposes of this chapter, the term "sojourners" includes all types of people planning to stay in a second culture for any length of time for any purpose. They may be people who are in the predeparture or in the postarrival stage of their trip.

2. The terms "adapt" and "adjust" and their derivatives are used interchangeably in this chapter.

3. "Effectiveness" is defined as the degree of satisfaction host-culture members experience while interacting or working with a sojourner (Ruben, Askling, and Kealey 1977).

4. "Deep culture" refers to those dimensions of culture that are fundamental to culture such as commonly held assumptions, patterns of thinking, values, etc. that operate significantly beyond the individual's conscious awareness.

REFERENCES

Adler, Peter S. (1975). "The transitional experience: An alternative view of culture shock." *Journal of Humanistic Psychology* 15, no. 4: 13-23.

Anderson, Bruce G. (1971). "Adaptive aspects of culture shock." *American Anthropologist* 73, no. 5: 121-25.

Baker, T. L. (1976). "The weakening of authoritarianism in black and white college students." *Sociology and Social Research* 60, no. 4: 440-60.

Brein, Michael, and Kenneth David (1971). "Intercultural communication and the adjustment of the sojourner." *Psychological Bulletin* 76: 214-30.

Brislin, Richard W. (1981). *Cross-cultural encounters: Face-to-face interaction.* Elmsford, NY: Pergamon Press.

Crisler, D. A. (1977). "New family constellations: Dimensions and effects of systematic culture shock." Doctoral dissertation, San Diego: School of Professional Psychology.

Foster, George (1962). *Traditional cultures and the impact of technological change.* New York: Harper and Row.

Gama, Elizabeth M., and Paul Pedersen (1977). "Readjustment problems of Brazilians returning from graduate studies in the U.S." *International Journal of Intercultural Relations* 1, no. 4: 46-59.

Garza-Guerrero, A. C. (1974). "Culture shock: Its mourning and the vicissitudes of identity." *Journal of the American Psychoanalytic Association* 22, no. 2: 408-29.

Gosnell, P. Wayne (1979). "The university acculturator for international students: An empirically-based, multi-cultural communication training technique." Doctoral dissertation, University of Michigan.

Hall, Edward T. (1959). *The silent language.* New York: Doubleday.

Harris, Philip R., and Robert T. Moran (1979). *Managing cultural differences.* Houston: Gulf.

Higginbotham, Howard N. (1979). "Cultural issues in providing psychological services for foreign students in the United States." *International Journal of Intercultural Relations* 13: 49-85.

Juffer, Kristin A. (1983a). "Initial development and validation of an instrument to assess cultural shock adaptation." Doctoral dissertation, University of Iowa.

_____ (October 1983b). "Cultural shock: A theoretical framework for understanding adaptation." BUENO Center for Multicultural Education's Monograph Series 4, no. 1. University of Colorado Press.

_____ (October 1984). "State-of-the-art research on cultural shock." *Bulletin of Intercultural Interchanges.*

Lundstedt, S. (Ed.) (1963). "Human factors in cross-cultural adjustment." *Journal of Social Issues* 19 , no. 3.

Marsh, Harriet L. (1975). "Re-entry/transition seminars for overseas sojourners: Report on the Wingspread colloquium." *Topics in Culture Learning* 3: 39-51.

Nagler, S. F. (1977). "Ego and vicissitudes of culture change: Proposed theory of culture shock." Doctoral dissertation, Smith College.

Noesjirwan, J., and C. Freestone (1979). "The culture game: Simulation of cultural shock." *Simulation and Games* 10, no. 2: 189-206.

Oberg, Kalvero (1958). "Culture shock and the problem of adjustment to new cultural environments." Washington, DC: Department of State, Foreign Service Institute.

Perls, Fritz (1969). *Gestalt therapy verbatim.* New York: Bantam.

Ruben, Brent D., Lawrence R. Askling, and Daniel J. Kealey (1977). "Cross-cultural effectiveness." In David S. Hoopes, et al. (Eds.), *Overview of intercultural education,* Washington, DC: Society for Intercultural Education, Training, and Research.

Toffler, Alvin (1970). *Future shock.* New York: Random House.

Torbiörn, Ingemar (1982). *Living abroad: Personal adjustment and personnel policy in the overseas setting.* New York: John Wiley.

8

Independent Effectiveness and Unintended Outcomes of Cross-Cultural Orientation and Training

James A. McCaffery

INTRODUCTION

Despite the good intentions, high energy, and unquestionable commitment of most people in the field, cross-cultural orientation and training programs all too often do not succeed in their aims. The laudable, intended outcomes of cross-cultural training have been clearly articulated (Brislin, Landis, and Brandt 1983, for example, or Gudykunst and Hammer 1983), but *unintended* outcomes sometimes render these, at best, ineffective and, at worst, harmful. Because some outcomes *are* unintended, they are often not evaluated and go unnoticed by the people who administer and deliver programs. Instead, program evaluation and subsequent redesign efforts tend to focus on the obvious and trivial at the expense of more significant problems that are difficult to identify.

This chapter begins by identifying possible unintended outcomes in cross-cultural training and orientation programs. A model is then proposed that is intended to help make cross-cultural training more effective and to reduce undesirable outcomes. The specific aim of the proposed model is to assist persons in becoming independent in a second culture by focusing on skill building rather than only on information transmission. Finally, the limitations of this approach are discussed.

UNINTENDED OUTCOMES

Deemphasizing the Importance of Training

Until recently, most U.S. corporations ignored cultural issues when sending people overseas to work. However, some companies have now begun to conduct predeparture orientation for personnel going overseas for a significant period of time (one, two, or more years). (See Harris and Moran 1987.) The orientation may last a couple of hours or one day. It frequently involves reading some general literature about the country, viewing slides or pictures taken by people who have visited the country, meeting for discussions with someone who has held the position previously, and sharing a list of do's and don't's. It is explicitly organized to help the departing person avoid obvious mistakes by learning something about that culture.

However, there are also some unintended outcomes communicated by such a program. There is a message that the orientation is really not very important. If it were, it would be allocated more time and be accorded a more important role in predeparture activities. Such an orientation can also unintentionally communicate that learning "enough" about another culture is easy, that it can be done in a short period of time, and that picking up some do's and don't's is all one has to worry about.

Stereotyping

When an orientation is as limited as the one described above and includes previous sojourners giving advice, it inevitably produces numerous unhelpful stereotypes. As Kealey and Ruben (1983) and Barna (1982), among others, have pointed out, stereotyping is one of the major obstacles to intercultural effectiveness.

I recently heard the following statements from a person who conducts cross-cultural training for a U.S. company in the Middle East:

> You know, they just don't have a sense of humor. You have to watch out where you drive, because they don't care about getting their cars dented a lot. People are aloof, and it is hard to make friends there.

The point is not whether these statements are right or wrong, but that they are stereotypes. On an implicit level, they encourage the listeners, the participants in the program, to see stereotypes as legitimate and perhaps even to generate stereotypes of their own. Moreover, such stereotyping predisposes sojourners *not* to see people in the host culture as individuals, to say nothing about the specific biases that are communicated.

Unrealistic Expectations

There is no activity specifically included in the orientation described above which involved expectations, and this means that expectations are generated, confirmed, or disconfirmed unreflectively and implicitly. A number of authors have suggested that expectations play a significant role in cross-cultural adjustment and effectiveness. Kealey and Ruben (1983), for example, suggest that realistic predeparture expectations are an important predictor of overseas success.

Stereotypes create expectations, as do exhortations like "You will love it there" or cautions like "Make sure you never ask a French person for directions because you will never get them." Whether positive or negative, unchecked or unexamined expectations can be very damaging. After all, if I have been told that I will "love it there" and go abroad only to find that I *don't* like it, I will not only feel sad or frustrated by that, I may also feel that people lied to me during the orientation or tried to oversell the country to get me to go in the first place.

Trainee Dependency

Another example of unintended outcomes derives from Peace Corps training. Over its twenty-two-year history, the U.S. Peace Corps has had extensive cross-cultural training programs and approaches. To its credit, it has realized the importance of the cross-cultural dimension and has invested more in development of training programs than any other agency, company, or university. Some of the training has been highly successful, especially when compared to other organizations. However, a number of years ago the Peace Corps was also plagued by an unintended outcome of major importance.

It was the goal of Peace Corps cross-cultural training to prepare volunteers to become independently effective within the host culture. In order to do this, much of the training was carried out in the country to which the volunteers were to be assigned. Along with an abundance of reading materials, cross-cultural training included a variety of activities—anecdotal discussions with ex-volunteers from that country, presentations by knowledgeable resource people from the national university, trips to important places in the country, participation in local events and holidays, and sometimes "live-ins" with host families. The program may have taken five to ten days of the eight-to-ten-week preparation period. Also, there was a heavy emphasis on language, which tended to reinforce the importance of the cultural dimension.

Certainly the message communicated with this kind of approach was that cross-cultural training was important. However, the program also produced dependent volunteers rather than independent, culturally effective volunteers. There were at least two reasons for this outcome. First, even though the trainees were living in-country, they were still being trained to study the culture, to observe, and to learn by depending on others. Implicitly, they were being taught to rely on expert knowledge about the country and were becoming used to the Peace Corps providing "answers" to cross-cultural questions and problems. In subtle ways they were becoming intellectually dependent on the Peace Corps training structure.

This factor, combined with a training environment described below, produced very dependent trainees. For a variety of convincing operational reasons, trainees were housed at Peace Corps training centers where training administrators were responsible for food, shelter, and some kinds of transportation. Thus, if problems arose (e.g., if the food were bad, the sheets dirty, a window broken, or a dispute occurred), the trainers or training administrators were there to solve the problem. This, of course, created an environment in which trainees became dependent on the Peace Corps for food and shelter, two especially powerful needs when one first arrives in a different country.

It is somewhat ironic that this situation became a no-win game for the training staff. If they were efficient and ran a tight ship, responded quickly and appropriately to ongoing needs and crises, they created increased dependence. On the other hand, if the training center was not well run, it created frustration, complaints, and bitterness in the temporary training community.

Admittedly, the trainee-living situation was not the fault of the cross-cultural training program. However, the training environment influences training outcomes. By the end of training, this sense of dependence, both physical and intellectual, was easily transferred to the Peace Corps office in-country. This led many Peace Corps directors to complain that volunteers "aren't like they used to be—they complain all the time, they don't get out into the countryside, they hang out with each other too much, and they spend too much of the time in the office." However, after examining their training programs closely, some directors realized that it was their own programs that were inadvertently producing the dependent behavior that they were criticizing.

This outcome also occurs in many orientation programs for international students on university campuses. International students are sometimes brought to the campus early for the orientation program and often live together in the same dormitory, eat together, and go to their classes together. Orientation activities are frequently like the ones described above in the Peace Corps cross-cultural training program. The group may then stay together in the same dormitory for the year.

In this situation students may complain (very politely) that they are not getting to know Americans, that people are unfriendly, that their English is not improving, that the dorm is not good, or that the program administrator is not sympathetic. The program administrator, on the other hand, may see the students as clannish, unadventuresome, ethnocentric people who are not able to adjust very well and who are too dependent. The parallel with the Peace Corps cross-cultural training example seems clear: the combination of orientation structure and environmental conditions has again helped to produce the unintended outcome of dependent (and unhappy) international students. Of course, there are other factors which contribute to this condition, but it is clear that the orientation starts the process.

Negative Expectations

In addition to the specific examples spelled out above, there is one more basic area which needs examination. It is possible that some of our most popular (and fundamental) concepts and descriptions are causing unintended outcomes. Consider the following language: culture *shock*, *survival* techniques, and *coping* skills. Are we somehow unintentionally communicating to sojourners that the best they can hope for is to survive, cope, and avoid being shocked? The language used, however accurate and descriptive, certainly conjures up a hostile and alien environment.

Are there ways to describe the same phenomena without the linguistic harshness? One way is to focus on the concept of adjustment rather than shock. Janet Bennett (1977), for example, has suggested that the disorientation people experience as a negative part of cultural change can be converted into an opportunity for growth if it is viewed as a type of transition, similar to that which people experience in other life-change situations. (For a review of other research on adjustment and culture shock, see Church 1982.) Perhaps the concept of survival should be eliminated altogether from our lexicon and be replaced by, say, "being effective abroad."

This is not meant to imply that we should dispense intellectual rose-colored glasses. Indeed, Paige and Martin (1983) believe that trainers are ethically required to make clear to sojourners that cultural transitions are quite often difficult or painful. But it seems that there must be ways to describe certain concepts without predisposing people to expect disaster upon arrival in another country.

It is important to emphasize here that ineffective cross-cultural orientation or training does not result because administrators are ineffective, or trainers are lazy, or resource people are not knowledgeable, or because people in the field do not care or are not committed. Indeed, I find quite the opposite to be true, especially in terms of the deep caring and commitment I have often observed in people who work in the cross-cultural area. Unfortunately, good intentions are not enough. In situations such as those we have just considered, the power of unintended negative outcomes may far outweigh the positive value of what was communicated.

THE PROBLEM

The root of the problem is familiar: cross-cultural training is not seen as a discipline and, as a result, it is rarely approached holistically or systematically. Paige and Martin (1983), among others, have noted the lack of accepted academic avenues for would-be trainers and of a specific knowledge base for the discipline. Most of us got into the field because we traveled or liked other cultures or felt we were badly prepared when we first went overseas. Others enter it academically by studying anthropology or sociology. Almost all of us thus come into the field through the "side door," and most are only temporarily in the field or work in the field only occasionally—in addition to our "real" work. Because we do not approach it as a discipline, we tend to equate effective intercultural work with sound information dissemination, lively anecdotes, and short cross-cultural visitations.

In effect, we start in the field as cultural "experts," which causes us to view training as transferring to others a certain body of knowledge or facts rather than the *processes* through which this knowledge was derived. (Of course, our field is not unique in this: the teaching of history or science has been plagued with the same problem, the reduction of the discipline to "facts" or the "scientific method.") We rarely get to a point where we consider adult education principles, training techniques, educator/trainer styles, the relationship between method, content, and environment, and the overall aim of cross-cultural training and orientation.

There is an additional important factor which exacerbates this situation: cross-cultural work looks deceptively simple but is in reality exceedingly complex. My colleagues and I have a great deal of experience in the education and training field. We do organization development and management development, we help engineers write training manuals, we teach human resource development courses, we consult with teams that are having serious problems working together, and we do a range of cross-cultural training and consulting. Reflecting on it all, we have concluded that the cross-cultural work is the most difficult of all.

What we are faced with as a field, then, is undertaking a very difficult activity—the design and delivery of cross-cultural orientation and training—without the benefit of the kinds of systematic models that exist in and give guidance to other disciplines.

A NEW MODEL

There are many objectives in cross-cultural training. These range from such concrete goals as language mastery, competence as a teacher, and psychological adjustment to more comprehensive goals, such as fostering intercultural understanding and providing assistance to other cultures. (Brislin, Landis, and Brandt [1983] and Kealey and Ruben [1983] provide good overviews of the aims and objectives of the field.) Another popular aim is to help people assimilate into a different culture. Whether appropriate or not, this is the aim of some of the cross-cultural work being done with Asian refugees who have arrived in the U.S. over the last several years. Helping people learn to participate in another culture without necessarily assimilating is another cross-cultural training aim. This one might be particularly relevant to international student exchange programs or, again, to the Peace Corps.

All of these aims, and others like them, are legitimate; however, they are limiting in nature. They do not provide a vision of the real power and enablement that can result from cross-cultural training and orientation.

Skills and Independence: A New Training Goal

There is a need for a new model in the cross-cultural training field, one which approaches the work holistically and systematically and which, because it does, will help increase our ability to identify and achieve important explicit outcomes and reduce the number of unwanted inadvertent ones. The model has three imperatives which must be integrated: (1) a basic and clear cross-cultural training aim needs to be identified, (2) an educational methodology needs to be described which is consistent with that aim, and (3) educators and trainers need to design and deliver their programs in a style that is congruent with and that reinforces the methodology and educational aim.

AIM

The aim proposed for this new model is to move people toward developing/enhancing the skills they need to become independently effective cross-cultural sojourners.

This aim is enabling and intends to move people toward cross-cultural self-reliance. It is an ambitious aim—an emancipatory aim—for it subsumes (or could subsume) the other aims mentioned earlier. After all, if one has the skills necessary to be independently effective in another culture, then one can make one's own choice about the degree of assimilation one wishes to attain and about other important adaptation issues.

In order to achieve this aim, training and orientation programs must be skill-based. They must focus on "learning how to learn" rather than on learning a particular fact or set of information. The latter produces dependency on the trainer for information, for right answers. What happens, then, when the trainer is not there, or a new situation crops up that has not been "covered," or a different culture is encountered? Skill training, on the other hand, allows a sojourner to develop the means to deal with new situations after the program has ended.

Certain cross-cultural skills and principles can readily be identified and learned. There is nothing magical about them. We all have a valuable reservoir of skills, habits, traditions, and knowledge that can be utilized in "crossing" cultures because we have all grown up in a culture and have developed ways of being relatively effective and happy within it. Effective cross-cultural training identifies prior experiences and skills, builds on them, helps adapt them, and introduces new skill areas to individuals who may not have had access to some of them.

The following are some sample cross-cultural skill areas which I developed with Dan Edwards (1978, 1981) for use by the Peace Corps:

Managing Transitions. This skill area deals with those skills and techniques that can be used to help assess and manage expectations, to reflect on the culture which one is leaving, to deal with any unfinished business (emotional as well as financial), and to develop a practical, concrete strategy for entering another culture (i.e., the first day or week or several weeks in-country). An especially difficult part of this skill area is reflecting on one's own culture; most people do not have a solid, explicit sense of the meaning and practicalities of their own culture. There is much that is taken for granted, and many faulty assumptions are made. These can have a profound effect on one's ability to enter a different culture. Overall, this skill area is aimed at facilitating an effective leave-taking as well as a skillful entry.

Gaining Fluency. This skill area can be subdivided into two somewhat distinct clusters. The first might be labeled "everyday-life skills," and the second, communication skills.

Everyday-Life Skills. Some examples of everyday-life skills are as follows:
- Observation: looking critically and carefully at what is happening in cross-cultural interaction situations
- Self-reflection: reflecting on how one's own presence in a situation may be altering it; examining how one's own cultural values and filters might be affecting interactions or interpretations
- Transactions: refining and adapting appropriate behavior relative to daily transactions (getting taxis, changing money, buying vegetables, bargaining, learning time systems around appointments); learning skills to discover how transactions work

- Saying no: assessing consequences of saying no in different situations and refining and adapting skills and tactics for doing so

  (We found this area to be particularly important, since, if people do not feel they can say no, they often begin trying to avoid entirely those situations in which they might wish to say no. This results in increasingly less contact with the host culture.)

- Responding to ambiguity: realizing when one is in an ambiguous situation and choosing personally appropriate responses that are within culturally acceptable parameters

Communication Skills. Useful communication skills include the following:
- Initiating conversations: finding topics of mutual interest and of appropriate linguistic complexity in cross-cultural interactions
- Active listening: this includes paraphrasing, summarizing, restating, reflecting feelings, and testing for understanding
- Nonverbal: learning to read facial expressions, hand gestures, body language, and the use of proximity

  (For further discussion of the communication strategies and skills that promote cross-cultural effectiveness, see Ruben [1977] and Gudykunst and Hammer [1984].)

Developing Knowledge about the Culture. Overall, the aim of this skill area is to enable people to develop the knowledge they need about a culture when they need it and as substantively as they need it. It is entirely different from the approach used in many cross-cultural programs wherein participants are given too much information about a subject, often at the wrong time. The skill area has two subareas:
- Gathering information: refining and adapting skills in areas of observation, question asking, simple researching, and developing data from reflecting on actual experience
- Filtering/validating information: identifying and using alternative sources of information, checking and measuring the perspective of information sources, dealing with conflicting data, recognizing when two or more "truths" may exist simultaneously, and making reasonably valid judgments based on imperfect and/or incomplete data

  These cross-cultural skill areas exemplify the kinds of skills that can be taught or trained in order to reach the aim that is proposed in this chapter. Because the aim contains the language "move people toward," it recognizes that an orientation or training program might not be able to reach the objective completely. Indeed, in a short orientation, the movement might be rather small, but it will be there (if the other elements in the model are consistent with the aim).

Above all, the proposed aim provides clear direction for cross-cultural trainers, teachers, and designers: anything that moves people toward independence is consistent with the aim, and any activity which does not should be avoided. More specific program goals, content, method, training or teaching style, and educational environment all can be assessed to determine congruency with the overall goal. If this is done rigorously, unwanted, unintended outcomes should be significantly diminished, if not altogether eliminated. Of course, there may be times when one chooses to do something which is inconsistent with the aim, but if this model is used, that choice will be *conscious*, and any negative impact will be known beforehand and accepted.

The aim, then, provides a framework for choice and for action. It is intended to be as useful for a half-day orientation as for an in-depth two- or four-week cross-cultural training program. The skills learned will be transferable from one context to another, and the ultimate outcome for participants will be greater independence. The next part of the chapter will examine the methodology which is congruent with the aim and the emphasis on skill building.

METHODOLOGY

The methodology most consistent with the aim stated above is experiential and learner-centered.

The methodology currently used in most cross-cultural orientation and training programs is inconsistent with the proposed aim. (Gudykunst and Hammer [1983] provide a good overview of training methods.) There tends to be an overreliance on lectures, presentations, question and answer sessions with "experts," and the dissemination of written materials. This methodology is especially seductive, because the closer one gets to going abroad, the more urgent one's needs for specifics and certainty become, and this approach helps create the illusion of certainty in what is a very ambiguous process. The methodology is inadequate also because it does not recognize the value of each participant's personal knowledge in the learning. Finally, and most importantly, it focuses on information dissemination rather than skill development.

This is not meant to imply that, say, information dissemination is somehow an ill-advised activity in the cross-cultural training arena; indeed, it can be quite valuable. However, it depends on how it is done and how it fits with an overall methodological pattern which is indeed consistent with the skill-development aim. What might such a methodology look like? A methodology which is consistent with the proposed aim needs to be based on the following assumptions:

- Participants must be actively involved in the learning process, as opposed to being passive recipients of information or knowledge.

- All participants need to be seen as being able to contribute to the learning process, both their own and others'. Even if people have not traveled, they have inevitably had some cross-cultural experience, although they may need assistance in seeing it as such. In any event, people make their own meaning, and that needs to be legitimized as a valued part of the individual and group learning process.

- The training curriculum must incorporate a variety of educational approaches in order to accommodate the variety of ways in which people learn. (See Kolb's [1974] discussion of differences in learning styles.)

- Learning is most effectively brought about when the more specific learning goals and objectives have relevance and meaning for the participants in terms of their own lives, what they already know, and their professional and personal goals.

- The primary learning activities need to focus on skill development, and information dissemination must be seen as a subset of skill development. Learning is meaningless if it is confined merely to the acquisition of facts and figures. The acquisition of information must be supplemented by an understanding of why this information is important and how this knowledge "fits" or can be utilized productively.

- To achieve optimum learning, there must be a sense of mutuality between trainer or teacher and participant in terms of shared responsibility for movement toward program outcomes as well as contributions to the learning process.

These fairly standard adult education assumptions are nevertheless rarely applied to cross-cultural orientation and training situations. With the training model we are discussing, they need to serve as the base which undergirds the methodology. Furthermore, even though these assumptions have been drawn from principles of adult education, they constitute a sound approach when dealing with students, even secondary school students, who might be in a student exchange program. The methodology itself has been derived from an experiential training model.

The Experiential Approach

Experiential training is exactly what the name implies—learning from experience. The experiential approach is learner-centered and allows the individual trainees to manage and share with their teachers responsibility for their own learning. Effective training strategies which incorporate experiential learning provide opportunities for a person to engage in an activity, analyze this activity critically, abstract some useful insight from the analysis, and apply the result in a practical situation. (Gudykunst and Hammer [1983] provide a brief historical review of the experiential approach.)

A graphic representation of the model is presented in figure 1 below.

Figure 1

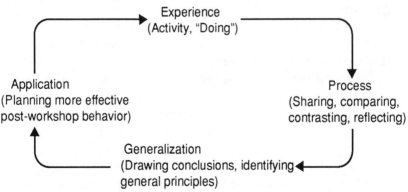

It may be applied to cross-cultural training in the following ways:

The *experience* phase is the initial activity and the data-producing part of the experiential learning cycle. This phase is structured to enable participants to become actively involved in "doing" something. Doing,

in this instance, has a rather broad definition and includes a range of
activities like the following:

- Case studies
- Role plays
- Simulations
- Games
- Lecturettes

- Films and slide shows
- Skill practice
- Completing an educational instrument
- Living with a family from another country

This sample list indicates that the range of training techniques varies
from the more passive and artificial (lecturette) to the more active and
real (living with a family). Exactly which technique one chooses as an
educational activity at any given moment would depend largely on the
session goals.

Once the experience phase is completed, the trainer or instructor
would guide the group into the *process* part of the cycle. During this
phase, participants reflect on the activity undertaken during the experience phase, and they share their reactions in a structured way with the
whole group. This may occur on an individual basis, in small work
groups, or in a full training group. Individuals share both their cognitive
and affective reactions to the activities in which they have engaged. In
addition, with trainer assistance, they try to link these thoughts and
feelings together in order to make a whole which gives meaning to the
experience.

The trainer's role as facilitator is very important during each phase
of the cycle. During the process phase, he or she should be prepared to
help the participants think critically about the experience and to help
them verbalize their feelings and perceptions as well as draw attention
to any recurrent themes or patterns which appear in their reactions. The
trainer's role involves helping the participants to conceptualize their
reflections on the experience so that they can move toward drawing
conclusions.

The *generalization* stage is that part of the experiential learning cycle
in which the participants extract conclusions and generalizations which
might be derived from, or stimulated by, the first two phases of the cycle.
During this phase, participants are helped to "take a step back" from the
immediate experience and discussion and to think critically in order to
draw conclusions that might be generalizable to "real life" or to a
particular theoretical construct. This stage is perhaps best symbolized by

the following questions:
- What did you learn from all this?
- What more general meaning does this have for you?

The trainer or instructor structures this part of the experiential learning program so that participants work alone first and then are guided in sharing conclusions with each other so that they may serve as catalysts to one another. In addition, the trainer helps to facilitate this step by:
- Asking and helping individuals to summarize in concise statements or generalizations what they have learned
- "Pushing back" at people to help make their thinking more rigorous
- Relating to each other the conclusions reached and integrating them into a theoretical model
- Making sure, within reasonable time boundaries, that everyone who wishes to share significant insights gets a chance to contribute
- Helping the group compare and contrast different conclusions, identifying patterns and legitimate areas of disagreement

After participants have done some focused work on generalizations, they are guided into the *application* stage. Drawing upon insights and conclusions they have reached during the previous phase (and other phases), participants incorporate what they have learned into their lives by developing plans for more effective behavior in the future. In an ideal educational or training event, participants would be able to apply what they have learned immediately after the workshop ends. The applications that they plan may relate to their profession, their personal life, or their student efforts, depending on the background and needs of specific participant groups. Techniques used to facilitate the application stage include the following:
- Individuals work to develop action plans which put "thought into action."
- Participants review each other's plans and provide consultation and help as appropriate to each other.
- Some individuals share parts of their plans with the whole group in order to create a sense of synergy.
- Participants identify other learning needs.

One way the trainer assists during this process is by helping participants be as specific as possible in developing their own application plans.

It is important to stress two other points about the experiential model. First, the exact nature of each phase of the model is driven by the goals of the training or orientation session/program. Once the goals are defined, then the session can be designed using the model as the framework. Second, theory can enter in two different places—either before the experience, in which case the experience becomes a way to test the theory or try out the skills implied by it, or after, when it is interwoven into the generalization phase as participants develop their own "theory." When this is added to the "picture" of the model, it looks like figure 2.

Figure 2

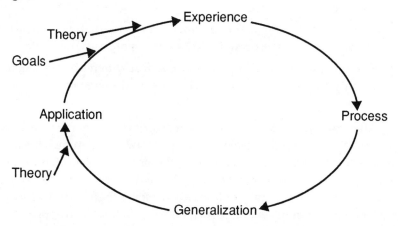

In order for this model to be effective, it needs to be rigorously applied, both in the design and delivery stages. Experiential training or learning is referred to often in the educational and training worlds; yet the phrase is frequently misused in practice, where it seems to mean letting people participate in a presentation, having a question-and-answer session after a lecture, or conducting a role play or case study *by itself* without the subsequent steps in the model. Most frequently, the generalization and application stages are simply left out; as a result, the power of experiential learning is significantly diminished or is negated altogether.

Although the model, when correctly explained, looks very clear, the way it works out in practice is not always so clear. There are transitions between phases, and occasionally, especially if the trainer is going too fast, the group will return to a phase until it is "finished." Also, individuals in the group may not approach the learning process in such a linear fashion, and that is perfectly legitimate. The model is meant to serve as a guide for the trainer or instructor who is trying to design and carry out an educational experience for a group.

The experiential model is especially suited to cross-cultural skill training because most of the techniques are active and involving and get participants to practice and try things out. It can be used for a culture-general approach (skills and knowledge that will help people move from culture to culture effectively) or a culture-specific approach (skills and knowledge aimed at helping people achieve effectiveness in country X). The experiential model implicitly helps people move toward independence because it *asks them to reflect on their experience, draw conclusions, and identify applications*. The effective instructor or trainer does not do this for participants. Thus they are not spoon-fed, nor are they led to be dependent on cross-cultural experts. Of course, this model requires a special trainer or instructor style for it to be implemented effectively, and it is to that subject we now turn.

TRAINER/INSTRUCTOR STYLE

The training style most congruent with the above aim and methodology is that of facilitator.

To be a trainer or instructor who uses the experiential model means that one must adhere to the adult education assumptions spelled out above and clearly understand and be able to utilize all aspects of the experiential model as we have described it. In addition, one must have a training style which is congruent with those assumptions and with the experiential model. Training style, in this case, means how one actually approaches trainer/instructor interactions in educational settings. An appropriate style for this model might be labeled "facilitative," and trainer behaviors include the following:

- Assesses needs
- Develops goals
- Creates/delivers design
- Provides initial structure

- Creates environment for shared course management
- Asks questions
- Creates interactive environment
- Provides feedback
- Manages group process
- Evaluates jointly
- Learns with group
- Provides appropriate theory inputs
- Provides appropriate cultural information

When done well, this kind of training looks very easy. It is not. The trainer or instructor must always strive for a balance between taking too much control or too little, between giving too much information or too little, and between legitimating participants' own learning or challenging them to consider other factors, theories, and points of view. Another trainer dilemma involves structure; although the trainer provides initial structure, there are opportune moments when participants ought to make important instructional decisions. It is sometimes difficult to distinguish those moments from the times when the trainer ought to decide. It is also difficult at times when the trainer notices that participants appear to be on the wrong track or are ignoring an important theory or a significant piece of cultural information. How does the trainer intervene without changing the basic relationship between trainer and participant and, in the process, recasting it in the expert-to-student mold?

It takes a great deal of study, practice, feedback, in-depth educational-process knowledge, and work with the model in order to do it effectively. Unfortunately, many in the cross-cultural field are not aware of the model and the instructor skills necessary to practice it, or they do not reach levels of competence in it. This results in some common trainer mistakes: overtelling; anecdotal training which, although often entertaining and humorous, is not particularly educational; leading people toward conclusions that the trainer has already reached ("Don't you think that..." or "Isn't it better if..."); telling participants what they will learn from their experiences in another culture or, even worse, telling them, when they are actually overseas, what they are learning from living abroad; and, finally, the most common mistake probably involves thinking about training as what one is going to "tell" or "give to" participants.

Although difficult, a facilitative training style is consistent with the educational assumptions and experiential training model delineated above and, if put in practice competently by trainers, will result in building skills and achieving the basic cross-cultural training aim.

Limitations to the Model

Some have argued that this model is too "Western" or "North American," and that different cultures have different learning styles, and I myself for many years believed this to be true. Some years ago, however, my colleagues and I gradually (and very carefully) began to introduce this kind of approach into our international training, and we found it to be extremely effective. Ironically, we discovered that the variable which seemed to cause people to accept or not to accept certain methodological approaches was more likely to be educational level than cultural background.

To expand on this a bit, we found that people with college degrees, especially those who had gone directly on to graduate school, were most resistant to experiential learning *regardless* of culture. On the other hand, those who had been away from formal education for a significant period of time, or had never gone to school in the first place, seemed to thrive on experiential training. It is easier, for example, to get two rural Kenyan farmers to participate in a simulation than two Canadian Ph.D. agronomists. The "educational culture" of participants, then, must be considered when applying this model (of course, one's general cultural conditioning may reinforce educational culture and thereby make someone even more resistant). However, the model can still be used; it simply means that the program may need to start by using educational methods which are more familiar to participants and then gradually move to more experiential methods.

Another potential problem involves the issue of how much skill training can actually be done in, say, a half-day orientation. The answer is obvious—not much. However, if the basic approach used is consistent with this model, participants will still be "moved" more toward a "learning how to learn" orientation rather than developing a dependency on expert knowledge. However small that movement is, it is better than no movement at all.

A third problem is the apparent and misleading simplicity of many cross-cultural skills. People often look at them and think that everyone already does those things—people listen, they find taxis, they ask questions, and so on. Although it is true that people do have these skills, nevertheless, when they are applied in cross-cultural settings, the rules change just enough in many cases to diminish people's effectiveness. Moreover, some people do not use some of these skills at all or do not use them effectively within their own culture.

Finally, some skills are really very complex. For example, developing knowledge about a country is really an epistemological undertaking rather than a skill. This is difficult to teach, and it is a difficult activity for participants to examine and undertake in an explicit manner. In these circumstances, people may look for excuses not to do it, or they may do it only at a subconscious level, or they may genuinely think it is "too simple." This means that cross-cultural skill training is much more difficult to do than is commonly envisioned, and it takes more effort to rationalize, to show benefits, and to forge links from one activity to the next.

The final problem to be discussed is related to the issue of complexity. To learn and apply this model takes a greater amount of experience, educational competence, and effort than is generally present in the field. It takes seeing cross-cultural training and orientation as a discipline that, in fact, must be learned and practiced rather than something which is done occasionally. This new seriousness about cross-cultural training as a discipline, however, does not alter the fact that the focus must change from content expertise to process expertise.

REFERENCES

Barna, LaRay M. (1982). "Stumbling blocks in intercultural communication." In Larry A. Samovar and Richard E. Porter (Eds.), *Intercultural communication: A reader.* Belmont, CA: Wadsworth.

Bennett, Janet M. (1977). "Transitional shock: Putting culture shock in perspective." In N. C. Jain (Ed.), *International and Intercultural Communication Annual* 4: 45-52.

Brislin, Richard, Dan Landis, and Mary Ellen Brandt (1983). "Conceptualization of intercultural behavior and training." In Dan Landis and Richard Brislin (Eds.), *Handbook of intercultural training* 1. Elmsford, NY: Pergamon.

Church, Austin (1982). "Sojourner adjustment." *Psychological Bulletin* 91: 540-72.

Gudykunst, William B., and Mitchell R. Hammer (1983). "Basic training design: Approaches to intercultural training." In Dan Landis and Richard Brislin (Eds.), *Handbook of intercultural training* 1. Elmsford, NY: Pergamon.

_____ (1984). "Dimensions of intercultural effectiveness: Culture specific or culture general?" *International Journal of Intercultural Relations* 8: 1-10.

Harris, Philip R., and Robert T. Moran (1987). *Managing cultural differences* (2d ed.). Houston: Gulf.

Kealey, Dan J., and Brent D. Ruben (1983). "Cross-cultural personnel selection: Criteria, issues, and methods." In Dan Landis and Richard Brislin (Eds.), *Handbook of intercultural training* 1. Elmsford, NY: Pergamon.

Kolb, David A. (1974). "On management and the learning process." In David A. Kolb, I. M. Rubin, and J. M. McIntyre (Eds.), *Organizational psychology: A book of readings* (2d ed.). Englewood Cliffs, NJ: Prentice-Hall.

McCaffery, James A., and D. Edwards (1978). *A model for pretraining and assessment of Peace Corps volunteers.* Washington, DC: U.S. Peace Corps, Center for Assessment and Training.

_____ (1981). *Cross-cultural training for Peace Corps volunteers.* Core Curriculum Resource Manual Series. Washington, DC: U.S. Peace Corps.

McCaffery, James A., D. Edwards, and E. Salt (1981). *The role of the volunteer in development.* Core Curriculum Resource Manual Series. Washington, DC: U.S. Peace Corps.

Paige, R. Michael, and Judith N. Martin (1983). "Ethical issues and ethics in cross-cultural training." In Dan Landis and Richard Brislin (Eds.), *Handbook of intercultural training* 1. Elmsford, NY: Pergamon.

Ruben, Brent D. (1977). "Human communication and cross-cultural effectiveness." In N. C. Jain (Ed.), *International and Intercultural Communication Annual* 4: 95-105.

9

The Missing Linkage: The Process of Integrating Orientation and Reentry

Bruce La Brack

ORIENTATION

Human beings have been wandering around the globe and going back home again for millennia. Until recently their preparation for either leaving or returning was usually anecdotal, based on stereotypes, factually incorrect, or notable by its absence. As a consequence, intercultural encounters involving people from different backgrounds have historically been too often marked by mutual suspicion or varying degrees of hostility and misunderstanding. The resulting ethnocentric attitudes and perceptions did little to advance cultural understanding, encourage respect for difference, or prepare people to interact productively with others whose lifestyles were significantly at variance with their own. At least it could be argued that until modern times most people lived in relatively constricted social worlds and could afford the luxury of prejudice and ignorance. Today such complacency in the presence of cultural difference can neither be justified nor tolerated. One antidote to insular thinking which has proven remarkably effective is study abroad. Moreover, it is important for those involved in promoting study abroad to realize just how much more effective and relevant the overseas experience can be made by providing participants a well-designed orientation prior to immersion. Further, it will be argued here that upon their return these same students should be offered an equally thoughtful and structured setting within which they can analyze both their foreign experience and the impact of reentry into their own society.

We have only recently emerged from a period which future practitioners will undoubtedly look back upon as the Dark Ages of training, marked by ethnocentric and Eurocentric assumptions. This bleak period, before orientations were taken seriously, would seem to be behind us. Truly massive efforts have been made since World War II to gather data and generate orientation techniques which make predeparture intercultural training relevant, effective, pragmatic, and interesting. Further, research continues to both substantiate the value of such training and improve the process in at least two ways. First, it has been proven that properly designed and conducted orientation programs do assist participants to achieve positive intercultural adjustments as well as to attain personal goals (which in turn reflects well upon the sponsoring agency). Second, research itself has played a key role in generating theory and evaluating training techniques (see chapters by Grove and Torbiörn and by Martin, this volume). Although the application of these research findings seems to be lagging behind their publication, it should no longer be continually necessary to justify either the value of cross-cultural training programs or the need for them.

There is a relatively substantial body of literature on the subject of orientation, and there are many examples of programs which have worked for both general and highly specialized target populations. In spite of all this, and while acknowledging that conditions and support of intercultural training have seldom seemed better, there remain some fundamental, underlying assumptions regarding orientation that are impeding what seems to me to be the next logical and necessary step, i.e., linking predeparture orientation and training with postexperience analysis and integration.

What follows is an account of a specific undergraduate program as it developed within the University of the Pacific (UOP) over a sixteen-year period. Specifically, we will show how it evolved from a voluntary, single-country, noncredit, orientation-only course for one college in the university into a multicourse-linked set of variable-credit orientation and reentry offerings serving the entire university community, including foreign students. In recounting the genesis of specific programmatic aspects of what we call the Cross-Cultural Orientation and Analysis of Overseas Experience courses, the original rationales and techniques used to encourage students to view their time abroad as an ongoing process of change and growth will be examined. Although designed for U.S. undergraduates, the theoretical basis and overall structure which links orientation and reentry may be easily generalized for application in a variety of contexts.

The key term above is "process," which will be discussed shortly. First we must consider why offering predeparture orientation alone, even though it is important and necessary, is insufficient if we wish to develop a holistic understanding of what study abroad is about and to provide our students with an integrated intercultural experience.

Failure of Orientation in Isolation

Among study-abroad professionals, there is a fundamental failure to provide a linkage between orientation and reentry. The majority of orientation programs are currently conducted as though they existed in a vacuum, separate from the rest of participants' lives, be they students in the midst of their academic careers or businesspeople on the way to overseas assignments. For students, the year abroad is seen, probably unconsciously, as a stage of development, an activity which has a life span of its own, beginning when the individual enters the foreign milieu and ending with the return home. Understandably, advisors and inter- cultural trainers are concerned with promoting a successful time over- seas and therefore work hard to prepare the students for the impending immersion into a new social setting. For their part, few students possess an accurate view of what to expect, although many believe they do. Our students often have some prior exposure to travel abroad and arrive at orientation with what we see as a superficial sophistication about things cross-cultural. Further, they are eager to get on with the trip, often treating orientation as an imposition or, at best, a preview of coming attractions. Both perspectives miss what I feel is the main point not only of the imminent intercultural experience, but of the entire educational process that they (students and faculty alike) are involved in.

Orientation should ideally be part of a much larger undertaking which involves inculcating values and transmitting knowledge. More importantly, it should be constructed so as to encourage students to think laterally, synthesize, and make educated, intuitive leaps of imagination which serve to draw together and integrate diverse types of experience.

To conduct orientation as though the process it is part of will end when they have a good year abroad and return home is no longer adequate. To do so is to miss a major opportunity to advance the students' understanding of themselves and their personal experiences by placing them intellectually into a much larger philosophical and academic framework.

Another problem lies in the home-culture-as-familiar/foreign-culture-as-new-and-exciting dichotomy. Going to a new environment needs preparation; returning home is simply returning to the familiar. Yet, the fact is that a growing body of research on the subject of reentry and readjustment upon returning home suggests that the problems encountered in returning can be as substantial and disorienting as the culture shock experienced in leaving. The reverse culture-shock data clearly show that for some, home can be—at least for a while—as different and strange as another country (Martin, this volume).

Culture Learning vs. Tourism

The current situation did not arise out of design. It is a modern-day survival of earlier attitudes toward the purpose, meaning, and goals of foreign travel. It reflects, at least at a psychological level, a fundamental sojourner pattern which dates back to post-Renaissance Western Europe and is typified by the walking tour or Grand Tour. The Grand Tour arose as a pleasurable finale to a liberal education of British gentlemen and had little to do with cross-cultural contact and much to do with social credentialization. Unfortunately, many of our overseas programs still appear to be imprisoned by this mindset.

There are four major and important differences between a traditional walking tour of the Continent by nineteenth-century British upper-class undergraduates and contemporary American study-abroad programs and participants. First, the sojourn came at the end of British students' education, not in the middle. Second, no predeparture preparation whatsoever was given the British students, as their neoclassical education (including Greek and Latin) was considered completely adequate. Third, seldom was any genuine effort made by the British student to participate in the local culture, whereas there is strong pressure on the modern study-abroad student to adapt to and participate in the life of the host country. Fourth, the continental tour was intended as a capstone to a liberal education and represented a conclusion. After the tour was over, the student expected to enter adult public life and settle down.[1]

This scenario is in vivid contrast to the one that has been played out by typical returning American undergraduates who, as a result of their experience, may change majors, departments, and friends. At the very least, they have a period of from one semester to two years on campus to attempt to put their time abroad into a larger educational context. Where the overseas experience for the British generally marked an end of cross-cultural interaction (barring colonial service or commercial interest abroad), for contemporary American students, one hopes, it marks only a beginning of interest in and knowledge about international affairs.

Centrality of "Process"

What we greatly need today is to construct bridges between the orientation and reentry experiences, between the pre- and postsojourn ruminations, which use the actual overseas experience as a behavioral/social text to be deciphered, analyzed, and finally melded with the student's ongoing academic pursuits and personal development. The entire notion of orientation as a one-time, rather static set of prescriptions, simulations, and do-don't lists needs to be revised, using the more dynamic and inclusive idea of orientation and reentry as twin reflections of the intercultural process.

Those of us who teach these courses conceive of "process" in a number of ways. First, it is a flow of experience which, although divisible intellectually, is actually a continuum of experiential learning that needs to be understood in its entirety, though particularly at points or stages of transition. Second, the process includes fostering personal growth and self-understanding as a part of the students' academic training. Finally, process is understood to include the interaction between the student's role as learner/informant and the faculty/trainer's role as facilitator. In other words, a reentry course should both guide and reflect. It should present students with alternative adaptive strategies while at the same time promoting an open-ended exploration of current roles in society. It should promote examination of past reactions to culture contact and change. This is surprisingly easy to do if built into a linked orientation/reentry program, because the concepts and exercises which turn out to be extremely useful in orientation as preparation for going abroad are the same ones which can assist in smoothing the return. As will be seen, the preparation for reentry can and should begin during orientation, where the groundwork can be laid for integrating the students' intercultural learning upon their return. Before-leaving exercises, which are in some degree created by the students themselves, are highly individualized and relevant and retain their saliency regardless of when the student returns.

Historical Origins of the UOP Program

In 1975 the author arrived at Callison College of the University of the Pacific to act as the resident anthropologist, teaching cultural anthropology classes and preparing students to participate in the college's ongoing overseas programs. Although not specifically designated to be a training ground for Asian specialists, Callison had, since its inception in 1965, been one of three internationally oriented "cluster colleges" within the university: Raymond College stressed Euro-American studies, Covell was a bilingual unit concentrating on Latin America, while Callison focused upon non-Western/Asian studies. From the beginning the Callison faculty felt that a year of participant observation in an Asian atmosphere would facilitate cross-cultural learning, increase global awareness, and provide opportunity for intercultural exchange. In order to allow maximum time to reflect upon the experience and to encourage spontaneity and openness, it was decided that the entire sophomore class would go as a unit to Asia. The original destination was India (1965-1974), later shifting to Japan (1974-1980).

The freshman year became, in a literal sense, a continuous preparation for a mass exit the following fall. The sense of community and common destiny which arose among classes each year was remarkable. As the sophomore class went abroad, the junior class returned (as many as seventy per class) and served as resources of information and role models for the freshmen preparing to go. The discontinuity of having one entire class year abroad was balanced by the camaraderie which would eventually bind the freshmen, the veteran juniors, and the worldly seniors.

All students were required to participate in an orientation for the year abroad and to pass a standard course in cultural anthropology. The anthropology requirement allowed the person conducting the orientation to assume that the entire class would have been exposed to a basic sociocultural conceptual framework. Since everyone was going to the same destination, the orientation tended to be culture-specific. It met for less than eight hours (sometimes for as little as two three-hour sessions), though two years later it was upgraded to a required twenty-one-hour, two-unit credit course.

As the freshmen who had just gone through orientation entered their overseas year, the juniors came home. Almost immediately there was a succession of students with serious looks on their faces coming in "to talk about their experiences." It became evident that despite all the planning and preparation in orientation, the reintegration of returning students was going to be neither automatic nor free of tension. What I came face-to-face with were varying degrees of reentry shock, something I myself had experienced when I returned to the United States from India in 1970. Unfortunately, I was not familiar with either the theoretical underpinnings or the behavioral dynamics of reentry, and the research literature available in 1976 was not much help. Within one year, the student interest and demand were strong enough to begin bringing returnees together informally, meetings which evolved quickly into a permanent course on reentry.

Like orientation, the reentry course was at first an informal, non-credit, voluntary seminar, but within two years was upgraded to a two-unit credit course. By 1977, the sequence for every class was set, every member was required to take orientation, cultural anthropology (which only I taught at that time), and the reentry seminar. Thus, I had a built-in population with which I would have recurrent contact over at least three years. Although this fortuitous circumstance was initially unplanned, it is clear in retrospect that the twin factors of recurrent contact over a long period (pre- and postexperience) and the intense, year-long student experience abroad combined to provide a nearly perfect laboratory within which to experiment with training techniques, linkages between phases, and the application of theory to practice. It was during this early period that I decided to begin a longitudinal study of the effects of overseas living and study. Simultaneously, I decided to make a concerted effort to link the two components, orientation and reentry, and to use the experience abroad as the raw data for students to research and study such topics as paralinguistics, language acquisition, identity formation, culture shock (and reentry shock), and an analysis of their own reactions and value shifts.

In the curriculum design, I had to begin to think of orientation and reentry as one package, not separate entities tacked on at the beginning and end. What was dealt with in orientation would undoubtedly come up again in reentry. The important difference is that what was abstract theory in orientation would have been transformed by the overseas stay into direct (and even painful) experience in reentry. For example, there would be continued interest by students in exploring and defining "Who am I?" During the orientation these questions were being asked by freshmen who were often confused, anxious, and naive. Their ideas about "the other" were often stereotypical, while their awareness of their own "Americanness" ranged from nonexistent to active denial. In reentry, the

"Who am I?" was pursued by junior-year returnees who had become much more reflective, even introspective, self-reliant, and questioning about what it had meant to be an "American"—or more specifically what it meant to be a Nisei from Hawaii studying in Taiwan, a Catholic living in a Buddhist/Shinto community in Hokkaido, a woman in a male-dominated Iberian homestay, or an American among South Asians.

In other words, questions about identity were a constant; what changed after the experience abroad was the sophistication and complexity of the elements which were going into the equation. This was paralleled by increased linguistic competency and sensitivity to nuance, understanding and appreciation of the arts, awareness of mutual cultural boundaries, recognition of value conflicts and ethical dilemmas, ability to "read" proxemic/kinesic gestures, and a myriad of additional insights which form the substance of intercultural knowledge. All of these topics are normally dealt with in orientation, but arise again in much more powerful and informed incarnations upon a student's return. The questions are: what do these changes represent; how can trainers maximize their positive, long-term effects; and how can reentry contribute to orientation (and, of course, orientation to reentry)?

Developmental Theory and Training

That students often undergo significant changes while abroad comes as no surprise to anyone familiar with the types of transformations which may occur as a result of intercultural experience, even if the students themselves may not recognize the extent of such changes until weeks or months after return. Until recently, there have been few comprehensive conceptual frameworks which have accurately described these states and their characteristic behavior and psychology. For years the success of programs was often measured by the number of participants. The success for students seems to have been based on an "enjoyment quotient." Teachers looked for some evidence that the student had attained a "more international" attitude. There was little serious examination of how he or she arrived at a particular point and even less of where they may have started from, developmentally speaking.

Although a variety of developmental theories are currently being applied to intercultural learning stages, one in particular has had an influence on our program design and is noted here both as a powerful theoretical tool for evaluation of student attitudes and as an influence upon curricular design. While first reading Milton J. Bennett's chapter

"Towards Ethnorelativism: A Developmental Model of Intercultural Sensitivity" (this volume), I was struck by how closely the description of the seven ethnocentric stages (organized under "denial, defense, and minimization") paralleled typical student responses in cross-cultural orientation, while the six ethnorelative stages (organized under "acceptance, adaptation, and integration") were frequently echoed in the responses of students in the reentry classes. Building on the work of William Perry in the areas of intellectual and ethical growth, Bennett has applied a developmental schema to the intercultural arena in ways that clarify how a person "thinks about the world" and "the other" at various stages. But it is more than a classificatory system because it recognizes that the process itself is dynamic and people can move forward toward relativistic thinking or revert to ethnocentric postures. Which direction a person moves toward is influenced by a large number of internal and external factors, but the important point is that by understanding a person's current attitudes toward intercultural interaction a trainer can assist individuals to reflect upon their presuppositions, attitudes, and behaviors. If indicated, the trainer can suggest alternatives for consideration which are likely to prove more practical and personally satisfying. Critically, this model implicitly acknowledges that the entire process is an ongoing one which has potential applications over a lifetime.

By not theoretically limiting growth potential to a period of orientation or focusing excessively on the actual overseas experience, the model provides points of evaluation and encourages the possibility of enhancing one's understanding as part of a reentry process. In other words, it can be applied at any point in the intercultural process as both a diagnostic tool and a point of departure for program design. By serendipity, the UOP model of linking orientation and reentry evolved over the years into a channel through which individuals could experience many of these cognitive transformations; however, the path could have been shorter and the results somewhat more quantifiable had such a developmental model been available in 1975. Developmental models are now available, and these theoretical orientations can be directly and immediately incorporated into training designs and used to anticipate student reactions, overcome resistance, and prepare a range of appropriate exercises according to the stage the audience has reached. Any model based on categories must be used with care lest it be applied too rigidly. Nevertheless, they are useful conceptual and diagnostic tools. This is one wheel we can stop reinventing; now we can concentrate on refining and applying it to training programs.

Of course, it is not always clear which techniques will be most effective in assisting specific individuals to achieve higher stages. How to translate developmental theory into practical applications is the job of the training designer. Further, intercultural sensitivity and competence have been achieved by individuals for centuries *without* the benefit of formal education or training programs; yet, even in such self-enlightened cases these people often report that a great deal of their understanding about their own culture as well as any contrast cultures came *after* the fact, that is, postexperience—and without the benefit of prior orientation. It is clear that although relativistic thinking can be derived from experience alone, it can be more effectively and predictably fostered within intercultural programs, particularly if it is consciously built in to linked orientation and reentry exercises. From the data I began compiling in 1977 on our returning study-abroad students, the striking and inescapable conclusion was that the overseas experience, preceded by orientation, was only the beginning of an ongoing learning process. In recognition of this fact we have since 1988 retitled the orientation and reentry courses. They are now Cross-Cultural Training I and Cross-Cultural Training II, symbolizing our belief that they are two halves of a single process. For the sake of clarity, in this account we continue to differentiate them by using their earlier titles, Orientation and Reentry.

Left to their own resources and devices, the majority of students are perfectly able to reintegrate themselves upon return to school in some functional manner. Most of them probably perform the necessary academic tasks and conduct their personal lives adequately without a reentry seminar. A few of the most highly motivated and thoughtful are certainly able to combine their experiences with current course work in genuine, creative ways. But most, I suspect, don't do so efficiently in isolation and in the absence of any applicable frame of reference. This point is crucial. Rather than deal directly with temporary problems related to homecoming and seek ways to integrate their academic and overseas experiences, many, if not most, I'm sure, simply compartmentalize the year abroad. In this "shoebox effect" the time abroad is mentally put away to be taken out and examined occasionally. I felt it important to prevent that. I also wanted to prevent the development of a "what I did in my year/semester overseas" syndrome. What is for many students the most personal and intense experience of their lives can devolve into a kind of exotic vacation or, worse, a nostalgic topic for cocktail party conversation. One manifestation of student awareness of these mindsets is the fear many students express over the possibility that they might "lose" the experience because they either are having trouble fitting it into subsequent academic and personal contexts or fail to see the relevance of experiential learning to textbook theories. Therefore, another clear function for a reentry program should be to expand the students' understanding of their international experience and to show them how to connect it with both their ongoing coursework and their personal lives. In short, orientation, the overseas experience, and reentry should be developmentally linked. To this end, we have found that the deliberate and systematic coupling of orientation and reentry is not only logical but enormously productive.

Linking Orientation and Reentry—the Program to 1985

The most direct and productive way we found to link orientation and reentry was to arrange the presentation of topical areas in both courses in such a manner that the same general subject matter was dealt with twice. Of course, in Orientation such materials were given at an introductory level and, more often than not, were presented in a lecture format with stages, definitions, or critical incidents dominating over more experiential modes. It is necessary in initial meetings to present the material in this more cognitive, abstract manner as "concepts" because there is rarely an experiential base to refer to. By the time the students reach the reentry course these same topics, which were once largely conceptual, are now quite real. The returnees have lots of experience to process and feelings to explore. Since both courses run roughly the same length of time (seven weeks/one three-hour meeting per week), it is possible to devote roughly equal time to a particular topic, once as "theory" in Orientation and again as "personal experience" in Reentry. For example, take the concept of culture shock.

Culture Shock/Orientation

Just as you can't really describe the taste of a hot fudge sundae to someone who has never experienced one, it is difficult to actually convey just how disorienting entering another culture can be to a student without any cross-cultural experience. What you can do is place culture shock in the much larger referent of cultural adjustment and change. This can be approached in a number of ways. The culture-shock session at our university begins with a lecture giving the definition of culture shock, listing causes, noting the range of possible reactions, discussing how to recognize them, and offering ways to minimize stress. The students then view a half-hour film from the Going International series[2] which looks at culture shock as experienced by businesspeople and their families. In addition, the students are assigned two articles on the subject to be *studied*, not just read.

Prior to this session the students have been asked to prepare a short (four-page) paper on either "Problems I anticipate abroad and what I can do to prepare myself to meet them" or "What I will miss most about America and what I am most looking forward to about being overseas." During the session in which these papers are handed in, a rough tabulation and item analysis is done on them and then common elements or themes put on a blackboard and discussed. In addition to building rapport, this exercise helps lower apprehension for the individual student who may have been feeling alone in his or her concerns. It also gives the instructor data to refer back to later when the culture-shock issue comes up for discussion.

Another source of data for the culture-shock session—as well as serving to help the students become aware of their unconscious patterns in daily life—is a log each student is asked to keep of a typical day in his or her life. They are expected to record in minute detail everything that happened (when, where, what time, with whom, in what, etc.) from waking up to going to sleep. This log does not need to be handed in, but is kept by the students for their own reference. The list of things they did is discussed in some detail, however, to show how maintaining that same routine might be difficult, culturally unacceptable, or simply impossible in another country. For example, the person who started the day off with no breakfast and a twenty-minute shower which "they couldn't wake up without" might be informed that if Japan is his or her destination, this will cause problems on a number of fronts. First, there may well be no shower; and, in any event, most families take their bath (*ofuro*) in the evening before retiring (often in a predetermined order of family members), and the water is usually heated then for bathing only. Furthermore, while you might skip breakfast in the U.S. out of habit or laziness, it is likely that the wife of your homestay family will be up before everyone else preparing breakfast for the entire family (now including you) because it may be the only meal which the family regularly eats together. There are further concerns about nutrition and the energy needed for a typically long commute or to perform well in school. To not eat, or at least not sit with the family at breakfast, may be a serious breach of etiquette. As such examples are multiplied, the students begin to see how their normal routines are culturally specific and idiosyncratic constructs which may conflict with the normal routines of their French, Japanese, Brazilian, German, etc., hosts.

All of this leads naturally into the discussion of culture shock and is brought up again when we raise the question of what happens when cultural difference and behavioral ambiguity replace habit and certainty. This includes how people felt when they participated in the cultural simulation classic, *Bafá Bafá*[3] (again, played two weeks before discussing culture shock). The combination of lecture, videotape, personal activity log, the list of fears and goals, and cultural simulation activities eventually gives substance and reality to the abstract idea of culture shock.

Giving these kinds of concrete and easily understandable cross-cultural contrasts in behavior and values creates a matrix in which students can place themselves, encouraging them to gauge for themselves how well they are prepared to enter a new cultural environment. More important, they can use their reactions as a reflection of the degree to which they are really ready to confront that new experience. It can motivate them to take seriously the training we offer, including culture-specific tips on ways they can further prepare themselves for study and living abroad. Of course, at this juncture it is primarily an intellectual exercise in empathy, sensitivity, data acquisition, and anticipation.

Reverse Culture Shock/Reentry

Reentry is another matter altogether. Reentry shock or reverse culture shock occurs, but the problem is that the return home is usually characterized by two unique elements: (1) an idealized view of "home" and (2) a taken-for-granted familiarity with the home culture which fosters the illusion that neither home nor the sojourner will have changed since she/he went away. This combination of mistaken attitudes frequently results in frustrated expectations, various degrees of alienation, and mutual misunderstanding between returnees and their friends and family. In this context, both initial culture shock and return culture shock can be discussed and compared in some depth and at great length. It is fascinating how materials gathered six to twelve months earlier during orientation can be used to get at not only the causes and results of overseas adjustment difficulties but to illuminate sources of ongoing readjustment problems upon the return home. The lists of problems they might encounter, which they drew up and discussed academically during orientation, can be compared to the *real* sources of frustration and conflict while overseas. Similarly, the daily logs of life at home which they are asked to keep can be compared to the reality of an actual overseas routine, discussing in detail the salient cultural similarities and differences. It is sometimes uncomfortable or even embarrassing for some students to realize just how naive or unrealistic some of their preconceptions were, and how baseless some of their fears. Nevertheless, such exercises usually lead to revelations about serious problems they experienced abroad in areas they had not foreseen (i.e., male/female relationships or concepts of friendship overseas). By using their own orientation papers (which were copied and kept by the instructor for Reentry), they can truly compare their postexperience self to what some have called their "former existence." Doing so in a supportive atmosphere with others who have their own failures and triumphs to report is an important step in dealing with any unresolved conflicts about the overseas experience as well as coping with current adjustments. In this way the relationship of before and after is made much more explicit.

Additionally, it creates what can be considered baseline data of a most personal kind. Eventually the students are able to place their highly idiosyncratic sojourns into larger analytical frameworks which incorporate the feelings and experiences of others. For the minority who experience particular difficulties in reentry, it gives solace that this too is another stage of development or a phase that will pass. This stance neither caters to a victim mentality nor discounts the validity of their condition. They can be shown through their own experiences that struggle is part of the process of growth, of an adjustment to life. As one student noted, "There is life after a year abroad, it's just different." By emphasizing the linkage between their orientation attitudes and their more sophisticated and realistic postexperience worldview, even those with doubts about how well they performed abroad can see real personal progress and take an honest pride in their new knowledge, skills, and understanding. Without the "before and after" comparative material, it would be much more difficult to construct the necessary timeframe and invoke the prior mindset, which allows the student to view the overseas experience as a continuum of events and an accumulation of ideas and behaviors. It makes being in the midst of a readjustment much more bearable as well as academically productive. It gets to the heart of the matter quickly, does it on an individual, specific basis, yet allows for the discussion of sophisticated and complex issues and concepts about the nature of culture, the results of international experience, alterations of value systems, and a host of related issues.

Topics of culture shock and reentry adjustment are thus psychologically, theoretically, and pragmatically interrelated through an examination of the students' own earlier work, an analysis of present feelings and
behaviors, and a discussion of relevant conceptual research on these topics.
We feel this reflects the reality and holism of the situation and creates the
continuity necessary to discuss cultural adjustment objectively while not
losing sight of the unique elements of every individual student's experience. Best of all, students told us it worked on all these levels.

Identity and Stereotyping

Another example of linkage between orientation and reentry is in the
area of identity and stereotyping. During Orientation we discuss how
human beings form their basic sense of self through enculturation to a set
of values which are historically derived and expressed in all aspects of
the culture, particularly language. As part of this section the students are
asked to list ten major values which they feel typify Americans and then
to rate to what extent those values apply to themselves. The major ones
are then listed on the blackboard and discussed in terms of ethnic
variability, regional differences, socioeconomic class, educational levels,
etc. This discussion is aided by reading assignments and handouts on
American values which range from turn-of-the-century compilations
through the 1920s and into the 1950s. They are also encouraged to use
Stewart and Bennett's *American Cultural Patterns* as a resource.[4] In this
way, concepts about both the persistence of core values and accommo-
dation to change are investigated. The aim is to show how, regardless of
the individualism stressed by so many, all humans are deeply and permanently influenced and molded by their childhood milieu. Simultaneously,
it illustrates how simplistic and reductionistic most stereotypes really are.
There is always someone in the class who resists being labeled an American,
but who is quite willing to ascribe uninformed stereotypes to others.

In Reentry this theme is raised again, only this time students are
asked to provide examples of stereotypes of the people with whom they
had lived and studied overseas. While they readily acknowledge the
existence of such stereotypes and can discuss their content, they are
much more personally reluctant to make facile judgments of people they
now know firsthand. "You cannot make that kind of statement about
everyone" is a typical stance. They are also asked once again to provide
a composite picture of the typical American. It is interesting that generally the American portrayal comes off much less idealistic and positive

than profiles done in Orientation, in part because of the behavior of Americans they witnessed while abroad. These types of discussions lead to clearer perceptions about the negative nature of most stereotypes, particularly about people one does not actually know or interact with.

A curious twist on stereotypes sometimes arises in Reentry. I call them "acculturation stereotypes," which refer to secondary attitudes and conceptions students pick up as part of identifying and interacting with their host culture. Examples include both anti-Arab and anti-Jewish sentiments from non-Jewish American students returning from studying in Israel, anti-English sentiments from American students returning from the Republic of Ireland, anti-Turk sentiments from study in Germany, anti-Algerian and Muslim sentiments from France, etc. In all such cases the students appear to have derived these attitudes as a kind of secondhand culture learning, picking them up from the social sentiments expressed among their overseas contacts rather than developing them as a result of actual interaction with the rejected culture group. This only proves that one can learn some negative things while abroad. When these surface in the reentry class, they can be discussed as another kind of stereotyping—which confirms two points related to reentry: first, without a reentry program you wouldn't know that your students have arrived home with some unintended and potentially unproductive attitudes; second, knowing that these secondary stereotypes can occur enables you to begin dealing with the possibility of orientation as part of the general discussion of stereotyping.

Further, students are asked to provide examples of how they were stereotyped by others while abroad, what the content and expectations of these images were, and how they felt about being lumped into some, usually negative, archetypical cultural category. Of course, everyone hated it. It is interesting to hear returnees' reactions to being stereotyped and categorized as "one of those Americans," particularly because so many of them were resistant in the orientation to the idea that Americans shared a coherent and deeply embedded set of assumptions and values. Although they still resist being labeled in stereotypical ways by others, they are much more willing to concede that the idea that certain behaviors and values manifested by Americans are cultural rather than individual has more than a grain of truth in it. Even those who had initially seen themselves in Orientation as rugged individualists realized in Reentry that they did take a full load of American cultural baggage abroad with them. Yet, in almost inverse proportion to the extent of their efforts to fit in and be sensitive to local customs, they resented being stigmatized as Americans. Being stereotyped abroad was a new and unpleasant experience. To reduce it, some would avoid tourist areas, even pretending not to understand English so as not to be identified as an "ugly American." Some even claimed on rare occasions to be Canadian or British to avoid unpleasant confrontations over political or social issues with locals they did not know.

I have written elsewhere about another, related phenomenon I identify as "dual ethnocentrism,"[5] which often characterizes the immediate postexperience period. The major manifestation of this is the willingness of the students to rise to the defense of their "adopted" culture and the behavior of its people (because they now really want to empathize with and understand it at a much deeper level) along with a countertendency to lump Americans more readily into categories than before they left, including making more negative judgments about them. This diminishes over time as they feel less threatened or as the need to justify why they went to Poland, or Nepal, or Japan is reduced. In any case, the linking of predeparture images they previously held with the more real experiences gained by actual residence in the country is a useful tool to reduce their reliance on gross cultural generalizations or characterizations encompassing entire national personalities. There may be composite national personality and culture profiles which are valid, but such academic abstractions are a far cry from the more subjective and uninformed blanket assertions which one hears from ethnocentrics. The students become significantly less willing to accept such stereotyping from others and much more reluctant to engage in it themselves, while still recognizing that "American" can constitute a valid, generalizable category. Without the linkage it would be considerably more difficult to compare the before and after. As it is, some students try to minimize their earlier views by laughingly noting, "What did I know?" Indeed, that is the point!

Almost all our students readily admit they sometimes now feel "more American" than they ever did before the overseas sojourn, although not in a jingoistic or ultranationalist sense. They report simply realizing the extent to which their ideas, values, and emotional reactions were preconditioned by being raised in a specific nation (class, religion, etc.) with English as their primary language. Culture is eventually recognized neither as a prison nor a form of behavioral predestination, but as an underlying guide to morals and behavior which is subject to modification. Culture is then used as a concept in Reentry to extend discussions on what "American" really means and how to compare and contrast other societies and cultural varieties in a nonjudgmental way. Culture has become much more real and tangible, less of a straitjacket and more of a useful, definable heritage.

There are other similar and related linkages between orientation and reentry, such as the role of language and paralinguistics in culture learning and communication, the importance of knowing the history and general background of the chosen country (particularly politics, religion, and economics), the multiple roles of the student overseas (foreigner, student, American, homestay/family member), value shifts and substitutions, dealing with different academic systems and teaching styles, and how to be a well-informed informant. Each of these is discussed in Orientation in such a way that they can be taken up again in Reentry and reviewed in the light of actual observation and interaction. It is a most fruitful joining of the theory of orientation with actual overseas experience and the current concerns during readjustment back home.

In addition to the exercises and discussions, each member of the reentry class must write a twenty-page (minimum) paper analyzing his or her own reentry. Over fifteen years we have gathered over four hundred of these papers, and they represent an invaluable source of information on shifting attitudes, ranges of experience, and personal reactions to study abroad by young college students. As one might imagine, the resistance to this particular requirement is terrific, but once finished the students are honestly grateful that they were made to reflect at length. Further, they now have another very personal benchmark which documents this stage of their intercultural development. Students have written back to us years later requesting copies because they had lost theirs, and it was a valuable record for them. Of course, where we have their permission to do so, we can use excerpts as appropriate in the orientation. These written records provide a permanent, archival record of our students' experiences and tell us what has and has not worked along the way of the entire process from orientation through reentry.

Early Attempts to Utilize Foreign Students

Once the orientation and reentry class patterns were established we sought ways to add a foreign flavor to these gatherings. Initially we turned, as many programs do, to international students on our campus. We were aware of the potential dangers of free-form intercultural discussion without adequate preparation and safeguards. Therefore, the first international student participants we approached were well known to the instructors and were selected for being outspoken, articulate, and friendly (although not uncritical of things American). They were briefed on the goals of the exercises and a range of likely responses from the American students. To be honest, they were often primed as devil's advocates, particularly when we felt they could carry it off with grace and good humor. We stressed that their responses should be their own and reflect their personal cultural backgrounds. They were encouraged to discuss honestly their perceptions and conflicts with what they saw as the "American Way."

There are several techniques which proved useful in provoking American student response in the orientation, some of which used American returnees and international students together, while others employed only the international students. One example of the latter type involved a panel of four to six international students for about an hour of discussion during the American values session. First, we set the scene for the interaction through a half-hour of exploration of "What is American about American culture." Because the international students were chosen for their outspokenness and ability to articulate their ideas, their characterizations often did not agree with the self-perceptions of the class. However, the class was not allowed to interrupt or challenge at this stage. After the international students and American returnees had finished (around five minutes apiece), they were then asked to tell what American practice, belief, or custom had been most strange to them when they first arrived and how they viewed it now after more experience in the U.S. This exercise was often quite enlightening to the Americans, who usually found it difficult to understand the framework from which a Saudi Arabian, for instance, evaluates American family life, or how the Japanese view labor relations, or the nature of the Indonesian Muslim's concern for religion. When the international students were finished, they left the classroom for about fifteen minutes while the Americans discussed what they had just heard. The range was predictable. A few empathized, but most were at least mildly offended and felt that the foreigners really didn't understand the U.S., or if they did—and didn't like it—wondered why they came to the U.S. to study. One or two would suggest they could leave anytime. At this point the Americans were reminded that in a very short time they would be in exactly the same situation as these students. They would be foreigners themselves. Did they really feel they knew their prospective country any better? Did they have any fewer preconceptions? Were they not likely to misinterpret behavior? Of course, it was further pointed out that most of them probably did not speak any foreign language as well as these international students spoke English (many of them had had only a year or two of the language of the country they were going to, some none at all).[6]

The international students were then brought back in, and the Americans were invited to question them about their country, their perceptions of Americans, or anything else. The international students had been warned in advance that there might be some hostility, and most enjoyed engaging in a bit of mild provocation. More to the point, they often had much of value to say about what it meant to be an international student in America and what kinds of barriers and prejudices they may have faced. For several years this exercise was quite successful in opening up broad areas for discussion and making the American students more sharply aware of a number of issues, not the least of which was the whole complex process of being a stranger in a strange land. While we recognized the value of having foreign peers model some of the attitudes and behaviors the Americans would soon be facing abroad, we did not at this time use them as fully as we could have, certainly not to the extent we eventually found so synergistic and mutually beneficial.

Up to 1986, international students had been used only sporadically in the reentry seminar, but there had been some indication that it would be appropriate to use them at certain junctures in the course. For example, several weeks into the seminar we began discussing the students' individual experiences overseas, concentrating on what they had learned and how they had learned it. That is, they first discussed mistakes and cultural faux pas, then reconsidered under what circumstances they found it necessary or advantageous to change their ideas or behavior. I always ended the first hour or so of such discussions with a question: "Can you think of a situation, circumstance, or event which still puzzles you? Something which doesn't make sense in any cultural framework you are familiar with?" The students were usually able to recollect some unusual or downright strange event which happened to them, which they had witnessed, or which was related to them. Occasionally, I would invite some international students from the more popular study-abroad sites (France, Britain, Germany, and Japan among others) both to respond to the event which occurred in their country and to try to explain it to the American students. In some cases, a reasonable, culturally based explanation was possible. Where this was the case, we all learned from the example, and the message—that we needed to understand an alternative frame of reference—was reinforced. In others, the international students have been equally puzzled, considered the behavior rude, or attributed it to foreign influences on the society. In this case, a number of points which were equally true could be made: that variation within culture is great, that individual personality has to be taken into account, simply that the bizarre is not limited to any one cultural group. In turn, the international students could ask questions about the U.S. which still bothered them, and the Americans, now veterans themselves of overseas experience, could try to give answers or join the international students in attempting to figure them out.

This exercise led to interesting discussions of American and foreign cultural mores and customs without anyone getting defensive and with most marveling at the myriad ways human beings can respond to or interpret common events. Of course, it also allowed the various groups (French speakers, Japan-program veterans, returnees from Latin America, etc.) to reminisce about aspects of life abroad which they missed, as well as the difficulty of translating some phrases, ideas, or idiomatic expressions to outsiders. Each cultural interest group did likewise, creating a nice interchange, putting the students in a focused situation which was nonthreatening, and allowing a little indulgence in one-upmanship. The greater lessons were still there, however, to be revealed in the attempt to decipher singular, personal cultural happenings.

Although not intended as a therapy group, the reentry class does provide a supportive forum to explore common conflicts students may be having in the areas of family/friend relationships, attitudes toward schoolwork, general boredom with resumption of old roles and responsibilities, etc. Moreover, their evaluation of their own performance while abroad can be enhanced by giving them samples of how other travelers tried (and often failed), both in their endeavors abroad and in their own readjustment back home. This process can be furthered by providing materials for reading outside class in which anthropologists, sociologists, colonial officials, and travelers detail their own shortcomings and more humbling cross-cultural adventures.

For example, I have the students read Jean Briggs's autobiographical account of living with the Polar Eskimo, *Never in Anger*[7]. This text alone serves an important role in lowering students' negative self-evaluations, if they exist, by showing them that a trained and sensitive female graduate student conducting research for her Ph.D. made the same kind of cultural errors of judgment and experienced the same frustrations as the students. Briggs's book is a manual of common problems in living in another culture, including language difficulties, personality conflicts, tensions over diet and food sharing, violations of personal space, and the other trials and tribulations one experiences when trying to fit into a social setting one enters as if a child. She expresses all relevant emotions including anger, fear, loneliness, petulance, and frustration as well as the joy of discovery and the satisfaction of learning another cultural repertoire. Since none of the students is even vaguely familiar with the specific cultural setting, no one is able to raise the facade of pseudo-expert on the society. This allows them to empathize with Briggs and to see the parallels they share with her experience. It has never failed to trigger a flood of interesting and revealing anecdotes through which the class can relate common problems and even comical events in an atmosphere of mutual amusement or commiseration. At the end of the session in which Briggs is discussed, I sometimes distribute Laura Bohannon's delightful "Shakespeare in the Bush,"[8] her account of how the Tiv in Nigeria reinterpret "the Bard" to conform to local standards and beliefs.

Finally, the book *Survival Kit for Overseas Living*[9] formed the last link in this earlier version of the orientation/reentry pairing. In the first class of Orientation, Kohls's book was assigned and read throughout the course, chapter by chapter, in a sequence designed to fit with each week's topic. Since *Survival Kit* is a concise and relatively comprehensive overview of the sojourn to come, it has proven a popular handbook over the years, most students carrying it abroad with them where they report referring to it often. For the last session of reentry they are assigned to write a five-page critical analysis of *Survival Kit*, suggesting what they would add to it, how they might rearrange it, etc. In other words, they arrive at a point where the same book which seemed so wise and well-organized (and, of course, it is), a book from which they sought wisdom and ways to cope, becomes the subject of a dissection. They have gained the confidence, knowledge, and ability to critique the manual they had depended on, and feel confident doing so. Moreover, their suggestions are often sophisticated and reveal a good understanding of cross-cultural dynamics and the entire process of intercultural learning. It was gratifying to see them come so far in a two-year period. Perhaps best of all, the criticism is not based on some need to find fault with the text, but rather from their desire to share some of their hard-earned experience with others so their sojourns might contain fewer hassles and more rewards. Indeed, some of the ideas from these sessions have been incorporated in Orientation; for example, the suggestion that the session on paralinguistics and general body language be expanded. Interestingly, many students proposed adding a section on reentry to *Survival Kit* several years before Kohls did so in his second edition. At that stage of the program's evolution, the Kohls's exercise completed the feedback loop which began with the first anxious session of Orientation and ended with the celebratory last session of Reentry. Each reentry class has the potential to provide excellent, timely, culture-specific, student-focused data which can be almost instantly applied in both courses. Thus, every orientation course initiates a sequence which is brought to closure only when the same students return and suggest ideas for refining future orientation courses.

To reiterate our earlier ideas about process, the product of our cross-cultural training is in large part the quality of our students' experiences. We are not ultimately responsible for their success or failure, but we should be held accountable for preparing the best set of orientation and reentry courses we can. These must take into account the level of intercultural development of the students at each step in the cross-cultural process and offer them both challenges and support. It seems most successful to us and them when they are not only able to analyze their personal experiences, but are also able to apply those lessons in much wider contexts, including offering substantial and valid advice to their peers. At this point they are able to draw out universal implications from individual experiences and are able to integrate study-abroad experiences with what they learn in other courses and activities. In other words, the university integrates the programs in order to allow the students to integrate their experiences into their academic work and into their lives. In doing so they also almost automatically arrive at the realization that the concept of process lies at the heart of all experience. They become less likely to compartmentalize events in the future and more likely to think in broader frameworks, particularly when conflicting values and viewpoints are involved.

It is a fine irony for those of us who had been involved in the design and teaching of the program for many years, and had stressed so much the dynamic nature of process, that external circumstances in the late 1980s contributed to extensive and fundamental alterations in both Orientation and Reentry. More about that later.

Enter the International Students as Experts and Novices

In 1986, significant and far-reaching changes in the orientation programs were proposed by several members of the supervising team. Orientation remained a credit-bearing course required for all UOP students participating in overseas programs. What they proposed was to go much further in involving international students in the orientation, so that they became not simply informants or examples of contrast cultures, but integral members of the class. The reasoning was impeccable. The University of the Pacific, like most other universities, holds a number of "international student orientation events" at various times throughout the school year, including the following: the initial intake interviews; campus familiarizations; class registration with its emphasis on academic survival and logistics; periodic issue-oriented briefings (e.g., immigration regulations); and cultural lectures (for instance, American culture as reflected in its holidays).

Didn't it make sense to combine American and at least some of the international students into a single orientation? Were they not both undergoing an orientation to a foreign culture? Would not both groups bring interesting, diverse cultural backgrounds and quite different personalities to the classroom and make it truly multicultural? Was there not the potential for meaningful cultural dialogue and at least the opportunity for cross-cultural friendships to develop? I must admit that my first reaction was the flashing before my eyes of at least an equal number of disastrous scenarios including: great potential for mutual stereotyping; irreparable misunderstandings; problems in course design and content; differences in learning styles and expectations; loss of reentry continuity (as international students would not, of course, take the reentry class); and many other equally unattractive possibilities. I projected that not only might such outcomes be undesirable for the international students, but could have an impact upon the entire program.

These concerns proved groundless. Happily, the international students have been fully incorporated into the UOP orientation for over five years. While there were some tricky technical and cultural difficulties that had to be worked out over time, the transition progressed relatively well with the added benefits proving more important than the inevitable difficulties. It was a slow evolution as we worked out the details of curriculum, timing, and staffing, but the results were very satisfactory.

Although the main focus of this chapter is on the linkage between orientation and reentry for American students, the addition of international students to the orientation experience altered the very nature of the course. It is necessary to give the reader some idea of the various changes which were instituted and an idea of the impact they had upon the scope and content of the course—if only in the way the class atmosphere changed for American and international students alike. Moreover, some of our lessons might prove useful to others contemplating such a step. We will start with those elements which worked well and move on to those which were not so successful.

First, the work load to handle a projected forty-five to sixty American students and another ten to twenty international students each semester in terms of logistics alone (duplicating and distributing papers, counseling individual students, etc.) was such that we felt that an additional teaching assistant (T.A.) would be useful. As class size grew over the years, we had begun to employ as a teaching assistant an American student who had overseas experience and was a veteran of orientation. We now felt that we needed not only to regularize that position but to add an international student T.A. mentor as well. This has proven quite useful, particularly in semesters when the student was rather obviously "foreign," such as when one of our most delightful and perceptive Malaysian students agreed to be a T.A. and just happened to be a strict Muslim female who maintained the traditional dress, including long skirt and head covering. When we came to sections of the course dealing with value orientations and contrasts of traditional vs. modern lifestyles, she was able to explain her religious commitment and perspective in a charming and articulate way. For many Americans it was a most enlightening encounter, perhaps the first time they had heard firsthand a reasonable explanation for and defense of practices they heretofore found incomprehensible. Americans could ask questions directly and continue the discussion on breaks or after class, which they often did. The international T.A. thus played a role in class participation and modeled the behavior we wished to elicit from international students. Also, from the moment the international students entered the class, there was someone they could approach for advice who would understand their situation and position on campus.

If the international T.A.s perform well they become much more than helpers in logistical matters because they serve as "culture brokers" and act in such various roles as translator, intermediary, counselor, tutor, and "representative" for the international student group. Naturally, an international student T.A. will have a sensitivity to the issues facing the international students which comes from their own direct experience, but they must also be able to empathize with the American perspective and respond appropriately.

Pedagogical changes were also necessary. For example, the exercises had to be rethought so that they took into account everyone's viewpoint and allowed the greater variation in perspective now represented in the class to emerge. Even language style and vocabulary had to be considered. For example, a number of the instructors tended to speak rather quickly and to use slang expressions. Both of these tendencies quickly became potential liabilities, although we were able to turn them into at least tolerable assets. Speaking more slowly and enunciating more clearly, and announcing to the class why this was being done, was appreciated by the international students and taught American students that they had to do the same when they asked international students questions in class or made general statements to the group—a skill the students would find useful overseas. The use of slang was handled more formally. One of the T.A.s or a faculty member would undertake to keep a record of any slang, obscure references, or technical terms which were used in lectures. At an appropriate time the entire class would be asked if they knew what these meant. While most of the Americans did (though some did not), often none of the international students understood. In either case it gave the Americans a chance to explain the word or phrase in question. It also frequently resulted in Americans realizing just how nonstandard some of their language is and how hard some idioms and phrases are to translate. Moreover, to some of the American students the slang used by the professors would be unfamiliar, illustrating how different generations, social and educational classes, ethnic groups, etc. can influence language use and how it can vary within a single culture. The class was not designed to focus much on sociolinguistics, yet the presence of nonnative English speakers in the class often acted as a natural language laboratory, giving all students a glimpse of the complexity, flexibility, and levels of ordinary speech. And it occurred in ways which would not have happened naturally in a monolingual, English-only setting.

One big change for instructors teaching such a mixed class is the necessity of speaking simultaneously to two groups whose interests are quite divergent. It is a constant challenge to keep the interest levels of both groups high while dealing with materials which on the surface apply to only one of them. This can be accomplished in a number of ways, such as having the international students discuss culture shock when introducing the subject to Americans. Conversely, when discussing cultural aspects of college life, which international students may have a hard time understanding, the values embodied in them can be drawn out by asking the American students to comment on and explain them. But make no mistake, it is a very fine line to walk for three hours at a time, and the stress instructors feel is very different from that in a normal class session. The rewards for a teacher who does it well are commensurate. In some situations where the integration of the subject matter cannot logically or reasonably be accomplished, the class can be divided for a brief period, although it is wise to keep this to a minimum for obvious reasons.

In spite of such added complications, the addition of international students worked well at so many levels and in so many instances that it is impossible within this space to outline all the specifics. So let the following instances give some feeling for the whole. Once while watching the class from the back of the room during a discussion of body language, I was struck by how evident the small but important differences were between the general classroom deportment, dress, and posture of the international students and that of the Americans. For my own anthropological amusement I made a list of the differences I saw and put it away. A week or so later the discussion turned to academic behavior, ranging over such things as classroom etiquette in other countries, written and unwritten rules of academic culture, and the problems international students have with American informality, etc. It occurred to me that the list of behaviors which I had made the week before might serve some purpose, so I got it out. Here are a few things I had jotted down:

1. Feet propped on tables, soles of shoes showing to instructor
2. Feet placed upon books
3. Gum being chewed, drinks being slurped, even some food being eaten
4. Students talking among themselves in apparent disregard of the instructor
5. Waving hand or calling instructor's name when wanting to answer a question or make a comment.

The list included twenty more items, but for this illustration the first two are sufficient. I asked a Saudi male if he had noticed the behavior of the Americans. He said he had and it bothered him a lot at first. I asked what would happen in his university if that were done. He replied to a shocked group of Americans that he would be permanently expelled from school; such a serious show of disrespect was unforgivable. He continued to explain that feet on books also had religious connotations as writing was a gift from God, and to show such contempt for knowledge and sacred symbols was the mark of a barbarian. Needless to say there is no question that the student overstated the Middle Eastern cultural norms in question here, but his response provoked a spirited discussion, allowing several important points to be made. Views were exchanged on a wide range of topics including what certain behaviors mean cross-culturally, why they came to have that connotation, and how easy it is to inadvertently transgress different cultural boundaries without suspecting anything is amiss. Some international students then told of things they had done recently on campus that Americans thought exceptionally strange, and we discussed why Americans reacted so strongly and what values informed their actions. Thus the Americans gained a better understanding of foreign perceptions and values while international students learned that certain behaviors are likely to be misunderstood by Americans.

This type of impromptu analysis brought a number of intercultural truths home to everyone and allowed both groups to discuss actual or potential cultural gaffes in an atmosphere which consisted more of laughter than criticism. It mattered not that examples were drawn from world areas where no one was intending to study. It was much more important that the principles of the process were being interestingly illustrated with concrete behaviors than that the single specific "ethnofactoid" (as our students called the tidbits of cultural information that sometimes bounced meaninglessly around the room when a discussion began to meander) was under discussion. Certainly, the half-dozen students who were going to France that year might be forgiven for wondering about the utility of a discussion about Middle Eastern customs. The delayed-utility (or "who knows when this stuff will come in handy") aspect of cross-cultural training became apparent a year later when, in the reentry class, an American woman returning from France talked about how the discussion about Muslim attitudes that day in Orientation (and a subsequent one on the meaning of Ramadan), helped her better understand the perspective of Algerians and other Francophone African Muslims living near her in Paris. Naturally, one invites this type of returnee into some subsequent orientation class to express exactly that to students about to go abroad. Once again, making this type of linkage is impossible if you never find out what has happened to your study-abroad students and why it might be important for you, and others, to know about it.

Many additional examples could be cited such as the visceral impact upon American students when, during a discussion of culture shock, a woman and a man from Southeast Asia both described the emotional roller coaster they experienced in the first weeks on the UOP campus and the tremendous changes they confronted in everything from food to friendship. They became for a moment peer teachers of our students, whose direct experience was both a foreshadowing of what was to come for the Americans and a story from which valuable lessons could be learned. We found, over and over, that when we allowed the international students to make the main point from their actual experience, the impact was considerably more than when we talked theory or gave them our own "war stories."

Such activities helped make the international students more accessible to the American students and promoted more interesting dialogue than a teacher-led discussion alone. This type of synergy was possible throughout the course, but it was not always forthcoming. As in any classroom situation there were off nights, when there was a reluctance to discuss certain topics (sex, politics, etc.), a tendency for some students to monopolize the conversation, some incipient male chauvinism escaping from certain individuals, and the usual panoply of difficult situations which all teachers have to deal with regardless of the culture or composition of the class. In fact, having some problems and misunderstandings arise is an excellent way to demonstrate how to deal with conflict creatively in a cross-cultural context. It also provides opportunity to practice separating personal traits from cultural patterns. Some stereotyping did occur, such as the reticent Japanese, the fundamentalist Arab, the shy Filipino, the strident German, the stolid Swede, but the addition of international students was a great antidote to easy generalizations, and it humanized "the other" for everyone involved. Close friendships between Americans and international students were formed, and the entire tenor of the course was altered largely for the better.

However, before we paint too rosy a picture, there are some problems which must be mentioned. The integration of the class is never total, and mini-ghettoization can occur, particularly when one or two groups have a numerical preponderance in a particular class, which may be international students or perhaps a group of Americans who are members of the same fraternity or sorority. On the international-student side, the differences in length of time in the U.S. and language/academic backgrounds affected the ability of the instructor to pace the class and provide a balance between basic information and more advanced considerations. Of course, the experience level of Americans also varies enormously, from those who have not been outside the state of California to Americans who were essentially raised abroad and find more in common with international students than with their American peers. The so-called "global nomads" and "third-culture kids" who have grown up abroad may find the idea of an orientation insulting. Some international students find some Americans narrow-minded, geographically illiterate, spoiled, immature, and all too willing to give an opinion in an area of marginal competence. I guess we feel, more than we would like to admit, that such a situation reflects an accurate microcosm of the real world. We are better off talking to one another with a modicum of respect in a controlled situation than keeping to ourselves and nursing our separate perceptions. Like anything else, it is not ideal, but the bringing together of different realities has created a stimulating pedagogical setting. The drawbacks are minimal compared to the gains we get—in the intensity of student interaction, in the presentation of multiple viewpoints, in the provision of opportunities to question cultural values and practices directly with those holding them; in being able to provide a forum for intercultural analysis, and in linking the presentation of theory with the confirmation of individual experiential history. Furthermore, for those instructors who participate in the orientation, the experience of dealing with a range of culturally different students from diverse backgrounds is a useful and continual reminder that flexibility is required not only of the students but of the faculty as well.

Overall, we think that the addition of international students to what was once an exclusively American overseas orientation has yielded a number of benefits which would not have emerged otherwise, particularly in the validation by international students of the usefulness of a thoughtful, specific preparation for study abroad. Seldom have any of our students from abroad had any predeparture preparation whatsoever. Therefore, taking the orientation course with American students provides a unique academic and social setting which can promote a type of learning and sharing not provided before they arrived on our campus and which is unavailable anywhere else in the university. We have always believed that every American student should study abroad as a part of his or her undergraduate experience and have an appropriate orientation prior to going. We now feel that, whenever possible, the integration of international students into that process is beneficial to everyone involved. We were, and remain, concerned that the bringing together of the international and American students benefit both groups equally. From the comments on the course evaluations by the international students, which are mandatory, we believe they see themselves in positive roles as students, culture brokers, cultural interpreters, and representatives of their respective ethnic, national, religious, and political backgrounds, and as individuals—in other words, in the same kind of roles we hope our American students will occupy when they are abroad.

Another innovative activity we have developed is to designate one period "An American Social Event," a dinner for international and American students at a faculty home. This occasion is used as a mirror to reflect American written and unwritten rules of hospitality. These are discussed and debriefed for a couple of hours after the dinner. It has been most successful (and enjoyable) in raising consciousness of basic cultural differences in everyday behavior: Who is a guest? How does one respond to an invitation, if at all? What time does one arrive and leave? Is a gift brought? If so, what kind? How does one act? What does one do about food restrictions or attitudes toward liquor? What is correct dress? How does one reciprocate? How are differences in status among the guests handled? This exchange of ideas and beliefs about common human hospitality illustrates to the students the variability as well as the similarities of customs in a friendly setting and gives the international students valuable insights into American culture without their having to worry too much about social faux pas. Further, they share their traditions with each other, learning a number of new approaches to living and entertaining in addition to the American way. Again, the faculty also learn a great deal about the international students, and this information can be used to further enhance the orientation course. The dinner party thus both transmits and generates information which is useful in a variety of training contexts.

Institutional Impact

Like everything else in the world, the orientation and reentry classes do not take place in a vacuum. They were and are firmly embedded in an institutional matrix and subject to all the vicissitudes which affect such organizations. Two major elements which directly involve any such internationally oriented programs are the composition of the student population itself and the administrative structure of the university. Changes within both the university and the orientation and reentry courses themselves accelerated greatly after 1986, resulting in greater complexity in terms of acquiring additional staff, course sequencing and credit changes, recruitment, curriculum revisions, administrative accountability and structure, study-abroad advising, interunit coordination, and the incorporation of international students into the orientation. Considerably more change within UOP cross-cultural programs took place between 1985-1990 than in the prior decade. We now turn to an overview of these changes.

By the 1980s the exploratory ethos of the sixties had been replaced by a more preprofessional and career-oriented mentality among college populations generally. UOP's student demographics reflected this and resulted in a dismantling of Callison College. Our Asia-based overseas programs, which had been administered by an on-site director and had stressed homestays and a combination of language study, academic courses, and internships, were replaced by more standard year-abroad or semester-abroad programs. Under a newly formed Office of International Programs (OIP), the university eventually expanded the number and diversity of overseas study opportunities, offering some one hundred overseas study sites in over forty programs. The impact on Orientation and Reentry was immediate, beginning with the obvious changes that a greater range of student destinations, motivations, and academic backgrounds would entail. In both courses this situation resulted in a consideration of a much greater number of cultures and behaviors, most noticeably in Reentry where the range of student experiences was delightfully staggering in its diversity and complexity.

It was through the OIP, with quasi-departmental status, that the orientation and reentry courses were offered for several years. However, in 1987 the administration decided to constitute a new, autonomous, degree-granting undergraduate School of International Studies (SIS) under whose administrative control the OIP would operate. The destinations of the students changed radically, shifting away from the single-country programs of Callison in India and Japan. The tendency after 1980 was toward more traditional, primarily Western European, destinations as the demand for intense, year-long programs in Asia decreased. However, we retained diversity in our offerings by maintaining or generating study-abroad links with less developed world areas including sites throughout Asia, Africa, and Central and South America as well as a variety of internships, parliamentary fellowships, and work-study options. These changes required minimal structural alterations to the basic, linked framework. Dealing with a larger variety of cultures and overseas centers caused some additional burden on the instructors, but the goals and techniques remained largely intact. The loss of the three-year contact sequence, common during the pre-1980 Callison program, lessened to some degree the close personal contact and overall continuity. Nevertheless, the institution of the requirement that all School of International Studies students take both the orientation and reentry courses provided a core group which would continue to benefit from the two-course linkage and give it some stability. While all UOP students going abroad are required to take Orientation, Reentry is optional (for reasons of campus politics) for all but SIS students. Yet about one-third of any reentry class is normally composed of students taking it voluntarily. This results in less disjuncture and more effective carryover than seemed probable at one time, given the demands of both courses.

Because of the above factors there has arisen some endemic, if predictable, friction between some academic departments and even administrative units of the university. Because the impact of these somewhat unusual schedules and requirements has not fallen equally upon all units, there have been bureaucratic difficulties. To be honest, the entire process of establishing the orientation and reentry courses as legitimate, academically sound curricular offerings has been fraught with logistical compromises and philosophical differences of opinion. These will probably arise in any institution which attempts to link the orientation and reentry sequences, particularly if they are (1) required of all students, (2) offered for credit, or (3) perceived as infringing on other units' territory or historical sphere of influence.

To faculty and administrators who support international travel and study for their students (and themselves), the litany of concerns about the merits and liabilities of intercultural study abroad is a familiar one. It does not appear to vary substantially from one campus or program to another. Dr. Donald Green compiled a survey paper[10] based on a sample of over one thousand students, faculty, and administrators of Pennsylvania universities, and the top ten criticisms he found expressed were:

1. Lack of apparent academic credibility
2. Lack of prerequisites, especially of language capability, for participation in the program
3. The awarding of nearly all A's and B's to participants
4. Favoritism in selecting faculty and student participants
5. Programs benefiting only a select few
6. Fear that international education pirates away much-needed funding from more traditional, already established programs
7. Alleged air of secrecy surrounding international education and study-abroad programs
8. Complaints of faculty having little input into the development of international educational exchanges and study-abroad programs
9. Fear that international education poses a threat to faculty and to academic departments

10. Fair-haired faculty and administrators use international education programs and their coordination as excuses for paid foreign vacations.[11]

Suffice it to say that most of these specters have been raised at the University of the Pacific and probably elsewhere. How directors respond and faculty counter such assertions will vary. There is no reliable guide on how to avoid such charges, and perhaps they should be seen as opportunities to educate and inform skeptics and critics alike about the nature, benefits, and integrity of orientation and reentry. They are academically valid pursuits. Most importantly, it is necessary for internationalists in these discussions to demonstrate the same qualities which we insist upon from our students headed overseas: patience, sensitivity, the ability to respond thoughtfully and nonargumentatively to hostile questions, flexibility, and the ability to compromise.

It is incumbent upon all concerned with offering such preparatory and postexperience programs that these programs be academically defensible and current with the latest theoretical and practical training advances. After a couple of years the results should become self-evident, both in student response and more objective measures of achievement and adjustment. The intimate linking of orientation with reentry is the best way of ensuring that students maximize their overseas sojourn as well as accomplish a reentry which utilizes and integrates the experiential learning with their ongoing, postexperience, academic and personal life. Students are our products. It only makes sense to offer them the greatest chance possible, not only to go abroad but to return and subsequently contribute to the furtherance of their, and our, international programs.

The constant necessity to justify and validate our overseas programs is somewhat analogous to the students' attitudes as they progress over the path of pre- and postexperience courses. Initially, there is often a passive (or not so passive) resistance to Orientation on the part of American students because: (1) they are forced to take a course in order to go overseas, (2) they already know all that stuff because they have been overseas, or (3) it's too much work. This attitude of hostility changes early on for some while others continue to resist. In general, we deal with this by acknowledging the hostililty in the first session and further explain that, at one level, we really don't care how they feel because it is: (1) a requirement, (2) they need it whether they think they do or not, and (3) how they adjust to the regimen of the class is often a good indication of how they will react to the demands of another culture—and we will be observing them behaviorally as well as academically. This doesn't totally alleviate the hostility but does mute it. For most, our position eventually makes sense and they cooperate. I suppose that is all one can ask. When programs must be defended it is not unusual for a similar pattern to develop. That is, initial resistance on the part of some members of the faculty and administration who see the enterprise as either intellectually weak or indulgent can eventually be turned around, not by provocation but by persuasion. The strongest case can be made by the students, many of whom willingly testify to their own conversion from resister to advocate as they moved from orientation through the overseas phase to reentry and beyond. Such students are not only the product of the linked programs but the best arguments for both having and linking the programs.

CONCLUSION

The foregoing has been a review of the overall genesis of orientation and reentry at the University of the Pacific, which has stressed the rationale for their almost symbiotic linkage and the importance of viewing the entire pre- and postexperience preparations as one relatively unbroken learning process. As of fall 1991, over one thousand American students have completed orientation at UOP, of whom about two-thirds have subsequently taken the reentry course. To date, over one hundred international students have participated in the combined orientation course.

The courses have been taught by five faculty members[12] who have used similar, but not identical, methods and materials.[13] We value flexibility as an important element in the entire program and have often modified the model. We will continue to do so in the belief that no process as complex as intercultural adjustment can ever be adequately summarized in one theory or taught using only one type of training technique. Variety and experimentation are the twin engines which drive the intercultural vehicle. One thing we won't change is the belief, based on experience, that orientation linked to reentry has a synergistic effect, the sum being greater than the parts. We recommend it highly.

Finally, if the reader has not been able to intuit it from the text, those of us who are engaged in the process find it challenging, interesting, enjoyable, and frustrating. Kind of like going overseas—or coming home.

ENDNOTES

1. An elaboration of this comparison is available in the author's commentary, "Something More Than a Grand Tour," *Pacific Review* 68, no. 2 (October, 1980): 5.

2. This four-part series of half-hour videotapes from Griggs Productions of San Francisco is designed to acquaint overseas-bound executives and their families with the problems and delights of "Going International." With appropriate audience preparation and postviewing discussion, these films can be used quite effectively with a college student population in both orientation and reentry situations.

3. Bafá Bafá is a culture-general learning simulation in which two cultures are created (Alpha and Beta). Participants belong to one or the other culture and learn the appropriate language, gestures, rules of etiquette, and social values of it. Each group visits the other for a period of time trying to discover the other's rules and motivations. A very popular simulation, *Bafá Bafá* provides a mini-experience in intercultural communication and cross-cultural interaction and serves as a vehicle for stimulating discussions of culture learning, culture and personality, relative values, and emotional reactions to difference and stress. Available from its creator, Garry Shirts, through Simulation Training Systems, Delmar, CA.

4. Students have been given a range of readings in the past including the section "American Values" by Clyde Kluckhohn in *Mirror for Man* (New York: McGraw-Hill, 1949) and are given a handout of a list of values compiled by Robert Lynde in the 1920s. Students also have read Edward C. Stewart's article, "American Assumptions and Values: Orientation to Action" in *Toward Internationalism*, Elise C. Smith and Louise Fiber Luce, eds. (Cambridge, MA: Newbury House, 1979). They are strongly encouraged to read Stewart's short summary, "American Cultural Patterns: A Cross-Cultural Perspective" (SIETAR, Georgetown University, 1979), which is extensively elaborated upon in the book *American Cultural Patterns: A Cross-Cultural Perspective*, by Edward C. Stewart and Milton J. Bennett, revised edition (Yarmouth, ME: Intercultural Press, 1991).

   Another handout which has been used in the past includes *Cultural Assumptions and Values Affecting Interpersonal Relationships*, adapted from Stephen H. Rhinesmith's *Bring Home the*

World (New York: AMACOM 1975): 43-45, which is a type of "contrast-American" approach which contrasts American cultural behaviors with those at the opposite end of a behavioral spectrum to highlight the importance of cultural differences in a cross-cultural interaction.

Finally, there are a number of articles which can be assigned depending on class size, interest, and destination. The most useful to date include Seymour Martin Lipset, "A Changing American Character?" in *Culture and Social Character*, S. M. Lipset, ed. (New York: Free Press, 1961); Robin M. Williams, Jr., "Values and Beliefs in American Society" (particularly the subsection "Major Value Orientations in America"), chapter 11 of *American Society*, 2d ed. (New York: Alfred A. Knopf, 1960); and, of course, selected portions of Alexis de Tocqueville's *Democracy in America* (New York: Vintage Books, 1959).

5. See Bruce La Brack, "What Is the Result of International Experience for U.S. Students: Bi-Culturalism or Dual Ethnocentrism?," paper delivered to the International Society for Educational, Scientific and Cultural Interchanges, Los Angeles, March 19, 1981; and "The Rediscovery of America: Cultural and Psychological Factors in U.S. College Students' Reentry," paper delivered at the International Congress of Cross-Cultural Psychology, Istanbul, Turkey, July 6-10, 1986.

6. Before the integration of UOP international students into the orientation program, this exercise was used primarily to discuss the generalized role of being an international student in an unfamiliar cultural setting; however, it also stressed the need for American students to become knowledgeable about not only the country in which they were intending to study, but their own as well. With this dual goal in mind, we have in the past assigned Charles T. Vetter, Jr.'s *Citizen Ambassadors: Guidelines to Responding to Questions Asked about America*, Brigham Young University, 1983, and then assigned a five-page paper on "Questions about America I Would Most Likely Be Asked in the Country I Am Going to and How I Would Answer Them." This requires the students to search out cultural information about the U.S. and Americans and about their selected country and to use the information in constructing diplomatic and thoughtful responses. The exercise has been very successful in focusing on areas where the students' cultural knowledge is weak as well as making them aware that it is not just the content of their answers that is

important but also the form and tone the answers take. Although now somewhat dated, Vetter can be used with appropriate adaptation.

7. Jean L. Briggs, *Never in Anger: Portrait of an Eskimo Family*, Cambridge: Harvard University Press, 1970.

8. This classic tale has found its way into numerous anthropological and cross-cultural communication collections under various titles but is best known as "Shakespeare in the Bush," a delightful and insightful venture into parallel and divergent realities where a familiar story is given new, powerful meanings and symbolism. The article is read within a week or so of the session in which we do a value clarification exercise called Alligator River. The latter is a simple story with five characters; the students are asked to rank the characters from most to least admirable and give their reasons why. The point is to show how even within the same culture there will be a wide range of reactions and interpretations. What then can be expected in a foreign setting?

9. L. Robert Kohls, *Survival Kit for Overseas Living: For Americans Planning to Live and Work Abroad*, 2d. ed. (Yarmouth, ME: Intercultural Press, 1984).

10. Donald E. Green, "Student and Program Evaluation: A Neglected Dimension of Study Abroad Programs," paper delivered at the International Studies Association meeting, Washington, D.C., March 5-9, 1985.

11. Ibid., 11.

12. Over the years a number of people have been involved in the teaching of Orientation and Reentry, and the author would like to acknowledge them here. Dr. Cortlandt Smith, professor of Political Science, was present from the Callison College days and has greatly assisted and supported the evolution of the UOP cross-cultural training curriculum, both as an instructor in Orientation and Reentry (even taking Reentry for personal reasons after a particularly difficult return from a sabbatical of his own in England) and in his past capacities as director of the Office of International Programs and acting dean of the School of International Studies. Barbara St. Urbain, director of the Office of International Services since 1985, has been an active supporter of the orientation program, acting as liaison between the international students and the academic staff and participating regularly in the classroom. It was at her and Dr. Smith's

suggestion that international students were mainstreamed into the American student orientation. Anthropologists Longina Jakubowska (Europe and Middle East) and Deborah Rubin (Africa) have contributed their own international perspectives and extensive overseas experience to the courses since 1987 and 1990, respectively. Jo Ann Martin (Mexico and Latin America), currently at Earlham College, taught both beginning and advanced cross-cultural courses for us in 1987-88. For three years (1987-90) Helena Behrens, as director of the Office of International Programs, participated actively (from recruiting to participating in both cross-cultural training courses) in all phases of preparing our students to go abroad. Helena is now living permanently in Germany and we wish her well. The author extends his sincerest thanks to all of these individuals for their ideas and hard work and offers congratulations for a difficult job well done.

13. Different approaches by different instructors have resulted in a collection of course syllabi for both Orientation and Reentry which vary somewhat in assigned readings, exercises, and sequencing. We would be happy to supply, within reason, samples of such syllabi to interested individuals and institutions. Please send a self-addressed manila envelope (standard letter size or larger) to Dr. Bruce La Brack, School of International Studies, University of the Pacific, Stockton, California 95211 U.S.A.

10

A Culture-General Assimilator: Preparation for Various Types of Sojourns

Richard W. Brislin

INTRODUCTION

The cross-cultural training materials described in this chapter were designed to be useful in a wide variety of orientation programs regardless of the countries in which people will live or the roles they will assume (e.g., businessperson, international student, diplomat). Further, the materials were designed to be applicable to training programs aimed at improving communication and facilitating interaction among members of different ethnic groups within any one country. Since the basic unit of these materials is the critical incident, and since the materials were designed following suggested guidelines for culture-assimilator development (Fiedler, Mitchell, and Triandis 1971; Albert 1983), we are calling the result a "culture-general assimilator."

Rationale for Materials Development

The basic assumption behind the development of a generally applicable set of training materials is that there are extensive commonalities in the experiences of people who interact with culturally different others. These commonalities occur despite differences in the exact jobs people have or despite differences in the exact place where the intercultural interaction takes place. In preparing a broad overview of the wide range of issues and problems involved in cross-cultural encounters (Brislin 1981), I was struck by the similarities in the intercultural interaction literature even though the material was gathered from very different parts of the library. There are sections of the library where materials on international students can be found, another section concerned with the experiences of businesspeople, another on interpreters and translators, another on Peace Corps volunteers, still another on diplomats, and so forth. There were also materials in other sections of the library on interaction among citizens of one country, such as research reports on the adjustment of immigrants or the experiences of teachers and students in recently desegregated schools. Yet upon studying these materials, we found that the experiences of people are very similar. For instance, all have frustrations while trying to communicate with culturally different others. All have to make adjustments in familiar, habitual patterns of behavior to interact effectively with others. All observe behaviors which are difficult to interpret, and all experience confrontations with their prejudices. Further, looking at the encounters in a positive light, all people have the potential to grow and to develop as a result of their cross-cultural experiences.

To digress just slightly, these commonalities may explain why people who have interacted extensively with people from other cultures frequently form friendships with each other (Useem and Useem 1967). These friendships occur even when the cultures they experienced were different and they have no roles in common. For instance, a former Peace Corps volunteer in India may develop a friendship with a businessperson who worked in Sweden, and both may have extensive interaction with a social worker who works with refugee communities. A well-known principle in the study of interpersonal relationships is that similarity leads to attraction (Bryne 1971). The similarity in the experiences of people who have had extensive intercultural interaction is the commonalities under discussion throughout this chapter.

Given the assumption of commonality, it was thought that a set of materials could be developed which deal with the experiences, feelings, and thoughts that are typically encountered during cross-cultural interactions. There would be a number of potential benefits. One is that there could be more communication *across* the specialist roles of people who work with the various types of participants in cross-cultural interaction. Examples are social workers who design job programs for immigrants, international student advisors, Peace Corps trainers, and personnel officers in multinational corporations. Another benefit is that if common- alities could be pinpointed, they could form the basis for identifying widely shared *concepts* which all professionals in intercultural commu- nication would know and use. One reason why the study of intercultural communication and cross-cultural orientation has not advanced as fast as it might is the relative paucity of widely shared concepts. With few shared concepts, there is little possibility for serious conversations about, or for in-depth analysis of, people's cross-cultural experiences. If profes- sionals, in their discussions and presentations, go beyond the few rela- tively well-known ideas such as culture shock (Oberg 1958), U- and W- shaped adjustment curves (Gullahorn and Gullahorn 1963), and cultural differences in the use of time and space (Hall 1959, 1966), they have to be very careful to ensure that their audience is familiar with their terminol- ogy. Another benefit is that the identification of commonalities allows the participants in cross-cultural training programs to develop a frame- work which assists them in interpreting their forthcoming experiences. Often, participants in orientation programs complain that while the material presented was interesting and the staff well-prepared and concerned, the content was hard to organize in their minds. So much is presented that too great a burden is placed on information-processing skills and on the ability to remember specific facts. If the orientation program can be organized around a framework consisting of the feel- ings, thoughts, and experiences which people will almost surely have, then participants are likely to bring newfound knowledge to their cross- cultural encounters rather than to leave the knowledge at the training program site (Bhawuk 1990).

The Culture-Assimilator Format

The format chosen for the development of the training materials was that of the culture assimilator (Fiedler et al. 1971), also called the "culture sensitizer." Of all the various cross-cultural training techniques, the culture assimilator has been subjected to the largest number of empirical research studies (see Albert 1983; Cushner 1989 for reviews). In the past, culture assimilators were designed for people from one specific and named country who were (1) about to live in another specific and named country, or (2) about to interact with a specified minority group within their own country. For example, assimilators have been designed for citizens of the United States about to live in Thailand and for white, middle-class company employees about to interact in the workplace with newly hired African Americans. In an assimilator, there are approximately 100 incidents involving miscommunication and/or problematic interaction among members of different cultural groups, alternative explanations of the incidents, and discussions about the appropriateness of each alternative. Learning takes place as participants in a training program choose one or more of the alternative explanations and then find out the reasons for the correctness or incorrectness of their choice(s). Evidence exists (Malpass and Salancik 1977) to suggest that participants benefit from reading discussions of all the alternative explanations, both those that they choose as correct and those that they implicitly or explicitly label as incorrect. "Correctness of choice" is determined by a validation procedure in which members of the host or target culture give their judgments concerning the various explanations for any one incident. In the two examples mentioned above, the validation process would involve Thai nationals and African-American workers, respectively.

In the development of the culture-general assimilator, 106 incidents were written which attempted to capture experiences, feelings, and thoughts which virtually all sojourners encounter. These incidents were written to provide concrete examples of eighteen themes (to be discussed later), or commonalities, which the developers felt were central to an understanding of cross-cultural experiences. These incidents can also be grouped according to eight categories that reflect the social context of the cross-cultural interactions, or the obvious subject matter of the incidents. These categories can also provide the basis of various sessions within a longer training program.

host customs	the workplace
interactions with hosts	the family
settling in	schooling
tourist experiences	returning home

The more subtle, and perhaps more important, aspects of the incidents are discussed as the eighteen themes are introduced and explained. The distinction between the eight categories and the eighteen themes might be confusing. Basically, the eight categories allow the 100 incidents to be grouped into units which are familiar to workshop participants. The eighteen themes examine the underlying, more subtle aspects of the incidents, and these themes are very frequently *not* part of participants' vocabulary and thinking prior to the cross-cultural training program. One of the major assumptions of the culture-general assimilator is that if these eighteen themes *are* understood, they provide an effective framework for the sophisticated analysis of people's actual intercultural experiences subsequent to the training program.

For the development of a culture-general assimilator, the people who would constitute the validation sample could not be from any one country. Rather, the reasoning was that since a culture-general assimilator should be able to assist in preparing people no matter what their role and no matter where they will be interacting, then the validation sample should reflect this diversity. For this project, then, a validation sample consisting of sixty people was chosen with the following characteristics:

1. All had lived in another country for two years or more or had extensive interaction with minority groups within their own country for a similar period of time

2. All had (or have) jobs which necessitated extensive interaction with culturally different people, for example, Peace Corps volunteers, teachers in overseas schools, diplomats, overseas businesspeople, social workers involved in programs for refugees, international students, immigrants, and so forth

3. All were interested in reviewing their cross-cultural experiences and bringing them to bear on the assimilator materials, as shown by their willingness to volunteer the six to eight hours necessary to read and make judgments about the 106 critical incidents.

In addition, all members of the validation sample were over twenty-five years of age, ranging up to seventy-one, with an average age of forty-two. All continents except Antarctica were represented in the list of places where the people had lived. There were thirty-two females and twenty-eight males. Twenty-eight members of the sample had published articles in professional journals concerned with cross-cultural training and/or communication. For example, the editor of this book (R. Michael Paige) was a member of the validation sample.

More details on the nature of the validation sample's task can be found in the introductory chapter to the culture-general assimilator

(Brislin et al. 1986). Briefly, based on the responses to the appropriateness of the explanations for each of the incidents, 100 of the 106 original incidents were clear, unambiguous, and led to a consensus with respect to correct explanations. Thus the final culture-general assimilator is based on these 100 validated incidents.

Examples and Advantages of Critical Incidents

The best way to introduce these training materials is to examine and to discuss one of the 100 incidents. The decisions made at various points concerning the training materials should be clearer if they are applied to a specific case. In an actual training program, participants would read the following incident, ponder the question, and judge the adequacy of all the alternative explanations. It is best to judge the adequacy of all the alternatives since successful cross-cultural communication involves rejecting incorrect explanations as well as making appropriate conclusions.

LEARNING THE ROPES

Henry Connor had been working in a Japanese company involved in marketing cameras. He had been in Japan for two years and was well respected by his colleagues. In fact, he was so respected that he often was asked to work with new employees of the firm as these younger employees learned the ropes. One recent, young employee, Hideo Tanaka, was assigned to develop a marketing scheme for a new-model camera. He worked quite hard on it, but the scheme was not accepted by his superiors because of industrywide economic conditions. Henry Connor and Hideo Tanaka happened to be working at nearby desks when the news of the nonacceptance was transmitted from company executives. Hideo Tanaka said very little when he heard. That evening, however, Henry and Hideo happened to be at the same bar. Hideo had been drinking and Henry overheard him vigorously criticize his superiors at work. Henry concluded that Hideo was a very aggressive Japanese male and that he would have difficulty working with him again in the future.

Which alternative provides an accurate statement about Henry's conclusion?

1. Henry was making an inappropriate judgment about Hideo's traits based on behavior that he observed.

2. Since, in Japan, decorum in public is highly valued, Henry reasonably concluded that Hideo's vigorous criticism in the bar marks him as a difficult coworker.

3. Company executives had failed to tell Henry and Hideo about economic conditions, and consequently Henry should be upset with the executives, not Hideo.

4. Henry felt that Hideo was attacking him personally.

Rationales:

1. For Alternative 1, trainees would read:

This is the best answer. When observing the behavior of others, a very common error is to draw conclusions about the traits or qualities of those others. Here those judgments (called attributions) are that Hideo is aggressive and hard to work with. There is much less a tendency to take into account the immediate factors in the situation which could also cause the behavior, such as the frustration upon hearing bad news. Interestingly, if Henry had been asked to interpret his *own* behavior had he gotten angry, he would undoubtedly have said something like, "Well, wouldn't you be angry if a plan you had worked hard on ended up being rejected?" In addition, vigorous behavior in bars is an acceptable outlet in Japan. People are not supposed to make permanent conclusions about others based on the "bar behavior" they see. But in analyzing the behavior of others, there is much less tendency to take into account such immediate factors of the situation or social context. This error—making trait judgments about others and not taking situational factors into account—has been called the fundamental attribution error (see Ross 1977) and is probably more prevalent in cross-cultural encounters, since there is so much behavior that is new and different to sojourners. When abroad, sojourners often make more attributions about people and events than they would in their own countries. Even though Henry has been in Japan for two years, there will still be many new experiences that call forth judgments or attributions from him.

2. For Alternative 2, trainees would read:

Certainly a common observation about Japan is that decorum is highly valued. Yet people do become angry and upset. Rather than jumping to a conclusion, it is usually better to go beyond the common observation or stereotype (in this case the frequently noted value placed on proper decorum) and to analyze in more detail the specific instance. If a person has been exposed only to the common observation, then he or she is ill prepared for behaviors (which will inevitably be encountered on a long sojourn) that are at odds with the general observation. An important point is that vigorous behavior in bars is an acceptable outlet in Japan. Permanent conclusions should not be made based on "bar behavior," Japanese hosts tell us. Please choose again.

3. For Alternative 3, trainees would read:

   Henry and Hideo, if they are capable professionals, should know about industrywide conditions on their own. While Hideo might be expected to take into account these conditions before his reaction to the nonacceptance of his plan, a highly abstract and nonimmediate thought like "industrywide conditions" rarely wipes out the frustration of seeing hard work leading to no visible reward. Please choose again.

4. For Alternative 4, trainees would read:

   This could be part of the interpretation. There is a strong tendency on the part of people, upon seeing the negative behavior of others, to wonder if they somehow were involved. Since Henry had been working with Hideo, such feelings would be natural. During cross-cultural experiences, this tendency is probably stronger. Since Henry and Hideo have not worked together long and are still learning things about each other, Henry is not going to be able to readily interpret all of Hideo's actions. Since he is not intimately knowledgeable about Japanese culture after two years there, he will be motivated to wonder even more if he is somehow personally involved. Because of felt personal involvement, any of Henry's final conclusions will be even more intense. There is another explanation which focuses on a mistake Henry could be making in his thinking. Please choose again.

A striking fact about the incident is that even though it was designed for a culture-general assimilator, it deals with behavior taking place in a specific country. Indeed, this is true for all 100 incidents—they take place in specific countries, although in different countries for different incidents. There are a number of reasons for choosing to specify settings. One is that the critical incidents are much more interesting to read if the settings are noted, characters created, a plot line developed, and conclusions reached involving a misunderstanding between people from different cultural backgrounds. In pretest work with training participants, people were uncomfortable if a more general setting was indicated, such as "an Asian country." People asked, "Which one?" Another reason is that specifying the exact country sometimes helps people to choose correct responses or to eliminate inappropriate responses. Actual cross-cultural interaction involves figuring out problems and trying to discover the reasons for communication difficulties in specific other cultures. Knowing the exact place where the assimilator incident takes place adds an air of specificity and reality to the exercise. In the case of countries like Japan, readers, even though they have not lived there, often have some knowledge of the culture because of the country's frequent mention in the popular press.

Consequently, the choice was made to create incidents which take place in a specific country. A very important point, however, is that correct responses to the 100 incidents rarely demand knowledge of a particular aspect of the country's culture. In the above incident, for example, there are two good explanations (numbers 1 and 4), but neither involves an aspect of culture or behavior specific to Japan. Rather, the correct explanations, as well as the discussions of the incorrect alternatives, involve issues typical of any extensive cross-cultural interaction. In this incident, these issues include (1) overreacting to colorful incidents, (2) the trait-situation distinction, (3) the fundamental attribution error, (4) avoiding stereotypes, (5) acceptable outlets for aggressive feelings, and (6) feeling personally attacked. These are the sorts of issues which could be discussed in any training program where these materials are used.

In creating the 100 incidents, the developers tried to appeal to people's basic interest in human relationships. A major complaint about many cross-cultural training programs, voiced by both participants and trainers, is that the materials have little meaning for the participants. Given that participants have not had much cross-cultural experience prior to training, material depicting life in another culture often seems irrelevant. Of course, trainees see the relevance *after* some actual cross-cultural experience, but this fact does not help the administrators of pre-experience (usually called predeparture) training programs. The developers of the culture-general assimilator attempted to tackle this problem by creating incidents in which the characters have problems to which the trainees can relate. In the incident presented above, for instance, the assumption was made that everyone, at one time or another, has been tempted to react too quickly to colorful incidents, or has felt personally attacked by someone else. Trainees can thus relate to the characters in the incidents and learn about cross-cultural interaction by analyzing how these common human experiences are played out when people are interacting across cultural boundaries.

There are other advantages to materials based on critical incidents. The incidents, since they depict real people attempting to make a good cross-cultural adjustment, are inherently interesting. Workshop participants want to know what happened to the people depicted in the incident. Readers of this chapter, for instance, would undoubtedly be frustrated if there were no analysis of the four alternative explanations for the critical incident reviewed above. Further, the incidents capture problems which the participants will actually experience during their cross-cultural interaction. Any of the critical incidents can form the basis of role-play scenarios, should workshop participants want to play out the encounters during the orientation program and then discuss their reactions. Of course, such an approach would take place only in workshops where the administrators are comfortable and experienced with this more active approach to cross-cultural orientation (see Landis and Brislin 1983 and Bhawuk 1990 for discussion of various approaches to orientation). Much information about cross-cultural experience comes out of discussions of the incidents. Participants learn such information relatively painlessly as they attempt to discover whether their choices regarding correct and incorrect alternatives match the analyses of the experienced, sixty-member validation sample. Finally, participants can retain a copy of the 100 incidents and explanations so that they can be referred to after the workshop so as to help in the interpretation of their actual cross-cultural encounters.

The Themes around Which the One Hundred Incidents Were Developed

As discussed previously, a major assumption is that there are commonalities in people's cross-cultural experiences. To explore these commonalities in the 100 critical incidents, eighteen themes were identified which are central to understanding people's cross-cultural interactions. These eighteen themes were gathered in the development of several publishing projects designed to provide broad and extensive treatment of both cross-cultural interaction and cross-cultural orientation programs (Brislin 1981; Landis and Brislin 1983), and longer discussions can be found in those sources. These eighteen themes provide a framework for the analysis of specific experiences people have during their cross-cultural interaction. The eighteen themes themselves are grouped according to three broader categories: emotional experiences, knowledge areas, and the bases of cultural differences.

Emotional experiences brought about by encounters with cultural differences.

1. Anxiety. Since people will encounter many unfamiliar demands, they will be anxious about whether or not their behavior is appropriate.

2. Disconfirmed expectancies. People may become upset not because of the exact set of situations they encounter in the host culture, but because the situations differ from those which they expected.

3. Belonging. People want to feel accepted by others and want to feel at home, but they often cannot, since they have the status of outsiders.

4. Ambiguity. The messages people receive in other cultures are often unclear and give little guidance for decisions about behavior that is acceptable to their hosts.

5. Confrontation with one's prejudices. People discover that previous attitudes which they learned during their socialization in their own cultures simply are not useful when interacting in another culture.

Knowledge areas which incorporate many specific cross-cultural differences and which sojourners find hard to understand.

6. Work. Many cultural differences are encountered in the workplace, such as attitudes toward creative effort and the proper relationship between on-task time and social interaction.

7. Time and space. Varying attitudes exist regarding the importance of being on time to meetings, as well as to the proper space people maintain when interacting with each other.

8. Language. Perhaps the most obvious problem to overcome in crossing cultural boundaries is that of language differences. Attitudes toward language use, and the difficulties of learning language as it is actually spoken rather than from a book, are part of this knowledge area.

9. Roles. As a result of being socialized in their own culture, sojourners are accustomed to a set of generalizations regarding who plays what roles or performs what sets of related behaviors. Examples of roles are the family provider, the boss, the volunteer, the leader, and so forth. Large differences exist with respect to the occupants of these roles and how they are enacted in other cultures.

10. Importance of the group and the importance of the individual. All people act, at times, out of their individual interests and at other times, out of their membership in groups. The relative emphasis on individual and group allegiances varies from culture to culture. This dichotomy is also called "individualism-collectivism" (Triandis, Brislin, and Hui 1988).

11. Rituals and superstitions. All cultures have rituals to meet the needs of people as they cope with life's everyday demands, and people in all cultures engage in behaviors that outsiders can easily call superstitious.

12. Hierarchies: Class and status—the relative importance placed on class distinctions and the markers of high versus low status—differ from culture to culture. The amount of power people have is related to their status.

13. Values. People's experiences with such things as religion, economics, politics, aesthetics, and interpersonal relationships become internalized. Understanding these internalized views, called values, is critical in cross-cultural adjustment.

The bases of cultural difference, especially concerning how people in different cultures think about and evaluate information.

14. Categorization. Since not all pieces of information can be attended to, people group bits of information into categories for more efficient organization. People in different cultures place the same individual elements into different categories (e.g., who is a friend, what a good worker does), causing confusion for people accustomed to another set of categories. Stereotypes are categories that deal with people.

15. Differentiation. One result of increased interest in, or importance of, a certain knowledge area is that more and more information is *differentiated* within that area so that new categories are formed, for example, the kinds of obligations which accompany various types of interpersonal relationships or the ways one overcomes red tape. If outsiders do not differentiate information in the same manner as hosts, they may be treated as naive or ignorant.

16. In-group/out-group distinction. In-group refers to people with whom interaction is sought. Out-group members are held at a distance and are often the targets of rejection. People entering another culture have to be sensitive to the fact that they will often be out-group members and that there are some behaviors associated with in-group membership in which they will never participate.

17. Change and growth, as well as the possibility for self-improvement, involve new learning styles. Even though people desire change and improvement, the style in which they best learn new information differs from culture to culture and often from person to person.

18. Attribution. People observe the behavior of others and make judgments about the *causes* of that behavior. These judgments are called attributions. The same behavior, such as a suggestion for how a proposal can be improved, may be judged as helpful in one culture but insulting in another.

Each of these eighteen themes is examined in five or six of the critical incidents. In addition, there are essays on each of these themes which pull together and expand the various ideas which were introduced in the discussions of the 100 incidents.

Uses for a Culture-General Assimilator

The culture-general assimilator can be used in a number of ways and with various types of workshop audiences. It should be mentioned that this assimilator is not intended to replace culture-specific training. Take the example of people about to travel to other countries. There will always be a need for specific information about a country for those sojourners about to go to live there. For instance, if I were about to accept an assignment in Saudi Arabia, I would want to have detailed information about limits which will be placed on my behavior, support groups, avocations or interests which I can and cannot pursue, working conditions, key aspects of the culture which sojourners find difficult to understand, legal sanctions for misbehavior, the impact of American military presence, and so forth. But even in such a program, to prepare people for life in one country, a culture-general assimilator can play a complementary role to the culture-specific training. This and other uses of the general package will now be discussed. For convenience, the examples will be drawn from the experience of sojourners living abroad, though examples could also be drawn from different ethnic groups within the same country.

Culture-specific training. At times, financial considerations will work against a culture-specific program. There may not be enough people going to any one other country to make such training possible. For instance, study-abroad students at a university often fan out to a large number of different countries. The person in charge of training, such as the study-abroad coordinator or the international student advisor, may not have the funds for culture-specific training corresponding to each destination. At times, people (e.g., military personnel, businesspeople) know that they will be going abroad, but don't know until the last minute their exact country of assignment. In such cases, a culture-general assimilator can be very useful.

Even in cases where there are a large number of workshop participants going to one country, the culture-general materials can be helpful. For example, the general assimilator can provide an outline of what might be covered in culture-specific training, which is sometimes implemented by asking people who have lived in the specific country to talk and/or to lead sessions. But what do they talk about, and what is the content of their session? Although these resource people undoubtedly know a great deal, they sometimes have a difficult time deciding what to say and how to organize the presentation. But if they do go through the list of eighteen themes and examine the 100 incidents, they will undoubtedly be reminded of important *specific* information which they can cover. For example, they might be reminded about key problems in understanding the in-group/out-group distinction (Theme 16) in that country or specific work attitudes which sojourners should know about (Theme 6). Such resource people may also be able to modify some of the incidents slightly so that they are exactly applicable to the specific country. For instance, with minor modifications the full incident presented above can be used for culture-specific training designed for most Asian countries.

In longer training programs, the general assimilator can be used for sessions devoted to experiencing extensive cross-cultural interaction, while other materials can be used in sessions devoted to preparing for life in the specific country. One caveat has to be mentioned. If the materials are to be used as part of culture-specific training, participants must have some intellectual interest in the eighteen themes and in the potential generalizability of the 100 incidents. They must find it intriguing to examine the incidents and themes and make modifications so that they can apply the ideas to their own cross-cultural experiences. If trainees are looking only for specific advice that they can use tomorrow in their own precise jobs within their specific communities, then the culture-general assimilator is not the best material to use.

Professionals who work with a multicultural clientele. There are many professionals who deal with so many different cultural groups that a general training approach is most appropriate for workshops designed to develop their cross-cultural skills. Examples of such professionals are international student advisors, counselors who see clients from many different ethnic groups, teachers in multicultural school districts, social workers, college professors who attract students from different countries, and personnel officers in multinational organizations that send businesspeople to various countries. Workshops designed around preparing for extensive cross-cultural interaction are more appropriate for the training needs of these professionals than are culture-specific orientation programs. In addition, some people who are typically thought of as having experiences in one country actually have experiences in several. Businesspeople in multinational organizations may be sent on troubleshooting trips to offices in several countries. Students on study-abroad programs live in one specific country but often travel to others during vacation breaks and as part of their return trips to their own countries.

College students. Professors face a problem in teaching courses in the broad area known as international studies (Spodek 1983)—cross-cultural psychology, intercultural communication, international economics, transnational political organizations, multicultural education, and so forth. The problem is that the typical college student has had little cross-cultural or international experience. Many college students find attempts to introduce concepts such as the influence of culture on behavior overly foreign, dull, or irrelevant. The exceptions to the rule are students who have had a cross-cultural experience, such as former Peace Corps volunteers or participants in one of the youth exchange programs (e.g., Experiment in International Living, AFS International, Youth for Understanding). Professors have long applauded the interest and performance of such students in internationally oriented courses. One possibility is to use the culture-general assimilator with college students to determine if it can substitute for an actual cross-cultural experience. As mentioned previously, the incidents were written so that all readers could relate to them, given the basic concerns in human relationships being examined. The importance of culture is introduced in the discussion of each incident, so readers learn about cultural differences (and similarities) as they work through the assimilator.

Even though the lack of extensive cross-cultural experience among students is decried, many if not most have had some contact, however limited, with people who are culturally different. At times, the incidents will remind students of an encounter which they had previously not thought about, such as the presence of an international student in one of their classes or a chat with a minority-group peer. The assimilator, then, may draw out experiences which students had not thought important at the time they occurred. After learning about the importance of culture, students may be more interested in their internationally oriented coursework. It should be mentioned, however, that these curriculum suggestions have not yet been empirically verified. Current research at the East-West Center involves testing the suggestions in undergraduate courses.

Two research projects have explored the use of the culture-general assimilator in undergraduate college classes. In both studies, the research design included randomly selected experimental groups, whose members studied assimilator incidents, and control groups, whose members studied other material related to the goals of their course. Broaddus (1986) found that students using the assimilator developed greater empathy for people from cultural groups other than their own. Combining the culture-general assimilator within a cooperative group-learning framework, Ilola (1989) found that students were able to identify the underlying issues involved in intercultural difficulties after working with assimilator incidents and essays. They also showed much more sophistication in analyzing personal incidents from their own lives. In both studies, students exposed to the culture-general assimilator were better able to solve new intercultural problems to which they had not been exposed during their classroom instruction. Both studies also documented student enthusiasm for use of the culture-general assimilator as one of their texts. In a related study that again had experimental and control groups formed through random assignment, Cushner (1989) found that teenage students participating in an exchange program in New Zealand benefited in various ways from the analysis of the culture-general assimilator incidents and essays. They demonstrated better adjustment to a new culture, were more efficient at identifying reasonable outcomes when dealing with problems and were able to identify the means to achieve those outcomes, increased their understanding of the dynamics that mediate intercultural interaction and adjustment, and could apply that understanding to personal incidents in their own lives.

Returning study-abroad participants. There are several seriously underused resources on college campuses which, if better marshaled, could improve the institutions' international orientation efforts. One is the presence of international students (Mestenhauser 1983; Paige 1990). Another is the presence of returned study-abroad participants. Often, there is little attempt to build upon students' international experiences during their remaining time in college (e.g., during the senior year if study abroad was for the junior year). Consequently, returning students are both ignored and underutilized. A frequent complaint is that "no one is interested in hearing about anything I learned." In some cases, the benefits of the cross-cultural experience are undoubtedly lost due to the lack of follow-up attention.

Sometimes students could do more on their own, but their cross-cultural experiences are unintegrated, poorly understood, or confusing. Presenting them with the culture-general assimilator after their experiences may help them to integrate what they have learned. The eighteen themes, for instance, may provide a conceptual map which allows an organizational framework for their specific experiences. This after-experience recommendation follows from one of the more interesting points in the research literature on cross-cultural training: training can be more effective for people who have already had some cross-cultural experience (O'Brien, Fiedler, and Hewlett 1971). The probable explanation is that experienced trainees can better relate to the workshop offerings. They have experiences which make the training materials interesting, relevant, and meaningful. In the case of the culture-general assimilator, experienced readers should find stimulation in comparing their own experiences with those depicted in the 100 critical incidents and determining if the concepts presented in the assimilator aid in integrating their previously disparate thoughts and feelings.

REFERENCES

Albert, Rosita (1983). "The intercultural sensitizer or culture assimilator: A cognitive approach." In Dan Landis and Richard Brislin (Eds.), *Handbook of intercultural training* 2. Elmsford, NY: Pergamon. 186-217.

Bhawuk, D. P. S. (1990). "Cross-cultural orientation programs." In Richard Brislin (Ed.), *Applied cross-cultural psychology*. Newbury Park, CA: Sage.

Brislin, Richard (1981). *Cross-cultural encounters: Face-to-face interaction.* Elmsford, NY: Pergamon.

Brislin, Richard, Kenneth Cushner, Craig Cherrie, and Mahealani Yong (1986). *Intercultural interactions: A practical guide.* Beverly Hills, CA: Sage.

Broaddus, Darrell (1986). "Use of the culture-general assimilator in intercultural training." Doctoral dissertation, Indiana State University, Terre Haute, IN.

Bryne, Donn (1971). *The attraction paradigm.* New York: Academic Press.

Cushner, Kenneth (1989). "Assessing the impact of a culture-general assimilator." *International Journal of Intercultural Relations* 13: 125-46.

Fiedler, Fred, Terence Mitchell, and Harry Triandis (1971). "The culture assimilator: An approach to cross-cultural training." *Journal of Applied Psychology* 55: 95-102.

Gullahorn, John, and Jeanne Gullahorn (1963). "An extension of the U-curve hypothesis." *Journal of Social Issues* 19, no. 3: 33-47.

Hall, Edward T. (1959). *The silent language.* Garden City, NY: Doubleday.

_____ (1966). *The hidden dimension.* Garden City, NY: Doubleday.

Ilola, Lisa Marie (1989). "Intercultural interaction for preservice teachers using the culture-general assimilator with a peer interactive approach." Doctoral dissertation, University of Hawaii, Honolulu.

Landis, Dan, and Richard Brislin (Eds.) (1983). *Handbook of intercultural training* (3 vols.). Elmsford, NY: Pergamon.

Malpass, Roy S., and Gerald R. Salancik (1977). "Linear and branching formats in culture assimilator training." *International Journal of Iintercultural Relations* 1: 76-87.

Mestenhauser, Josef (1983). "Learning from sojourners." In Dan Landis and Richard Brislin (Eds.), *Handbook of intercultural training* 2. Elmsford, NY: Pergamon.

Oberg, Kalvero (1958). "Culture shock and the problem of adjustment to new cultural environments." Washington, DC: Department of State, Foreign Service Institute.

O'Brien, Gordon, Fred Fiedler, and Tom Hewlett (1971). "The effects of programmed culture training upon the performance of volunteer medical teams in Central America." *Human Relations* 24: 209-31.

Paige, R. Michael (1990). "International students: Cross-cultural psychological perspectives." In Richard Brislin (Ed.), *Applied Cross-cultural Psychology*. Newbury Park, CA: Sage.

Ross, Lee (1977). "The intuitive psychologist and his shortcomings: Distortion in the attribution process." In. L. Berkowitz (Ed.), *Advances in experimental social psychology* 10. New York: Academic Press.

Spodek, Howard (1983). "Integrating cross-cultural education in the postsecondary curriculum." In Dan Landis and Richard Brislin (Eds.), *Handbook of intercultural training* 3. Elmsford, NY: Pergamon.

Triandis, Harry, Richard Brislin, and C. Harry Hui (1988). "Cross-cultural training across the individualism-collectivism divide." *International Journal of Intercultural Relations* 12: 269-89.

Useem, John, and Ruth Useem (1967). "The interfaces of a binational third culture: A study of the American community in India." *Journal of Social Issues* 23, no. 1: 130-43.

11

The Intercultural Reentry of Student Sojourners: Recent Contributions to Theory, Research, and Training

Judith N. Martin

INTRODUCTION

> Almost every China survivor will tell you that everyone [at home] goes on missing the point, until you finally give up trying to make it and either go back to China or adjust in silence. This is what culture shock really means, either making your own peace, or leaving. Nothing is ever the same after you have gone "crazy" (Holm 1992, 20).

In a recent book, *Coming Home Crazy,* Bill Holm describes his feelings about returning to the United States after spending a year teaching English in the People's Republic of China. His interest in trying to understand the "craziness" of reentry is shared and evidenced by recent scholarly research and a concomitant increase in training materials. The intention of this chapter is twofold: (1) to describe recent theoretical and empirical contributions to this area of study and (2) to discuss training implications and resources based on these contributions. However, before describing theoretical contributions, there are several fundamental assumptions (regardless of the theoretical position taken) about the nature of reentry that should be noted.

First, the sojourner's readaptation to the home culture must be considered within the context of the entire sojourn. That is, cultural adaptation should be conceptualized as a process and reentry considered as one phase of the sojourn and one type of cultural adjustment (Koester 1983; Martin 1986a). Researchers have found that sojourners' reentry adaptation is significantly influenced by their experience in the foreign country (N. Adler 1976, 1981; Gullahorn and Gullahorn 1963; Uehara 1986), and trainers have also emphasized the importance of returnees' examining their experiences overseas in order to anticipate and meet the challenges of reentry (Koester 1984; La Brack 1986, this volume; Martin 1986a; Westwood and Lawrence 1988).

A second assumption is that the reentry transition is similar to other adult transition experiences. Regardless of the theoretical approach taken, most scholars agree that cultural adaptation (whether to foreign or home country) is similar to other adult transitions (e.g., domestic relocation, death of a loved one, new job) in terms of the challenges presented and the typical human responses to these challenges (J. Bennett 1977). Specifically, all transitions involve loss and change for the individual; there is the loss of the familiar (relationships, cultural frames of reference, etc.) and challenge of the new (new frames of reference, new relationships). In addition, all transitions present opportunities for personal and intellectual growth.

As many writers have noted, it is in resolving intrapersonal conflicts during the transition process that individuals are able to reach new levels of self-understanding and can broaden their cognitive horizons and their repertoire of responses. Both scholarly and popular literature have offered guidance in coping with loss and change and maximizing the potential of personal growth during such transitions (Brammer and Abrego 1981; Bridges 1980; Colgrove, Bloomfield, and McWilliams 1975; Gould 1978; Hopson and Hayes 1977; Kubler-Ross 1969; Sheehy 1974, 1981).

Third, recent conceptualizations of sojourner adaptation describe it as a complex phenomenon comprising cognitive, affective, and behavioral processes (Furnham 1988; Kim 1988; Searle and Ward 1990). It is not surprising, therefore, that few scholars have formulated comprehensive theories of adaptation that account for every aspect of the phenomenon. However, various theoretical perspectives have offered insight into particular aspects (Furnham 1988; Kim and Gudykunst 1987). For example, the traditional psychological focus has been on the intrapersonal (affective) fit with the environment (see review by Church 1982). Other scholars have focused on cognitive aspects—various learning outcomes of adaptation, e.g., self-awareness and cultural awareness (N. Adler 1976; P. Adler 1975, 1982) or on behavioral processes—how the sojourner's interaction with the environment plays a role in adaptation (Furnham and Bochner 1986; Martin 1984, 1986a, 1986b, 1986c).

Given these fundamental assumptions about the process of cultural adaptation, the following section describes recent theoretical approaches that explain how individuals manage loss, change, and growth—primarily in adaptation in the foreign culture but in the reentry phase as well. The first theories are grounded in psychological research and focus on understanding the intrapersonal psychological adaptation/response of the sojourner during the reentry phase. The second set of theories is more comprehensive and focuses on the role of communication in the reentry phase.

RECENT THEORETICAL CONTRIBUTIONS

Most traditional psychological investigations of sojourner adaptation have conceptualized adaptation as the sojourner's feeling of comfort or satisfaction reflecting the degree of congruence between the individual and the environment (see Church 1982; Furnham and Bochner 1986; Kim 1988 for literature reviews). Much of this research has focused on identifying problems experienced by sojourners and the variables that influence adjustment during their entry into the host culture and upon return to the home culture (Church 1982; Furnham 1988; Lonner 1986; Martin 1984; Uehara 1986).

Cognitive-Dissonance Theory

One useful framework for understanding the specific internal process of adaptation is that of the cognitive-dissonance theory. As noted earlier (Martin 1986b), it is useful to conceptualize culture shock and reentry shock as the individual's striving for internal consistency in dealing with conflicting cultural systems. That people strive for consistency in cognition, affect, and behavior is the basis of a number of sociopsychological theories, most notably the balance theory of Heider (1958), the cognitive-dissonance theory of Festinger (1957), and the congruity hypothesis of Osgood and Tannenbaum (1955).

Gullahorn and Gullahorn (1963) describe cultural adaptation as the adult sojourner's response to cognitive dissonance which occurs when individuals come into contact with new ways of thinking and behaving. They suggest that in dealing with cognitive dissonance, sojourners have three possible response patterns: to reject the new stimuli (attitude/value/way of thinking), to change their own thinking and behavior to adapt to the new stimuli, or to ignore it.

Janet Bennett (1977) also contends that culture shock may be viewed as a defense mechanism, a reaction to cognitive inconsistency. The cognitive inconsistency is triggered by the sojourner's inability to interpret the new environment, using the home culture's frame of reference, and can be exacerbated by the realization of the inappropriateness of trying to do so (see also Grove and Torbiörn, this volume). When this inconsistency is resolved by clinging to familiar views, it results in culture shock; when views are adjusted to fit the new cultural environment, the result is cultural adjustment.

Expectancy-Value Model

A related theoretical perspective suggests that the extent to which sojourners experience cognitive dissonance may depend on their expectations concerning the sojourn abroad. This perspective is based on expectancy-value theory (Feather 1967; Feather 1982; Feather and Simon 1971), which investigates the relationship between individuals' expectations and their subsequent behavior.

Researchers have noted the importance of sojourner expectations in adaptation to the foreign environment (Black and Gregersen 1990; Furnham 1988; Gullahorn and Gullahorn 1963; Hawes and Kealey 1981; Kealey 1989; Searle and Ward 1990) and especially in their return to the home culture (N. Adler 1976; Brislin and Van Buren 1974; Gama and Pedersen 1977; Martin 1984; Westwood, Lawrence, and Paul 1986; Westwood and Lawrence 1988).

While the sojourner expects to be on the margin of the foreign group, she or he expects to feel at home when reentering the home environment. However, the sojourner often finds that the home environment is much less familiar than expected and therefore experiences a feeling of strangeness in his or her own country. As Schutz (1964) noted:

> To the homecomer, home shows—at least in the beginning—an unaccustomed face. He believes himself to be in a strange

country, a stranger among strangers, until the goddess dissipates the veiling mist (106).

Applying the expectancy-value model to sojourner adaptation, Furnham (1988) suggests that the sojourner has expectations about the impending experience which are then fulfilled or unfulfilled. As shown in figure 1, fulfilled expectations lead to positive evaluations of the experience and ultimately to good adjustment; unfulfilled expectations lead to negative evaluations and poorer adjustment (Furnham 1988).

Figure 1:   Expectancy-Value Model of Cultural Adaptation

Preexperience	Experience	Evaluation	Outcome
Expectations	Fulfilled	Satisfied	Good Adjustment
Expectations	Unfulfilled	Dissatisfied	Poor Adjustment

However, only two longitudinal studies have applied this theoretical perspective to sojourner adaptation. First, Weissman and Furnham (1987) surveyed a group of Americans about their sojourn expectations and their mental health both prior to their departure and again while they were working in London. Weissman and Furnham hypothesized that unmet expectations would be associated with poor adjustment, i.e, poor mental health, and the results provided some support for this hypothesis; those sojourners reporting unfulfilled expectations were also more likely to experience psychological distress.

However, Weissman and Furnham speculate that respondents' expectations were fulfilled. This may have been due to self-fulfilling prophecy—that the overseas experience was as expected. Because of the limitations of the study (the small number of respondents, a lack of variation in the data, and a lack of representativeness of the sample), the results should be regarded as only suggestive.

The results of a more recent study comparing predeparture expectations of 238 U. S. students with their postreturn reports suggest a slightly different approach to expectations. Martin and Rohrlich (1991b) found, as did Weissman and Furnham, that most sojourner expectations were fulfilled, and these fulfilled expectations led to better adjustment. However, it was also found that when expectations were low and things turned out to be better than expected, better adjustment resulted.

The findings of this study indicate that it is important for sojourners to develop positive, realistic expectations. Expectations that are too positive or too unrealistic may lead to negative results.

Secondly, the study also revealed the difficulty of measuring expectations, since respondents reported they had not given a lot of thought to expectations prior to participating in the research survey. However, after returning from abroad, they were able to be more specific about whether or not their predeparture expectations were met. This brings into question the appropriateness of trying to measure the fulfillment of expectations objectively in a longitudinal design.

These two findings suggest that it may be appropriate to (1) expand the conceptualization of unfulfilled expectations to include those that are violated and (2) focus on violations of expectations as perceived by individuals *after their intercultural experience* in order to understand how expectations are related to adaptation. One useful theory that may be applied is *expectancy-violation theory*, used originally in investigations of nonverbal behavior. This approach focuses on how violations of expectations about another's behavior lead to positive or negative evaluation of that person (Burgoon 1983; Burgoon and Jones 1976; Burgoon and Hale 1988).

As shown in figure 2, this model expands the conceptualization of expectancy violation. As in the expectancy-value model, expectations may be fulfilled or unfulfilled, and those that are fulfilled lead to positive evaluations. However, unlike expectancy-value theory, not all unfulfilled expectations lead to negative evaluations and outcomes. Rather, unfulfilled expectations may be violated *either* positively or negatively. Expectations perceived as violated negatively do lead to negative evaluations. However, those violated positively lead to positive evaluations and outcomes. This model better explains recent research findings that violations viewed as positive have more positive consequences than those that are simply fulfilled (see Burgoon and Walther 1990; Black and Gregersen 1990; Martin and Rohrlich 1991b).

Figure 2:   Expectancy-Violations Model of Intercultural Reentry

Postexperience	Evaluation	Outcome
expectations fulfilled	positive	positive (good adjustment)

expectations violated	positive	positive
positively		(good adjustment)
expectations violated	negative	negative
negatively		(poor adjustment)

In a preliminary study based on this model, Lobdell (1990a) interviewed friends and families of adolescent sojourners about their expectations for the returned sojourners' reentry behavior. As a result of these interviews she was able to identify six areas of expectations concerning the returned sojourners' behavior:

1. attitudes and beliefs (e.g., expectations about returnees' attitudes—political, sexual, financial, family, religious)

2. social norms and rules (e.g., expectations for returnees' dress, appearance, eating habits)

3. role relationships (e.g., expectations about fulfilling the same roles they left—child, sibling, boyfriend, girlfriend)

4. effect of sojourn (e.g., expectations regarding their remaining in the U.S.)

5. communication patterns (e.g., expectations about their manner of speaking, the topics they would want to discuss, and their nonverbal behavior)

6. talking about the experience (e.g., expectations for how much and how often returnees would talk about sojourn).

In a second study, Lobdell (1990b) developed one scenario of violated expectations for each of the themes identified above. For example, the scenario of violated expectations of *attitudes and beliefs*:

Since your sibling/best friend has returned home, she or he questions the economic and political involvement of the United States in other countries. She or he discusses the fact that the United States has a lot of influence in the rest of the world, and that America is "too rich and too powerful," which is not good for other countries.

She then presented these scenarios to a sample of friends and families of sojourners and asked them a series of questions concerning the scenarios, including (1) whether they could imagine the behavior described in the scenario, (2) whether or not they viewed behavior in the scenario as a violation of their expectations, and (3) if so, how they would respond to and evaluate the sojourner if this behavior occurred.

The results provided some support for applying expectancy violation to the reentry context. Results revealed that respondents did perceive the scenarios as violations and that their evaluations of the sojourner were related to violations of expectations. However, the negative
violations did not provoke negative consequences, as predicted by the
model. That is, respondents indicated that they would not be embarrassed to be around the sojourner, would not avoid or spend less time
with him/her, etc. Lobdell suggests that the lack of significant relationship between evaluation and outcome may be due to the fact that the
findings were based on respondents' imagined behavior and not on
actual behavior. Specifically, individuals may not always accurately
predict their behavior, or the scenarios did not arouse the respondents
enough to elicit accurate cognitive-affective assessment of the situation.

Based on Lobdell's preliminary research and expectancy-violation
theory, one could also investigate returnees' expectations about reentry
relationships with colleagues, friends, and family. Using the model in
figure 2, researchers could use the following research agenda: What
reentry expectations are most salient to the sojourner? Obviously, the
returnee holds many expectations about the reentry experience, which
are either met or violated. Which expectations are most critical in
determining the success of the sojourner's adaptation and the personal
growth she or he experiences? Do the same themes hold for the sojourner's
friends and family?

Secondly, what are the consequences of reentry expectations that are
violated? There is some indication that fulfilled expectations and those
that are positively violated lead to positive evaluation of the experience.
However, as noted above, there are contradictory results concerning
negative violations. That is, Weissman and Furnham's (1987) and Martin
and Rohrlich's (1991b) results—that negatively violated expectations
lead to negative evaluation—were not supported by Lobdell (1990b).

Communication-Centered Approach

A more comprehensive theory of adaptation is proposed by Kim
(1988) and extends inquiry beyond the intrapersonal processes of cultural adaptation to include interpersonal (functional fitness) and intellectual (cognitive) outcomes. While cognitive-dissonance theories and expectancy theories focus on the relationship between expectations and
adaptation, Kim's theory focuses on the role of communication in resolving dissonance and dealing with unmet expectations. This theory, based

on general systems theory, conceptualizes adaptation as a stress-adaptation-growth cycle. That is, stress is caused by a lack of fit between sojourners and their environment; sojourners reduce this stress through interaction with the environment. As the sojourner responds to stress through communication/interaction, adaptation results in personal growth.

Strangers are capable not only of adapting to new cultures but also, more importantly, of growing and developing through the adaptive process. The psychological movements of strangers into new dimensions of perception and experience often produce forms of personality disintegration and stress, and yet temporary disintegration is the very basis for subsequent growth in the awareness of life conditions and ways to deal with them (Kim and Gudykunst 1987, 227).

The notion of stress as an important aspect of cultural adaptation is not new (Barna 1983; Dyal and Dyal 1981; Martin 1986a; Walton 1990; Weaver, this volume). Stress theory and its application in practical cross-cultural situations has also benefited from the psychological approaches of Selye (1974), the cognitive appraisal model of Lazarus and Folman (1984), and Holmes and Rahe's (1967) research on stressful life events.

The importance of interaction with members of the host culture and the social support of members of one's own cultural group has also been noted (Adelman 1988; Albrecht and Adelman 1987; Kim 1978, 1988). For example, Furnham and Bochner (1986) describe their concept of adaptation as the sojourners' acquiring requisite social skills that enable them to interact appropriately in the host environment. Others (Brein and David 1971; Gullahorn and Gullahorn 1963; Klineberg and Hull 1979) have emphasized the reciprocal relationship between interaction and adaptation—better communication skills lead to better adaptation, and better adaptation leads to increased interaction.

Specifically, the model comprises four interrelated components as shown in figure 3: *sojourner characteristics* reflecting an adaptive predisposition of the sojourners (e.g., cultural background, open/resilient personality, and preparedness for change); *host environment conditions* (receptivity of the host environment and conformity pressure); *sojourner communication* (the sojourners' communicative competence and the degree to which they communicate with members of the host culture and with members of their same culture or ethnic group, as well as their consumption of host-culture and home-culture mass media). These three components determine the fourth: *adaptive outcomes* (psychological health, functional fitness, and intercultural identity).

Figure 3: **Theoretical Dimensions and Constructs of a Systems-Based Theory of Cultural Adaptation (Kim 1988)**

1. Adaptive predisposition of the sojourner
   - Cultural/racial background (e.g., cultural similarity)
   - Personality attributes (e.g., openness, resilience)
   - Preparedness for change (e.g., education, preentry training, prior sojourn experience)

2. Host environment characteristics
   - Receptivity (e.g., openness to and acceptance of foreigners or people from the specific home culture of the sojourner)
   - Conformity pressure (e.g., formal and informal language policy, social segregation)

3. Communication of the sojourner
   - Communication competence (e.g., knowledge of host communication system, cognitive complexity, affective coorientation, behavioral competence)
   - Interpersonal communication with hosts (e.g., size/proportion of host ties, strength of host ties)
   - Mass communication with host (e.g., degree of exposure)
   - Interpersonal communication with same ethnic group (e.g., size/proportion of ethnic ties)
   - Mass communication of same ethnic group (e.g., degree of exposure)

4. Adaptation outcomes
   - Psychological health (e.g., absence of severe stress, absence of hostility toward host)
   - Functional fitness (e.g., congruent meaning system)
   - Intercultural identity (e.g., third-culture perspective)

Kim specifies (in a series of axioms and theorems) the exact relationship among the various components of the model. Generally speaking, sojourners with greater adaptive predisposition in a receptive host environment will interact more with host nationals and will ultimately be more successful in adapting in the host country. In a recent study, Rohrlich and Martin (1991) confirmed several propositions of Kim's theory and supported earlier research emphasizing the importance of sojourners' interaction in the foreign environment. However, these and other results suggest that the relationship between communication and adaptation is not necessarily linear, that sojourners with better communication skills may encounter more difficulties initially because of their intense interaction with the environment, but eventually they report more satisfaction and better adjustment (Kealey 1989; Rohrlich and Martin 1991).

Although Kim specifies that the model is not intended to explain reentry, preliminary investigation indicates that this framework could also be extended to the sojourners' readaptation to the home country (Rohrlich and Martin 1991). That is, as shown in figure 4, a reentry adaptation could also be conceptualized as a cycle of stress-adaptation-growth within the boundaries of the same three components—the sojourners, the host (home) environment, and the communication of the sojourners within the home environment—leading to the same adaptation outcomes (psychological health, functional fitness, and intellectual growth).

Although space does not permit a complete modification of all of Kim's axioms and theories, it does seem useful to describe how some of the elements of the model may be modified to fit the reentry context. The first two components, the adaptive predisposition characteristics of sojourners and their home environment conditions, would be directly applicable to the reentry context (see figure 4).

Figure 4:   Theoretical Dimensions and Constructs of a Systems-Based Theory of Reentry Adaptation

1. Adaptive predisposition of the returning sojourner
   - Cultural background
   - Personality attributes (e.g., openness, resilience)
   - Preparedness for change (e.g., reentry training, prior sojourn experience)

2. Home environment characteristics
   - Receptivity (e.g., openness, acceptance)
   - Conformity pressure (e.g., social segregation)

3. Communication of the returning sojourner
   - Communication competence (relearning communication system, cognitive complexity, affective coorientation)
   - Interpersonal communication with members of home culture (e.g., size/proportion, strength of home ties)
   - Mass communication consumption in home culture (e.g., degree of exposure)
   - Interpersonal communication with other returning sojourners (or members of former host culture) (e.g., size/proportion/ strength of ties)
   - Mass communication consumption of media from former host culture (e.g., exposure)

4. Readaptation outcomes
   - Psychological health (e.g., absence of severe stress, absence of hostility toward host)
   - Functional fitness (e.g., congruent meaning system)
   - Intercultural identity (e.g., third-culture perspective)

As shown, elements of the third component, sojourner communication, would be modified only slightly. The same aspects of sojourner communication competence would apply to reentry, i. e., being knowledgeable of the home communication system and being able to behave appropriately (having to relearn somewhat the system), managing cognitive complexity and maintaining flexibility and affective coorientation (being motivated to adapt and to fit emotionally with the environment).

Interpersonal communication (reestablishing ties and relationships with friends and family) in the home culture can be conceptualized in the same way as in the host country. Communicating with members of the home culture serves the same facilitative function as communicating with members of the host culture in the overseas context. Previous research, based on symbolic interactionism, suggests that the essence of reentering is understanding and internalizing personal change and that this is accomplished through communication with others. Martin (1986a, 1986c) has identified specific ways in which social relationships facilitate as well as inhibit the reentry process.

However, "communication with members of the ethnic culture" in Kim's (1988) model is modified more extensively. As shown in the theorems below, Kim emphasizes the importance of communication with persons from the same ethnic group in the overseas environment, suggesting that in the short term, these relationships are facilitative and provide support for sojourners during adaptation.

Theorem 13: The greater the sojourner's participation in ethnic interpersonal communication, the greater the initial short-term development of communicative competence in the host culture (77).

Theorem 16: The greater the sojourner's participation in ethnic interpersonal communication, the lesser the subsequent long-term development of communicative competence in the host culture (77).

This same principle holds true for the returnees' communication with others from their overseas culture or with other sojourners in general, so the "ethnic communication" is modified to "communication with other sojourners" or "communication with members of the sojourners' former host culture" in the reentry context. Communication with other returned sojourners or perhaps visitors from the sojourners' former host culture who may share the same worldview and give meanings in similar ways provides the same kind of support during the reentry. To restate Kim's theorem for the reentry context: The greater the participation in other returned sojourner communication, the greater the initial short-term development of home communication competence. On the other hand, the greater the participation in other returned sojourner communication, the less the subsequent long-term development of home communication competence. The same would hold for consumption of home- and host-culture mass media. One could thus modify the other theorems in the model to fit the reentry context.

Finally, the fourth component of the model—the readaptive outcomes—also applies, without modification, to the reentry context. Reentry adaptation can be conceptualized as comprising the intrapersonal psychological health, functional fitness, and the intellectual growth of the returnee.

In sum, applying this communication-centered perspective to the reentry context suggests several general research questions: Are the same general factors related to reentry adaptation, i.e., sojourner characteristics, the communication of the sojourner with members of the home environment, the receptivity of the home environment? What is the relationship of the communication/interaction of the sojourner with home family and friends during the sojourn experience? And how does it influence adaptation in the home culture upon return? What social or communication skills are required? Several preliminary research efforts have investigated these outcomes of reentry (N. Adler 1981; Wilson 1985).

Applying Theory to Training Contexts

Given these theoretical orientations and research findings, what are the implications for practitioners in designing and implementing reentry orientation programs? Conceptually, reentry training should be viewed as assisting participants to manage one kind of adult transition and should be viewed as part of a long-term process of cultural adaptation and learning. Sojourners should also be assisted in the three dimensions of adaptation: intrapersonal psychological adjustment, interpersonal skills leading to functional fitness, and cognitive learning. Overall, training should also help sojourners to integrate academic and professional as well as personal aspects of the experience during the reentry phase of the intercultural sojourn.

Orientation as Preparing for Transitions

Assuming the similarity between cultural adaptation and other transitions (including the transition to the foreign culture), trainers should encourage returnees to view the entire sojourn experience in the larger perspective of adult transitions. Bridges's (1980) discussion of three phases of change (letting go of the old, the neutral zone, and embracing the new) provides a useful conceptual framework and also gives useful guidelines for dealing with change.

Secondly, trainers can assist the participants in using their past transitional experiences in understanding the sojourn transition and in preparing for reentry. In preparation for the return home, sojourners should be encouraged to examine their experiences in the host country and reflect on the strategies they used for adapting to it (Koester 1984; La Brack 1986;

Westwood and Tillman 1984). For example, how did they respond to challenges of the new environment? By getting immediately involved? By making a few close friends in the host culture? What worked and did not work for them? It is likely that the same approaches/strategies that were effective in helping them adapt to the new cultural environment will also serve them well in readapting to the home environment.

Developing Expectations (Intrapersonal)

Based on research findings discussed above, reentry orientation, like predeparture orientation, should be conceptualized as helping sojourners develop positive realistic expectations (Furnham and Bochner 1986; Westwood, Lawrence, and Paul 1986; Westwood and Lawrence 1988). Sojourners should be encouraged to think about the reentry experience well before they return home. As described in La Brack's chapter (this volume), reentry orientation should be included in the predeparture orientation. While the topic of reentry need not be covered extensively, it should be noted in the predeparture training that the intercultural sojourn comprises the predeparture, overseas, and postreturn phases. A discussion of culture shock can also include mention of reentry shock and a recommendation that sojourners prepare for reentry during the overseas stay.

For example, research findings suggest that sojourners who maintain communication with friends and family at home while abroad, or go home from time to time (if on an extended sojourn), seem to adapt more easily to reentry (Brabant, Palmer, and Gramling 1990; Martin 1985).

In postreturn orientation, they should be encouraged to examine their own personal changes as well as changes which may have occurred in the home environment (social as well as physical). Recent research has documented the kinds of intellectual, attitudinal, and personal changes that are likely outcomes of the intercultural experience, especially for young U. S. sojourners (see Kauffmann et al. [1992] for a review of the literature). Understanding personal changes will lead to more realistic expectations and fewer negative violations of these expectations.

Another strategy is to examine literature describing reentry experiences of other sojourners. For example, the "Inventory of Reentry Problems," compiled by Asuncion-Lande (1976), was developed with the assistance of a group of international students studying in the U.S. The inventory identified difficulties in the following areas: cultural adjustment, social adjustment, linguistic barriers, national and political problems, educational problems, and professional problems. One of the most frequently mentioned violated expectations of returned sojourners, for instance, is the expectations that friends and family would want to hear about the sojourn experience, whereas it is the common experience of returnees that they do not.

Additional anecdotal descriptions of individuals' personal reentry experiences may be found in contemporary literature, e.g., Paul Theroux's (1986) "Yard Sale," Bill Holm's (1990) *Coming Home Crazy,* and the account of F. M. Boakari's (1982) returning home to Africa after years of study in the U S.

Developing Functional Fitness

Orientation should also assist students in developing the functional fitness aspect of reentry adaptation. Returned students have a tendency to isolate themselves during reentry, to assume that nobody understands them, especially if none of their friends has had a sojourn experience. However, they should be encouraged to share their experiences with their families. Research shows that for adolescent sojourners, communication with family can be helpful in reentry (Martin 1986a, 1986b). They should also seek opportunities for sharing experiences with friends and others, where they can act as cultural mediators (Wilson 1985).

Based on the communication-centered approach outlined above, returnees should be advised to form relationships with other returned students and international students, who may share the same international mindset (see La Brack's discussion in this volume of how international students can be integrated into reentry orientation).

Finally, students should also be encouraged to use the same communication skills and competencies that they used abroad to be successful at home (see Martin 1989a).

Intercultural Growth

Reentry orientation should extend beyond assisting students to adjust psychologically and functionally. First, as one way to deal with the challenges of reentry, many returning sojourners deny the existence of reentry shock and resist orientation. This has been documented and labeled by Brislin (1981) as the "hostility phase." It may also be that the term "reentry" has a negative connotation, or, as with predeparture training, there may be a resistance to admitting the possibility of encountering difficulties.

Secondly, psychological adjustment is usually only a small part of the demands placed on the returning sojourners, particularly those also making the transition from student to professional, as in the case of international college students returning home (Gama and Pedersen 1977; Gullahorn and Gullahorn 1963). There are often the demands of a new job or academic institution, new social relationships, and financial concerns. Therefore, reentry training should assist the students in integrating their experience overseas with the on-campus program of study (see Martin 1989b; La Brack 1986) or their professional goals (Pusch and Loewenthal 1988).

In our interviews with returning U. S. students, it was clear they felt that their colleges and universities did not assist them in their reentry (Kauffmann et al. 1992). They often felt that their institutions penalized them by not showing flexibility in transfer of credit, financial aid, registration deadlines, etc. In order to facilitate the student sojourners' reentry, academic institutions need to make it easier for students to incorporate an overseas experience into their college career. This may be accomplished in various ways, such as providing an integrated predeparture and reentry program (La Brack 1986), facilitating transfer of credit, and formally recognizing the overseas study experience as an academic experience.

RESOURCES FOR REENTRY TRAINING

There are a variety of excellent resources for persons interested in developing reentry programs for both international and U.S. student sojourners.

Reentry Training for International Students

Looking Forward/Looking Backward (Textbook)
Behrens, J. S., and W. F. Bennett eds. (1984). Lubbock, TX: Texas Tech University, College of Agricultural Sciences.

This textbook was developed for a course at Texas Tech University. It includes a theoretical framework and chapters on specific concerns of the returning international student (e.g., "Cultural/ Social Adjustment," "Technological Adjustment in the Reentry Transition," "Relevance of a U.S. Education to the Third World"). While the strength of this text is the emphasis on assisting in students' professional reintegration, it also includes exercises to assist international students in identifying and working through their own personal issues of reentry. The essay by F. M. Boakari recounts rather poignantly the personal and professional challenges he encountered on his return home to Central Africa after many years of professional preparation in the U.S. This text is useful both for participants and facilitators.

May be obtained from:
Office of International Affairs
Texas Tech University
Lubbock, TX 79409-5004
(806) 742-3667

Returning Home: A Program of Reentry (Videotape and Manual)
(1984)

This video and manual are designed for "persons assisting international students with the reentry process" and are based on the expectancy model described above. It is especially helpful for the neophyte trainer who has limited resources. The manual provides an excellent, though brief, introduction to this area of training (how to initiate and run a reentry program, program design and evaluation, a prototype program, and a bibliography). The video is a step-by-step portrayal of an actual half-day reentry orientation program and demonstrates how students, about to return to their home countries, are encouraged, in discussion-group format, to think about their return home. The discussion follows the format and rationale suggested in the manual.

An especially powerful exercise is the "Guided Fantasy" where students relax, sit with eyes closed, and answer a series of questions while visualizing their return home (e.g., who will meet them at the airport, what will they feel like, what will the weather be like, who will they be expected to see or what will they be expected to do once they are settled, what will their friends and family expect them to be like?). This exercise helps students clarify their expectations and the expectations of those at home and elicits insights that are otherwise difficult for sojourners to imagine prior to returning home.

May be obtained from:
Canadian Bureau for International Education
85 Albert St., Suite 1400
Ottawa, ON
K1P 6A4 Canada
(613) 237-4820

Helping Them Home (Manual)
Pusch, Margaret D., and Nessa Loewenthal (1988)

> This manual contains thirteen detailed training modules for both new and experienced workshop leaders.

Going Home (Workbook)
Denney, M. (1987)

> Designed to help international students reflect on and plan their transition from the host country to their home country. It contains checklists, handouts, and exercises and can by used by the individual on his/her own or in a workshop setting.

Professional Integration for a Smooth Passage Home (Video)
Graduate School USDA (Education for International Development) (1986)

> Designed for international students preparing for their return home. For use in a workshop setting. Contains specific suggestions to ensure professional success in the home country, e.g., maintaining contact with peers and colleagues in the U.S., developing professional networks in the home country, subscribing to journals in the field, etc.

The above three resources may be obtained from:
NAFSA, Association of International Educators
Publications Order Desk
1875 Connecticut Ave. NW, Suite 1000
Washington, DC 20009-5728
(202) 462-4811

Reentry Training for U. S. Students

There have been several prototype programs developed with the assistance of NAFSA. First, the program developed cooperatively by several institutions in the Philadelphia area in 1987 is described in an excellent report including suggestions for program planning, content evaluation, and resources:

A study abroad reentry conference: A model for regional cooperation (edited by M. L. McBride and P. C. Martin). Published by the Office of International Programs, University of Pennsylvania, Philadelphia, PA.

Other sources include descriptions of academic courses focused on the reentry experience, one developed at the University of Minnesota, described in an article by Koester (1984). Another course was developed at the University of the Pacific (see La Brack 1986 and this volume).

Coming Home Again: Absorbing Return Shock

This four-page description of reentry transition is part of a series of Infograms published by Brigham Young University. It includes helpful suggestions and lists of additional resources. It could be included in reading packets for any reentry training program.

May be obtained from:
BYU Kennedy Center for International Studies
Publications Services
280 HRCB
Provo, UT 84602
(801) 378-6528

There and Back Again: A Guide for Coping with Reentry
Rohrlich, Beulah (1989)

This thirteen-page booklet was developed by Syracuse University for distribution in their study-abroad programs, but could be sent to students abroad or included as supplemental reading in formal orientation programs. It includes very specific suggestions for dealing with various aspects of reentry (family, friends, country, school).

May be obtained from:
Division of International Programs Abroad (DIPA)
Syracuse University
119 Euclid Ave.
Syracuse, NY 13244
(315) 443-9417

There are also materials available for reentry orientation for adolescent sojourners, developed by national youth exchange organizations.

Planning and Conducting Reentry Orientations
Blohm, Judith M., and Michael C. Mercil (1982)

This is a how-to-manual with lesson plans, sample schedules, handouts, and flip charts, as well as background reading for those who conduct the orientation. There are also two pamphlets in their cross-cultural Horizons Series dealing with reentry.

May be obtained from:
Youth for Understanding (YFU)
Educational Services
3501 Newark St. NW
Washington, DC 20016
(202) 966-6800

Orientation Handbook for Youth Exchange Programs
Grove, Cornelius (1989)

This *Handbook* assists those who plan orientations for all phases of the intercultural sojourn, from predeparture through reentry. Approximately one-third of the book deals specifically with reentry orientation—for both exchangees and their families.

May be obtained from:
Intercultural Press
P.O. Box 700
Yarmouth, ME 04096
(207) 846-5168

Additional Resources

Austin, Clyde N. (1983). *Cross-cultural reentry: An annotated bibliography.* Abilene, TX: Abilene Christian University Press.

_____ (1986). *Cross-cultural reentry: A book of readings.* Abilene, TX: Abilene Christian University Press.

REFERENCES

Adelman, Mara (1988). "Cross cultural adjustment: A theoretical perspective on social support." *International Journal of Intercultural Relations* 12: 183-204.

Adler, Nancy (1976). "Growthful reentry theory." Unpublished paper. Graduate School of Management, University of California, Los Angeles.

_____(1981). "Reentry: Managing cross-cultural transitions." *Group and Organization studies* 6, no. 3: 341-56.

Adler, Peter (1975). "The transition experience: An alternative view of culture shock." *Journal of Humanistic Psychology* 15, no. 4: 13-23.

_____ (1982). "Reflections on cultural and multicultural man." In Larry A. Samovar and Richard E. Porter (Eds.), *Intercultural communication: A reader*. Belmont, CA: Wadsworth.

Albrecht, Terrance L., and Mara B. Adelman (1987). *Communicating social support*. Newbury Park, CA: Sage.

Asuncion-Lande, Nobleza (1976). "Inventory of reentry problems." In Harriet Marsh (Ed.), *Reentry/transition seminars: Report on the Wingspread colloquium*. Washington, DC: National Association of Foreign Student Advisors.

Barna, LaRay M. (1983). "The stress factor in intercultural relations." In Dan Landis and Richard W. Brislin (Eds.), *Handbook of intercultural training* 2. Elmsford, NY: Pergamon.

Behrens, Jacque Segars, and William F. Bennett (Eds.) (1984). *Looking forward/looking backward: The cultural readaptation of international students*. Lubbock, TX: Texas Tech University, International Center for Arid and Semi-Arid Land Studies.

Bennett, Janet M. (1977). "Transition shock: Putting culture shock in perspective." In Nemi C. Jain (Ed.), *International and Intercultural Communication Annual* 4: 45-52.

Black, J. Stewart, and Hal B. Gregersen (1990). "Expectations, satisfaction, and intention to leave of American expatriate managers in Japan." *International Journal of Intercultural Relations* 14: 485-506.

Boakari, Francis Musa (1982). "Foreign student reentry: The case of the hurrying man." *NAFSA Newsletter* 34: 33-49. Reprinted in J. S. Behrens and W. F. Bennett (Eds.) (1984). *Looking forward/Looking backward: The cultural readaptation of international students.* Lubbock, TX: Texas Tech University, International Center for Arid and Semi-Arid Land Studies.

Brabant, Sarah, C. Eddie Palmer, and Robert Gramling (1990). "Returning home: An empirical investigation of cross-cultural reentry." *International Journal of Intercultural Relations* 14: 387-404.

Brammer, L., and P. Abrego (1981). "Intervention strategies for coping with life transitions." *Counseling Psychologist* 9: 19-36.

Brein, Michael, and Kenneth H. David (1971). "Intercultural communication and the adjustment of the sojourner." *Psychological Bulletin* 76: 215-30.

Bridges, W. (1980). *Transitions.* Reading, MA: Addison-Wesley.

Brislin, Richard (1981). *Cross-cultural encounters: Face-to-face interaction.* Elmsford, NY: Pergamon.

Brislin, Richard W., and H. Van Buren (1974). "Can they go home again?" *International Education and Cultural Exchange* 9: 19-24. Also in Clyde N. Austin (Ed.), *Cross-cultural reentry: A book of readings.* Abilene, TX: Abilene Christian University, 1986.

Burgoon, Judee K. (1983). "Nonverbal violations of expectations: Explication and initial test." *Human Communication Research* 4: 129-42.

Burgoon, Judee K., and Jerry Hale (1988). "Nonverbal expectancy violations: Model elaboration and application to immediacy behaviors." *Communication Monographs* 55: 58-79.

Burgoon, Judee K., and Stephen B. Jones (1976). "Toward a theory of personal space expectations and their violations." *Human Communication Research* 2: 131-46.

Burgoon, Judee K., and Joseph B. Walther (1990). "Nonverbal expectancies and the evaluative consequences of violations." *Human Communication Research* 17: 232-65.

Church, Austin (1982). "Sojourner adjustment." *Psychological Bulletin* 91: 540-72.

Colgrove, M., H. H. Bloomfield, and P. McWilliams (1975). *How to survive the loss of love.* New York: Bantam.

Dyal, James A., and Ruth Y. Dyal (1981). "Acculturation, stress and coping: Some implications for research and education." *International Journal of Intercultural Relations* 5: 301-28.

Egbert, L., et al. (1964). "Reduction of post-operative pain by encouragement and instruction of patients." *New England Journal of Medicine* 270: 825-27.

Feather, N. T. (1967). "An expectancy-value model of information-seeking behavior." *Psychological Review* 74: 342-60.

_____ (1982). *Expectations and actions: Expectancy value models in psychology*. Hillsdale, NJ: Lawrence Erlbaum.

Feather, N. T., and J. G. Simon (1971). "Attribution of responsibility and valence of outcome in relation to initial confidence and success and failure of self and other." *Journal of Personality and Social Psychology* 18: 173-88.

Festinger, Leon (1957). *A theory of cognitive dissonance*. Stanford, CA: Stanford University Press.

Furnham, Adrian (1988). "The adjustment of sojourners." In Young Y. Kim and William B. Gudykunst (Eds.), *Cross-cultural adaptation: Current approaches*. Newbury Park, CA: Sage.

Furnham, Adrian, and Stephen Bochner (1986). "Culture shock: Psychological reactions to unfamiliar environments." New York: Methuen.

Gama, Elizabeth M. P., and Paul Pedersen (1977). "Readjustment problems of Brazilian returnees from graduate studies in the United States." *International Journal of Intercultural Relations* 1: 46-58.

Gould, R. (1978). *Transformations*. New York: Simon and Schuster.

Gudykunst, William B. (1988). "Uncertainty and anxiety." In Young Y. Kim and William B. Gudykunst (Eds.), *Theories in intercultural communication*. Newbury Park, CA: Sage.

Gullahorn, John T., and Jeanne E. Gullahorn (1963). "An extension of the U-curve hypothesis." *Journal of Social Issues* 14: 33-47.

Hawes, Frank, and Dan J. Kealey (1981). "An empirical study of Canadian technical assistance: Adaptation and effectiveness on overseas assignment." *International Journal of Intercultural Relations* 5: 239-58.

Heider, Fritz (1958). *The psychology of interpersonal relations*. New York: John Wiley.

Holm, Bill (1992). *Coming home crazy*. Minneapolis: Milkweed Editions.

Holmes, T. H., and R. H. Rahe (1967). "The social readjustment rating scale." *Journal of Psychosomatic Research* 11: 213-18.

Hopson, B., and J. Hayes (1977). *Transition: Understanding and managing personal change.* Montclair, NJ: Allenhald and Osmund.

Hu, L. T., and Paul Pedersen (1986a). "Reentry adjustment of returned Taiwanese students from abroad in engineering and related fields." Syracuse: Syracuse University.

_____ (1986b). "Research on the reentry of international students in engineering and related fields." Syracuse NY: Syracuse University.

Kauffmann, Norman, Judith N. Martin, Henry Weaver, with Judith Weaver (1992). *Students abroad, strangers at home.* Yarmouth, ME: Intercultural Press.

Kealey, Daniel J. (1989). "A study of cross-cultural effectiveness: Theoretical issues, practical applications." *International Journal of Intercultural Relations* 13: 387-428.

Kim, Young Y. (1978). "Toward a communication approach to the acculturation process." *International Journal of Intercultural Relations* 2: 197-224.

_____ (1988). *Communication and cross cultural adaptation.* Philadelphia: Multilingual Matters.

Kim, Young Y., and William B. Gudykunst. (Eds.) (1987). Cross-cultural adaptation: Current approaches. *International and Intercultural Communication Annual* 11, Newbury Park, CA: Sage.

Klineberg, Otto, and W. Frank Hull (1979). *At a foreign university: An international study of adaptation and coping.* New York: Praeger.

Koester, Jolene (1983). *Intercultural reentry from the viewpoint of communication.* Paper presented at the annual meeting of the International Communication Association, Dallas, TX.

_____ (1984). "Communication and the intercultural reentry: A course proposal." *Communication Education* 34: 251-56.

_____ (1985). *A profile of the U.S. student abroad,* New York: Council on International Educational Exchange.

_____ (1987). *A profile of the U.S. student abroad—1984 and 1985.* New York: Council on International Educational Exchange.

Kubler-Ross, Elizabeth (1969). *On death and dying.* New York: Macmillan.

La Brack, Bruce (1986). "Orientation as process: The integration of pre- and post-experience learning." In R. Michael Paige (Ed.), *Cross-cultural orientation: New conceptualizations and applications*. Lanham, MD: University Press of America.

Lazarus, R, and S. Folman (1984). *Stress, appraisal, and coping*. New York: Springer-Verlag.

Lobdell, Christine L. (1990a). "Differential effects of expectations in the context of intercultural reentry adjustment." M. A. thesis. Arizona State University, Tempe, AZ.

_____ (1990b). *Expectations of family and friends of sojourners during the reentry adjustment process*. Paper presented at the International Communication Association, Dublin, Ireland.

Lonner, Walter J. (1986). "Foreword." In A. Furnham and S. Bochner, *Culture shock: Psychological reactions to unfamiliar environments*. New York: Methuen.

Marsh, Harriet (Ed.) (1976). *Reentry/transition seminars: Report on the Wingspread colloquium*. Washington, DC: NAFSA: Association of International Educators.

Martin, Judith N. (1984). "The intercultural reentry: Conceptualization and directions for future research." *International Journal of Intercultural Relations* 8: 115-34.

_____ (1985). *The impact of a homestay abroad on relationships at home*. Occasional Papers in Cultural Learning No. 6. New York: AFS International/Intercultural Programs.

_____ (1986a). "Communication in the intercultural reentry: Student sojourners' perceptions of change in reentry relationships." *International Journal of Intercultural Relations* 10: 1-22.

_____ (1986b). "Orientation for the reentry experience: Conceptual overview and implications for researchers and practitioners." In R. Michael Paige (Ed.), *Cross-cultural orientation: New conceptualizations and applications*. Lanham, MD: University Press of America.

_____ (1986c). "Patterns of communication in three types of reentry relationships: An exploratory study." *Western Journal of Speech Communication* 50: 183-99.

_____ (Ed.) (1989a). *International Journal of Intercultural Relations* (entire issue on intercultural communication competence) 13: 227-427.

_____ (1989b). "Predeparture orientation: Preparing college sojourners for intercultural interaction." *Communication Education* 38: 249-58.

Martin, Judith N., and Beulah Rohrlich (1991a). "Relationship between study abroad student expectations and selected student characteristics." *Journal of College Student Development* 32: 39-46.

_____ (1991b). "Testing a model of sojourner expectations." Paper presented at the annual meeting of the Speech Communication Association, Atlanta, GA.

Mestenhauser, Josef A. (1988). "Adding the disciplines: From theory to relevant practice." In Josef A. Mestenhauser, G. Marty, and I. Steglitz (Eds.), *Culture, learning, and the disciplines.* Washington, DC: National Association of Foreign Student Advisors.

Osgood, Charles E., and Percy Tannenbaum (1955). "The principle of congruity in the prediction of attitude change." *Psychological Review* 62: 42-55.

Pusch, Margaret D., and Nessa Loewenthal (1988). *Helping them home.* Washington, DC: NAFSA.

Rohrlich, Beulah, and Judith N. Martin (1991). "Host country and reentry adjustment of student sojourners." *International Journal of Intercultural Relations* 15: 163-82.

Schutz, Alfred (1964). *Collected papers II.* The Hague: Martinus Nijhoff.

Searle, Wendy, and Colleen Ward (1990). "The prediction of psychological and sociocultural adjustment during cross cultural transitions." *International Journal of Intercultural Relations* 14: 449-64.

Selye, Hans (1974). *Stress without distress.* New York: J. B. Lippincott.

Sheehy, Gail (1974). *Passages.* New York: E. P. Dutton.

_____ (1981). *Pathfinders.* New York: Morrow.

Simon, J. G., and N. T. Feather (1973). "Causal attributions for success and failure at university examinations." *Journal of Educational Psychology* 64: 46-56.

Theroux, Paul (1986). "Yard sale." In Thomas J. Lewis and Robert J. Jungman (Eds.), *On being foreign: Culture shock in short fiction.* Yarmouth, ME: Intercultural Press.

Uehara, Asako (1986). "The nature of American student reentry adjustment and perceptions of the sojourn experience." *International Journal of Intercultural Relations* 10: 415-38.

Walton, Sally J. (1990). "Stress management training for overseas effectiveness." *International Journal of Intercultural Relations* 14: 507-27.

Weissman, Diane, and Adrian Furnham (1987). "The expectations and experiences of a sojourning temporary resident abroad: A preliminary study." *Human Relations* 40: 313-36.

Werkman, Sidney (1983). "Coming home: Adjustment of Americans to the U.S. after living abroad." *International Schools Journal* 5: 49-62.

Westwood, Marvin J., W. S. Lawrence, and D. Paul (1986). "Preparing for reentry: A program for the sojourning student." *International Journal for the Advancement of Counseling* 9: 221-30.

Westwood, Marvin J., and S. Lawrence (1988). "Reentry for international students." In G. MacDonald (Ed.), *International student advisors' handbook*. Ottawa, ON: Canadian Bureau of International Education.

Westwood, Marvin J., and George Tillman (1984). *Returning home: A program of reentry* (videotape and manual). Ottawa, ON: Canadian Bureau of International Education.

Wilson, Angene (1985). "Returned exchange students becoming mediating persons." *International Journal of Intercultural Relations* 9: 285-304.

About the Authors

Janet M. Bennett received her Ph.D. in communication, with an intercultural and organizational emphasis, from the University of Minnesota.

Her teaching and training interests include intercultural education, change, cultural diversity, adult learning, organizational development and training of trainers.

After spending two years in the Peace Corps in Micronesia she became intrigued with intercultural issues and convinced that culture represents a valuable resource in our educational and organizational contexts. She worked for twelve years as a division chair at Marylhurst College, and directed a nontraditional individualized degree program for reentry adult learners. Currently, she divides her time among college teaching, faculty training, diversity training and co-directing (with Milton Bennett) the Intercultural Communication Institute, a nonprofit operating foundation located in Portland, Oregon. The foundation sponsors the annual Summer Institute for Intercultural Communication, a professional development program for educators, trainers, counselors, and corporate managers.

Milton J. Bennett, Ph.D., has been active in the intercultural field since 1967. He served as a Peace Corps volunteer in Micronesia from 1968-70, and returned to complete his doctorate in Intercultural Communication at the University of Minnesota. While in Minnesota, he developed and conducted intercultural training for multinational corporations and international education programs.

In Portland, Oregon since 1977, Dr. Bennett has continued consulting and training through Communication Perspectives, a company he formed with his wife, Dr. Janet Bennett. They conduct professional development for university faculty and administrators, international student advisors, ESL and foreign language teachers, refugee caseworkers, corporate managers, health care professionals, and others in the private and public sectors. Currently, they design and conduct diversity programs for multicultural university campuses and for corporations with multicultural work forces.

In 1986, the Bennetts founded the Intercultural Communication Institute (ICI), a nonprofit, private operating foundation designed to foster an awareness and appreciation of cultural difference in both the international and domestic arenas. ICI maintains an extensive library, donates resources for educational purposes, and sponsors the annual Summer Institute for Intercultural Communication which draws faculty and participants from throughout the U.S. and abroad to three weeks of intensive professional development workshops.

Milton has been an Associate Professor in the Department of Speech Communication at Portland State University, where he created the graduate program in Intercultural Communication. He has published several book chapters and articles in academic journals, and he is co-author (with Ed Stewart) of the revised edition of *American Cultural Patterns*.

Richard W. Brislin is a Research Associate at the East-West Center in Honolulu, Hawaii. He organizes yearly programs for college faculty members who want to develop intercultural course work, and for cross-cultural trainers interested in expanding their skills.

Cornelius "Neal" Grove is a partner in Cornelius Grove & Associates of Brooklyn, NY, a firm that assists managers and professionals to meet the challenges of human, organizational, and national differences.

Kristin A. Juffer is a Research and Policy Analyst with the United States Information Agency in Washington, DC.

Bruce La Brack is Professor of Anthropology and International Studies at the University of the Pacific, Stockton, California. He holds a joint appointment in the Sociology / Anthropology Department and the School of International Studies where he is Coordinator of Cross-Cultural Training. He has conducted research in Japan and the United States on reentry issues, is on the faculty of the Summer Institute for Intercultural Communication, Portland, OR, and is the founder and principal of the International Training Group, a business consulting firm.

James A. McCaffery is Vice President of the Training Resources Group in Alexandria, Virginia.

Judith N. Martin is Associate Professor in the Department of Communication at Arizona State University.

R. Michael Paige is Associate Professor of International and Intercultural Education, College of Education, University of Minnesota.

Ingemar Torbiörn is Professor in the Department of Psychology at the University of Stockholm.

Gary R. Weaver is Professor in the School of International Service at American University.

Name Index

A

Abrego, P. 302
Ackermann, Jean Marie 178
Adelman, Mara 309
Adler, Nancy 139, 145, 302, 303, 304, 314
Adler, Peter 16, 27, 57-59, 60, 84, 139, 173, 207, 212, 303
Albert, Rosita 281
Albrecht, Terrance 309
Allport, Gordon 150
Althen, Gary 159
Anderson, Bruce 210
Askling, Lawrence 203, 205, 216
Asuncion-Lande, Nobleza 22, 315
Atkinson, Donald 119
Austin, Clyde 321
Ax, Elizabeth 22
Azrin, Nathan 140

B

Index

A